# KEYS TO SUCCESSFUL REMODELING

This book covers all aspects of remodeling, from foundations to finishing touches.

The first chapter presents the keys to a successful project and applies those keys to a typical case study: how it was planned, how it was done, and why it succeeded. The lessons learned can be applied to any remodeling project. The chapter also tells how to set priorities and add value to a home.

The second chapter gives an overview of rough construction, with checklists of specific points to help you judge the quality of a contractor's work.

The third chapter contains detailed how-to information on interior walls, trim, cabinets, and countertops.

The topics discussed in the fourth chapter—tile, painting, floors, wallpaper, fixtures, and appliances—may be either finishing touches or remodeling projects in their own right.

*This formerly ordinary living room was transformed with the addition of an arched passageway, new facing on the fireplace, new lighting, and a limestone-tile floor.*

# KEYS TO SUCCESS

*Not all remodeling projects are success stories. This one is. It's the experience of an imaginary couple who embarked on a quest to transform their aging home into a sparkling showcase—within a strict budget. This case study, which is based on typical real-life experiences, will teach you the keys to success for any remodeling project.*

## Starting Out

The homeowners started with an unoccupied, 1,800-square-foot, three-bedroom ranch house, just over forty years old. Although the house had a fine selection of "luxury" rooms—formal dining room, breakfast room, family room, and laundry—it had only one bathroom and a very small kitchen. The lot size was 19,000 square feet. The surrounding area was zoned for a minimum lot size of 10,000 square feet.

The homeowners began by establishing goals. They considered the existing house, the size of the lot, the location and orientation of the house on the lot, and the neighborhood.

The existing house had three obvious needs: an upgrade of the forty-year-old, poorly maintained interior; a second bathroom; and a larger kitchen.

The size of the lot allowed a significant amount of latitude. Local zoning restricted the square footage of the building to 40 percent of the lot size. The maximum permitted house size of 7,600 square feet was well beyond

the remodelers' needs and budget. The set-back limits—which specified that the building must be at least 10 feet from the property lines—left room to expand the house on the north, west, and south sides.

The house was at the end of a cul-de-sac, with the master bedroom on the west side, facing across a lightly traveled street to a park with tree-covered foothills beyond.

The neighborhood consisted mostly of forty- to fifty-year-old houses. In recent years many of these had been remodeled or replaced by new, larger single-family homes. The resulting well-maintained and improving area gave the owners confidence that an investment in remodeling would not be wasted.

Finally, the owners kept one consideration in mind throughout the project: how each change would affect the resale value of the house. This served as financial protection by preventing them from lowering the value of the house. It also helped them preserve their objectivity by allowing them to step back and view the project through the eyes of potential buyers.

## The Sequence

**1.** The owners had the interior of the house painted and the hardwood floors refinished before they moved in. This timing took advantage of the fact that the house was vacant. However, they were not able to arrange the ideal schedule, which would have been to paint first and then refinish the floors. Because the highly recommended floor refinisher was available for only a short period just after the close of escrow, the owners had to have the house painted after the floors were redone. This caused enough minor problems (such as trying to remove paint overspray from a floor finish that wasn't completely hardened) to make them emphasize proper scheduling for their later projects.

**2.** The next step, done immediately after the owners moved in, was to have the existing two-wire electrical service replaced with a three-wire service, which allowed the installation of 240-volt circuits for the clothes dryer and stove. In the process, they increased the size of the service entrance from 60 amps to 200 amps, providing reserve capacity for future electrical needs. They also gained incentive to replace the living room ceiling. Poorly installed to begin with, the ceiling—which consisted of acoustic tiles stapled directly to the joists—was made worse when the electrician stepped through it and left a 12-foot strip of tiles hanging by one edge.

## The First Mistake

**3.** The owners next planned a major addition to the north side of the house. This entailed enlarging the kitchen, converting one bedroom into a master bedroom suite, adding a bathroom, and placing a large pantry, mud room, and photo darkroom next to the kitchen. They revised the plan numerous times until it was as nearly perfect as possible. Then they rejected it and chose a completely different approach.

Why abandon so much time and effort? The owners concluded that the project was too expensive and time-consuming for a first attempt at remodeling. They also decided that the plan didn't make the best use of the lot space or the orientation of the building on the lot. By abandoning the overly ambitious plan, they avoided undertaking a project that could have dragged on for years, resulting in frustration and financial loss.

## Back on Track

**4.** Regrouping, the owners decided to approach their goals piecemeal. They developed a series of projects, arranged in a logical order, that would eventually produce the desired results.

**5.** The first project was easy and brief: replacing the bathroom vanity and medicine cabinet. The existing fixtures were so outdated and unattractive that they were unlikely to ever come back in style. The tub and toilet were inoffensive standard items that the owners left in place for the time being.

# Successful Remodeling

*Created and Designed by the Editorial Staff of Ortho Books*

Project Editor
## Alan Ahlstrand

Writer
## John Reed

Illustrators
## Ron Hildebrand
## Angela Hildebrand

Principal Photographer
## Kenneth Rice

# Ortho Books

**Publisher**
Robert B. Loperena

**Editorial Director**
Christine Jordan

**Manufacturing Manager**
Ernie S. Tasaki

**Editors**
Robert J. Beckstrom
Michael D. Smith

**Managing Editor**
Sally W. Smith

**Prepress Supervisor**
Linda M. Bouchard

**Editorial Assistants**
Joni Christiansen
Sally J. French

**Editorial Coordinator**
Cass Dempsey

**Copyeditor**
Elizabeth von Radics

**Proofreader**
Karen Stough

**Indexer**
Carolyn McGovern

**Separations by**
Color Tech Corp.

**Lithographed in the USA by**
Webcrafters, Inc.

**Consultant**
Edward J. Roberts

**Special Thanks to**
Dr. R. J. Allister
Mr. and Mrs. H. T. Birr
Deborah Cowder
Kirstie Bennett and Jeffrey
  Goldberg

**Architects, Designers, and Builders**
Names of architects, designers, and builders are followed by the page numbers on which their work appears.
Eric Haesloop, William Turnbull Associates: 11TR, 11TL
Jim Hagopian: 9
Glen Jarvis and Steve Smith Construction: 1, 3, 4–5, 11B, 14–15, 42–43
Daniel G. Smith & Associates, Architects, and Zanderbuilt: 10, 78–79

**Photographers**
Names of photographers are followed by the page numbers on which their work appears. All other photography is by Kenneth Rice Photography.

Alan Copeland: front cover, small photographs
Michael McKinley: 8B, 9
Kit Morris: back cover
Geoffrey Nilsen: front cover, large photograph; 8T

Address all inquiries to:
Ortho Books
Box 5006
San Ramon, CA 94583-0906

1  2  3  4  5  6  7  8  9
94   95   96   97   98   99

ISBN 0-89721-269-X
Library of Congress Catalog Card Number 94-65697

THE SOLARIS GROUP
2527 Camino Ramon
San Ramon, CA 94583

**Front Cover**
The key to successful remodeling is breaking the project into a series of discrete phases, then approaching each one as a separate job with its own budget, deadlines, skills, and materials requirements. Coordinating all of this activity and keeping the project on schedule is one of the most important tasks, and one in which the homeowner plays a vital role.

**Title Page**
This major remodeling project began as a simple, one-story ranch house in a neighborhood of larger homes. The careful design doubled the size of the house by adding upstairs living space while maintaining the charm and intimacy of a smaller home.

**Back Cover**
This kitchen remodel is near completion. The framing, rough wiring, rough plumbing, duct work, insulating, wallboard installation, painting, tile work, and most of the cabinet installation are done. All that remains are the finish wiring, appliance installation, and flooring installation.

# Successful Remodeling

## Keys to Successful Remodeling
Keys to Success **6**
Before You Demolish **12**

## Roughing-In
Demolition **16**
Foundation and Seismic Work **18**
Framing **20**
Roofing **24**
Doors, Windows, and Skylights **26**
Siding and Exterior Trim **33**
Heating **36**
Rough Plumbing **38**
Rough Wiring **39**
Insulation **41**

## Finish Carpentry
Interior Wall Surfaces **44**
Interior Trim **60**
Cabinets and Countertops **68**

## Finishing the Job
Tile **80**
Painting **90**
Floors **96**
Wallcoverings **98**
Finish Electrical and Plumbing **104**

Index **110**

# Adding to the Value of Your Home

It's likely that underlying all your other reasons for remodeling are financial considerations—improving the value of your home. This may not be a primary motivation, but it shouldn't be overlooked. Your home represents a tremendous financial investment that should not be neglected.

You need to take care of normal maintenance, of course, but you must also make improvements that keep your home up-to-date. Items that are considered basic maintenance—new paint or linoleum or weather stripping—don't add a great deal of value to a house. New buyers and appraisers expect a house to be well maintained and may see the new roof or carpeting you've just installed as part of routine care.

Extras such as swimming pools and saunas may not return their full cost either. It's practical to keep future buyers in mind when you plan a remodeling job. If you think you may sell your home in the future, reconsider plans that are unusually trendy or exotic. Such changes may actually reduce rather than increase the value of a house.

A well-planned remodeling project can provide an excellent return on your investment. Real estate appraisers say that certain types of remodeling provide better returns than others. Improvements that add space and utility to a home increase its value most. For example, the addition of a second bathroom or a third bedroom offers a reasonable return on investment. Modernizing kitchens and bathrooms is also advantageous.

For more information on the benefits of specific remodeling projects, consult local real-estate professionals. There are also many magazines and books available at local libraries.

---

To reduce costs, the owners selected fixtures that could be retained when the bathroom was completely redone at a later time.

**6.** The owners next turned to the kitchen, with a plan for expansion that didn't require major structural changes. The breakfast room adjacent to the kitchen was larger than necessary and was separated from the kitchen by a partition wall. Because the breakfast room was also next to the dining room—with a pass-through between the two—it doubled as a serving and warming area for food during large dinner parties.

The owners opened up the partition wall beneath the kitchen cabinets to create a pass-through, then placed new upper cabinets back-to-back with those on the kitchen wall. The kitchen countertop was replaced with one that extended into the breakfast room to cover the base cabinets on that side of the pass-through. As a final touch, they installed a small bar sink in the breakfast room side of the countertop. The changes gave the kitchen and breakfast room a more open appearance, more storage space, and improved traffic flow for moving food from the kitchen to the dining room.

**7.** The owners next scheduled a large, closely related group of projects: adding a master bedroom suite, a second bathroom, and a laundry; rewiring, reroofing, and insulating the house; and replacing the living room ceiling.

The largest part of the project was the addition to the west end of the house that included a master suite with a loft, the second bathroom, and the new laundry.

The design took advantage of the view of the park and foothills to the west. Unlike the owners' first design, which had placed the addition in a much-used area of the rear yard, the new design occupied an unused portion of the lot between the house and driveway. This left space in the rear yard for a lap pool.

The interior layout established the loft and master bathroom as private retreats off the master bedroom. It also placed the laundry near the master bathroom and bedroom, where most of the household wash was generated and stored. The need to roof the addition provided an opportune time to replace the aging composition shingles on the main house.

Before the house was rewired, the old roof and living room ceiling were removed. This simplified the task of replacing the old knob-and-tube wiring, as well as running the new circuits for the addition. Because all the circuits in the house passed over the living room en route from the service entrance, removing the ceiling gave the electricians easy access from below. It also eliminated the risk of an electrician repeating the earlier accident and stepping through the new ceiling. Having the roof off provided light, ventilation, and easy access to wiring in the outer walls.

Once the house was rewired, the new living room ceiling of wallboard was installed. The house was then insulated and the new roof was installed.

**8.** Building a new laundry freed up the old one. Since the old laundry was located next to the kitchen, the owners incorporated it and installed base and upper cabinets and a countertop. The existing laundry plumbing—hot and cold water and a drain—simplified the installation of a dishwasher and sink. The new cabinets provided pantry storage, and the sink allowed the area to double as a mud room.

**9.** Finally, the owners remodeled the original bathroom as the last project in the series. The existing arrangement of fixtures left more unoccupied floor space than was necessary; by rearranging them, the owners made room for a whirlpool tub. They also reversed the swing of the bathroom door to increase privacy.

## The Happy Ending

The lessons learned by these remodelers can be applied to any project.

First, carefully analyze what you have. The benefits and limitations of the house and its location are just as important as your budget when deciding which projects are feasible.

Second, start with small projects and graduate to more ambitious ones. Remodeling is a learning experience, whether you do all, some, or none of the work yourself. Experience gained on small projects can later be applied to larger ones.

Third, schedule the projects in a logical sequence. Try to keep inconveniences, such as loss of bathroom or kitchen facilities, to a minimum. Whenever possible, time projects so that work done on an early one simplifies later efforts. Group small projects together, when savings of cost and time will result.

*Top: Creativity can reduce the cost of luxury improvements; the low stone wall gives this portable spa the appearance of a built-in custom unit. Bottom: Outdoor lighting is an excellent project for a novice remodeler; it is inexpensive, attractive, and simple to install.*

# Setting Priorities

Remodeling projects can differ greatly in cost, complexity, and time required, but all have one thing in common: a general set of priorities. Following these will ensure that the most important tasks are done first.

### Protecting Health and Safety
Improvements that protect your health and safety should always be done first. These include such tasks as replacing dangerous wiring (especially aluminum wiring), eliminating cross-connections in plumbing lines, installing tempered glass in or near doors, and reinforcing broken or sagging structural members such as floor joists and rafters.

This category also includes home-security improvements: installing smoke detectors, fire extinguishers, and alarm systems; childproofing cabinets and electrical outlets and establishing emergency exits; improving outdoor lighting; and upgrading locks on all doors and windows.

### Controlling Costs
Projects that would lower general expenses should be done second. Costs can be lowered by reducing utility and maintenance bills and by preventing expensive future repairs. Projects in this category include installing double- or triple-pane windows, adding insulation and weather stripping, and repairing plumbing leaks.

### Doing Basic Repairs
Some simple jobs can bring about great improvements in the resale value and livability of a house. These include patching cracks in walls, eradicating mildew, caulking a tub or shower, caulking around window and door frames, refinishing a light fixture, removing stains from countertops, cleaning and buffing a kitchen sink, and replacing a toilet seat.

### Enhancing Appearance
This category includes painting, replacing wall- and floor coverings, installing a new front door, adding interior trim such as crown molding or a chair rail, removing plastic tub surrounds in favor of ceramic tile, adding a greenhouse window, and installing a skylight.

### Improving Function
There are many changes that can make a house function more efficiently, at prices high and low. In the kitchen, functional improvements range from installing a new dishwasher to completely redesigning the room. Elsewhere in the house, functional improvements include building an extra bathroom, basement storage shelves, a larger garage, and extra closets.

### Making Life-style Improvements
These jobs tend to be the most expensive but are some of the most effective and fun to do. Examples include adding a family room, expanding the master bath to handle the morning needs of two working people, turning a spare bedroom into a study, adding a deck, and installing a whirlpool bath or spa.

### Making Luxury Improvements
These projects include unusual and expensive changes that often yield a poor return on investment. Among them are such installations as an indoor pool, a billiards room, a sauna, ornate woodwork, or a kitchenful of commercial-grade appliances.

### Combining Priorities
Many remodeling tasks fall into more than one category. For example, a new roof can beautify the house as well as prevent water damage from leaks. Remodeling projects that accomplish several high-priority objectives will produce a better return on investment, and probably more satisfaction, than those that fulfill fewer, less significant objectives.

*Garage doors are available in a number of styles and materials, ranging from stamped metal with the look of wood panels, to insulated metal, to beautifully finished natural wood. Although replacing garage doors can be time-consuming, the doors usually come with thorough instructions that make this a realistic do-it-yourself project.*

This relatively new house didn't need extensive alterations, just more space. A simple but creatively designed sitting room addition was the answer. The use of matching tiles for the interior floor and fireplace (bottom) and the exterior deck (top) gives a sense of unity and spaciousness to the design. The tree in the foreground shades the south-facing windows and skylight during the summer but is pruned high enough to admit low-angle winter sunlight.

*Top: The back of this remodeled home (left) features an attractive deck that invites outdoor living and an updated exterior that blends with the character of the original home and neighborhood. The sunken sitting area (right) connects the deck outside, the remodeled kitchen, and the sunny eating area. Bottom: This simple alcove adds useful space to the kitchen; the shape of the bay window adds visual appeal and an open feeling.*

# BEFORE YOU DEMOLISH

*After you've decided what to remodel, there are still two essential steps that must be taken before any work can start. One is drawing up a set of plans. The other is planning the project. Professional contractors know that planning is the most critical step of any job—and often the most difficult. The following guidelines will help you with both steps.*

## Obtaining Plans

A full set of working drawings, with clear dimensions, structural details, and materials specifications, will guide the project through the planning and construction phases. Precise plans are necessary for negotiating contracts, estimating costs, obtaining permits, scheduling the project, ordering materials, and performing the actual work. Presenting design and drafting techniques is beyond the scope of this book, but whether you draw the plans yourself or hire a professional, figure that the process will take from three to six months or longer, depending on the size of the job and your level of involvement.

## Planning the Project

The main activities in project planning are deciding who will do the work, estimating costs, scheduling the project, and obtaining permits. Although you will have thought about these issues during the design process, your main efforts should not take place until after you have a completed set of working drawings.

## Who Will Do the Work?

Many homeowners do remodeling projects themselves; others prefer hiring a contractor to do some or all of the work. After reading this book, you'll have a good idea of the skills, tools, and experience required at each stage. If you plan to take an active role in your project, the following questions should help you determine your level of involvement.

### Doing Everything Yourself

This can be time-consuming and frustrating but it can also be highly satisfying. Do you enjoy physical work? Do you have safe and reliable work habits? Do you have the necessary tools and skills? Do you have the time? Will it matter if the project remains unfinished for weeks? Have you finished every project you ever started? Will other family members support you?

### Managing the Project

If you have business skills, you may want to be your own general contractor and hire subcontractors to do the actual work. Are you well organized, persistent, and clear about the details of the design? Are you

## Hiring Contractors

You may already be working with a design firm that provides contracting services, or you may have selected a contractor whose work you know. Otherwise you should solicit names of contractors from your designer, friends, neighbors, local suppliers, or trade associations. Your selection should be based on personal rapport, experience with similar jobs, references and recommendations, schedules, and cost. Use the following guidelines to help you in soliciting competitive bids.

• In your initial phone call to each contractor, describe the project briefly and mention that complete plans are available.

• Have ready a list of questions, such as degree of experience with similar projects, availability, names under which the contractor is (and has been) licensed, and status of insurance. You'll also want credit references, client references, and job sites you could visit.

• Check references by visiting job sites and completed projects. Ask the clients about the contractor's performance.

• Narrow your choices to three or four people and provide each one with a complete set of plans on which to base the bid.

• Request from each bidder a price quote, bank or credit references, verification of license, and a copy of the contract form.

• Set a firm date for receiving bids.

• Specify the materials and labor you plan to provide.

• If a bidder requests further information, answer the request in writing and send a dated copy, labeled Addendum, to every bidder.

• Review all the bids and forms carefully.

The low bid is not necessarily the one to choose. It may indicate low standards of work, inadequate supervision, or serious oversights. It is unethical to negotiate simultaneously with two contractors after you have received their bids, or to invite another contractor to compete after the bidding process has closed. Remember to notify all parties of your choice and of the winning bid price, and to thank everybody for participating.

free to spend time on the telephone and at the job site? Can you handle money, make payments promptly, and keep a budget? Are you comfortable negotiating with subcontractors and suppliers? Are you articulate, firm, and patient? Are you willing to be friendly but to stay out of the way? Are you prepared to take on the responsibilities of an employer

if you hire salaried workers or unlicensed professionals who are not family members (e.g., report wages to the IRS, withhold state and federal taxes, and carry worker's compensation insurance)?

### Performing a Trade

If you hire a general contractor, you may want to perform one or more of the trades. Are you experienced in a trade, such as carpentry, wiring, or painting? Do you have the proper tools? Can you make yourself available on demand, have your materials ready, and complete the work on schedule?

### Doing General Labor

Is there a significant amount of demolition, hauling, or simple alterations that you could do before a contractor takes over? Can it be clearly specified in the contract which tasks are the contractor's responsibility and which are yours? Are you available on short notice? Are you physically fit? Do you mind getting dirty? Will you take orders?

## Getting Permits

In most communities you will be required to obtain a building permit before starting construction. For remodeling projects, usually the homeowner is allowed to apply for the permit. Separate permits may be required for building, plumbing, electrical, and mechanical work.

Besides complying with the law, securing a permit has several other benefits. It validates any work you have done that affects the resale value of the house. It decreases the possibility that an insurance company would refuse a claim against fire or other damages of dubious origin. It gives you an incentive to plan the project thoroughly, and a sense of pride in your work.

Finally, and most important, the purpose of codes and permits is to ensure that you and your family will be living in a safe home.

The building permit will include a schedule of inspections. Generally, all work must be inspected before it can be covered up. A final inspection is made after everything is hooked up and ready to go.

## Estimating Costs

One of the most essential—and most difficult—skills in construction is estimating the cost of a project. For an accurate estimate you will need final plans and materials specifications. Do not rely on your own preliminary plans or on a designer's estimate of projected costs or on any contractor's price that is not a firm bid based on the final plans.

If you are hiring a general contractor or several subcontractors, their bids will be the estimate. Be sure that you understand what is and is not included in each bid. For instance, who will be responsible for removing debris? For purchasing and installing fixtures? For painting? If your plans do not specify such details as type of tile, brand of sink faucet, or quality of cabinet hardware, clarify whether the bids include a certain allowance for these items.

If you are acting as your own general contractor, you will have to do the estimate yourself. There are several methods for estimating costs, such as square footage multiples, national estimating guides, and comparing your project to similar projects of known cost. However, the only reliable way to estimate a job is to break it down into separate phases, itemize the materials and labor costs for each phase, total them up, and

add a reasonable contingency factor to the total. To price materials, make a complete list and shop it around at various suppliers.

Even with careful planning, a remodeling job is likely to incur many unexpected costs, which can add up over the course of a long project. They may include permit fees, employer expenses for hiring labor, tool rental, blade sharpening, power cords, lights, safety equipment, vehicle mileage, telephone, debris-box rental, dump fees, tarps, updating wiring or plumbing, patching around new windows or vents, delivery charges, and cleanup.

## Scheduling

To make a schedule, establish the sequence of construction then estimate the time needed to complete each step. No two projects are identical, but the following list is typical of most remodeling projects that don't involve major structural work.

### Preconstruction

1. Complete the design.
2. Obtain bids or an estimate.
3. Hire a contractor or subs.
4. Obtain permits.
5. Arrange for debris removal and materials storage.

### Construction

6. Clear out the rooms.
7. Seal them off from the rest of the house.
8. Remove appliances and plumbing fixtures.
9. Remove counters, cabinets, and built-ins.
10. Remove trim and molding.
11. Remove floor covering if necessary.
12. Remove lights and electrical fixtures.
13. Remove wall and ceiling materials.
14. Remove or alter walls; shore up bearing walls.
15. Repair subfloor if needed.
16. Complete rough framing for alterations.
17. Install new windows and exterior doors.
18. Install duct work.
19. Alter or install rough plumbing.
20. Alter or install rough wiring.
21. Get preliminary building inspections.
22. Install insulation and get inspection.
23. Repair or replace wall surfaces.
24. Install trim around doors and windows.
25. Paint ceiling, walls, and trim.
26. Install flooring (unless it is installed at end of project).
27. Install interior doors.
28. Install cabinets and built-in appliances as appropriate.
29. Install countertops.
30. Install baseboards and remaining (prepainted) trim pieces.
31. Install plumbing fixtures.
32. Apply wallcoverings.
33. Install light fixtures and electrical finish.
34. Install remaining built-in appliances.
35. Install towel bars and accessories.
36. Install floor covering (if not done).
37. Install movable appliances.
38. Clean up trash.
39. Touch up paint and stains.
40. Test plumbing and electrical systems.
41. Obtain final inspections.
42. Move in.

# ROUGHING-IN

*This chapter covers the phases of rough construction involved in a remodeling job. These are usually major tasks, and result in a weathertight shell with rough plumbing, heating, rough wiring, and insulation installed. Rough construction is the phase most often done by professionals.*

*The chapter provides an overview of how each task is performed and discusses aspects unique to remodeling. It also describes specific standards of workmanship that will enable you to judge how well your project has been done.*

*This kitchen addition included every aspect of roughing-in, from foundation work to new roofing. The combination of brick veneer and board siding, also used on the front of the house, helps integrate the addition with the existing building.*

# DEMOLITION

*In demolition you must reverse the construction process, working from finish to structure, from the exposed to the hidden. Hardware and finish materials are removed first, then the wall and ceiling surfaces. Mechanical systems are removed or rerouted, and finally the framing is torn out. Then the process is reversed.*

## Living With Demolition

If you plan to live in the house while work is in progress, try to minimize the disruption. Attitudes vary. The loss of kitchen, bathrooms, and private space disturbs some people, who may resent the dust, noise, and presence of strangers. Other people find every step of the transition to the new plan exciting and endure the hardships without complaint.

If you can, live somewhere else or go on vacation during demolition. If you must be there, set up at least one room that won't be disturbed. Keep your stereo, television, and computer equipment in that room and keep it sealed with tape and plastic against dust. If possible, use an upstairs room. If you stay directly under a room being demolished, you may have to cover the ceiling with plastic too, because dust could still seep in.

## Preparing for Demolition

There are several things to take care of before you start.

Demolition of foundations and framing, especially bearing walls, should be done by skilled professionals.

If power, water, or sewer connections are going to be changed, make sure the utility companies are notified and that your plans and their requirements are coordinated.

Check your insurance and that of all contractors or subcontractors. If someone you hire to work on your house is injured, you could be liable. Don't assume that your homeowner's insurance covers you; confirm it in writing.

If you are acting as contractor, plan on being on the job site during demolition. There will be enough work without repairing things that weren't supposed to be wrecked.

Have a debris box or site for waste, and plan to clean up as you work. Debris boxes come in various sizes and can be rented by the week. Have buckets, wheelbarrows, bags, ramps, or other means to get waste to a debris box or pile. Either arrange for someone to clean up constantly, or plan to stop every half hour to clean up the work site. Be aware that you are responsible for any cracks in sidewalks or water pipes caused by the weight of a debris box or the truck that hauls it.

Have a first-aid kit, telephone, and plenty of dust masks on-site.

If you plan to sell or refinance your house and a termite report is required, consider doing such remedial work now.

Have linoleum, vinyl, resilient flooring, plaster, and heat-duct insulation tested for asbestos (see page 17).

Determine whether framing to be removed is bearing or nonbearing.

Plan to save trim and hardware if you intend to match the existing surfaces. This can save a significant amount of money if you have the time to clean it and a place to store it.

## Starting Demolition

Mark all trim and hardware to be saved and talk with workers to find out whether they consider it salvageable. In your mind, how much is it worth? How much time should they spend on it?

Cover floors that will be saved with particleboard and tape the seams with duct tape.

Cover porous surfaces such as wallcoverings that you wish to save.

Seal off all heat registers or ducts to keep out dust and debris.

Seal off with plastic and tape all accesses to the parts of the house that are not being demolished.

Shut off electric power and then test to make sure it is off to all switches and receptacles in the area where you are working.

Shut off the water and gas to the work area.

Assemble protective gear (gloves, hard hats, dust masks, goggles, ear plugs, boots).

Assemble tools.

Give everyone involved in demolition clear orders to bend over any nails in a piece of wood before putting it down.

## Removing Finish Materials

Whether you want to remove a medicine cabinet or knock out part of the wall between the living room and dining room, all the planning and preparation you've done will pay off once you pick up your tools.

### Removing Wood Trim

First examine the trim and determine the original installation sequence. Then remove it in reverse order. If you want to save a piece of trim, pry it gently from the wall with a flat bar. If the wall or ceiling is to be saved, protect the surface by using a woodblock wrapped in cloth behind the head of the pry bar. You may need to score the paint with a utility knife. To remove the trim with minimal damage, try to locate the finish nails and drive them through the trim with a nail set. Immediately remove any remaining nails from trim to be saved—otherwise the pieces may be gouged or scratched before reuse. Often nails can be pulled through from the back or cut off with nippers so that the face isn't marred at all.

If you don't intend to save the trim, rip it off with a wrecking bar. Flatten the nails for safety and easier handling. If wood trim is glued as well as nailed in place, it is impossible to salvage much.

## Removing Doors and Frames

If you wish to salvage any hardware, remove it carefully first and tape screws or small parts together. Then dismantle the door from the frame by tapping out the hinge pins. Remove the trim and casings as just described. In some cases you can take out the jambs by prying from the bottom. If the finish floor interferes, an alternative technique is to cut through the side jambs and remove them in sections. If you intend to save the jambs, cut the nails holding them to the studs. If the nails are hidden by shim stock, tap it out with a chisel or flat bar. Once the nails are visible, cut them with a hacksaw blade or reciprocating saw with metal blade (bimetal blades aren't brittle and won't snap off), or place the V end of a pry bar over the nail and rap sharply with a hammer to shear off the nails. Then lift or pry the frame carefully from the rough opening.

## Removing Wood Siding

Exterior wood-siding boards are difficult to remove successfully so that they may be reused. Before spending time and money, consider whether you will have to buy new siding or get some milled to order. In either case it may be cheaper to buy it all rather than recycle some of the existing boards.

Wall shingles can be removed with a shingle hook. This tool is indispensable for removing shingles without opening up an area to the top of the wall. Remember, if you detect evidence of rot or termites during this process, the damage must be completely exposed and repaired.

## Removing Stucco

Stucco can be cut with a saw using a masonry blade. Follow the instructions provided with the blade. Wear goggles, ear protection, dust mask, and gloves. This is a tough, messy job. It is most useful if you are installing something in the wall that will fit exactly and no stucco patching will be necessary. If you will have to patch, you might as well break out the stucco with a hammer, which is faster. Depending on local code specifications, expose from 3 to 6 inches of wire lath to ensure a tight connection between the existing stucco and the new material.

The fastest way to break out stucco with a hammer is to start at the top of a wall and break out the perimeter of the area you wish to strip. Once you expose the wire at the sides, cut it and peel the stucco back from the top. Remember to leave 3 to 6 inches of wire exposed to lap over the new wire. Keep the size of sections you remove to about 3 feet by 3 feet. The weight of the stucco will help pull it away from the wall. Keep the piece under control and be wary of the many nails protruding from the backside.

## Dealing With Asbestos

Asbestos was used in many building products in the past, and without testing you often can't know if you or your family will be exposed during demolition. Since asbestos is hazardous only as airborne fibers, consider covering it up, which will be much cheaper than removing it in most cases. Building codes require stringent safety standards and specially licensed contractors to remove areas of asbestos building materials larger than 100 square feet.

Many common building materials include asbestos.

- Linoleum
- Vinyl paste
- Backing for linoleum and resilient tile or vinyl flooring
- Plaster
- Wallboard
- Taping compound
- Paper tape
- Heat-duct insulation
- Shingles
- Asphalt
- Acoustic tiles and sprayed-on acoustic texture

These materials must be tested for asbestos. For more information check with your local building and public health and hazardous waste departments.

## Removing an Old Roof

Portions of an old roof can be removed with a shingle hook. This eliminates the need to open up an area all the way to the ridge.

The primary tool for removing an entire shingle, roll-roofing, or built-up roof is the flat-bottomed shovel. Roofing suppliers often sell a shovellike tool that has serrated edges along the tip to cut nails.

Start near the ridge. On built-up roofs use a pick to break open a line along the ridge so that you can get the shovel underneath and begin prying up the material.

On wood-shingle or shake roofs, be sure to work your way down from the top so that debris won't fall through the open sheathing.

With shakes and shingles a crowbar often works better than a shovel. By running the flat end of the crowbar up under the shingles, then prying upward, you can remove a dozen or more at a time.

Tile can be removed by hand. Slate should be pried up with a crowbar.

To remove metal or fiberglass panels, use a crowbar to pry up the panels; pull the nails out.

Work carefully. Use safety ropes if necessary, because dust and debris make the roof surface slippery.

The best to way to dispose of the debris is to place a debris box close to the house, so you can dump the material directly from the roof into the box. If a debris box is not available in your area, a pickup truck can be used in much the same way, if you don't mind some dents and scratches. Protect the windows and siding of the house with tarps or sheets of plywood.

# FOUNDATION AND SEISMIC WORK

*Foundation work may involve strengthening, repairing, replacing, or extending a foundation. This is usually a job for professionals. They have the jacks, conveyor belts, jackhammers, and other specialized tools necessary for doing the work safely and efficiently.*

## Extending a Foundation

The first task in extending a foundation is laying out the perimeter with string lines. Normal batter boards and techniques for squaring the corners are used, unless the house itself is out of square. If the addition goes on a back corner of the house, where one of its walls becomes an extension of the existing side wall, the new walls and foundation must be in line with the side of the house, even if that side is not perfectly square with the back of the house.

When running the string line for that side of the addi-tion, sight along the side of the house and align the string visually, rather than square it a perfect 90 degrees from the back of the house. All other string lines and corners should be square.

Excavation for the new foundation is the same as with new construction, except that it may be impossible to get a backhoe or other large equipment into the backyard. In that case, digging by hand is the only solution.

The foundation for a room addition involves straightforward techniques for building forms, setting rebar, placing and curing concrete, and stripping forms. The complexity of the job varies with the style of the foundation, slope of the grade, accessibility, and overall size. The style of the foundation is generally the same as that of the house in order to maintain uniform floor levels. The following considerations are significant when joining a new foundation to the old.

• The new foundation must be physically tied to the old, usually with expansion bolts or rebar set into holes drilled into the old foundation. A rotohammer and appropriate masonry bit is used for drilling holes 7 inches deep and ½ to ¾ inch wide, depending on the size of the bolt. Drill every 24 to 36 inches along the edge of a slab. In a cross section of perimeter wall, drill at the three or four locations where rebar is called for in the plan. Blow out the holes with a tire pump or air syringe. Drive in expansion bolts with a maul, or set 28-inch sections of No. 4 rebar into the holes by packing a paste of slightly expansive cement around them.

• For a slab foundation all plumbing lines must be positioned and wrapped with a ½-inch layer of protective insulation where they will penetrate the slab. Any wood must be protected with metal flashing where concrete will be poured against it.

• When establishing the height of a perimeter foundation wall, calculate carefully based on the depth of floor joists you will actually use. The dimensions of new lumber may not match the dimensions of old, forcing the new foundation height to be different from the old.

• For a perimeter foundation enclosing a crawl space, an access hole in the new foundation and kneewall may be necessary, because the new crawl space may be inaccessible from the existing crawl space.

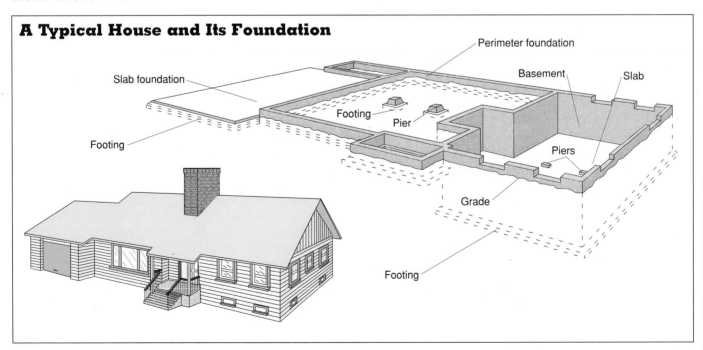

## A Typical House and Its Foundation

Slab foundation

Footing

Footing

Perimeter foundation

Basement

Slab

Footing

Pier

Piers

Grade

Footing

## Reinforcing the Foundation

If you add rooms on the second floor or change the bearing structure of the house, you will probably need to reinforce or replace parts of the foundation. Foundations that are cracking, settling, or turning also need repair, reinforcement, or replacement. This is best done with the advice of a structural engineer or architect and the help of a foundation contractor.

## Reinforcing the Structure

Houses are reinforced to prevent damage from earthquakes and high winds.

### Seismic Reinforcement

Seismic retrofits usually entail adding anchor bolts, metal connectors, and plywood shear walls. These strengthen the connections between parts of the house. Older houses simply sit on their foundations. In a large earthquake the frame can bounce or "walk" off the foundation. Kneewalls, which form the crawl space in some older houses, can buckle, allowing the building to collapse.

Builders of one-story houses often use ⅝-inch by 8-inch anchor bolts, whereas ¾-inch by 10-inch bolts are common for two-story houses. Bolts are spaced every 3 or 4 feet depending on local building codes. A structural engineer may specify a certain number in a particular part of the structure.

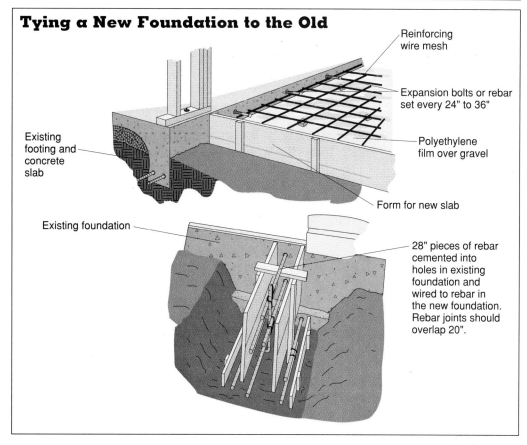

**Tying a New Foundation to the Old**

Reinforcing wire mesh

Expansion bolts or rebar set every 24" to 36"

Polyethylene film over gravel

Existing footing and concrete slab

Form for new slab

Existing foundation

28" pieces of rebar cemented into holes in existing foundation and wired to rebar in the new foundation. Rebar joints should overlap 20".

Many regions experience wind loads or seismic forces. One reinforcement technique is to strengthen a house with shear panels. These are simply sheets of plywood, or other panelized products rated for structural sheathing, nailed and blocked at all edges to increase the rigidity of the frame. Structural engineers will specify which walls need this treatment to ensure adequate protection for a given location and structure. If this is specified for your home, be sure you understand exactly what is required. If you are having the framing done, double-check that it was done correctly. Shear walls are covered with plywood from mudsill to top plate. All edges are nailed at 6 inches on center or less. Shear walls should

have a pair of 2-inch ventilation holes through the plywood in each stud bay. Cut out and block around crawlspace vents.

If joists rest directly on the mudsill, you may have to use angle iron to bolt the joists, mudsill, and foundation to each other. Metal plates are also used to put horizontal bolts in the foundation and mudsill. Six-inch and 9-inch framing clips are recommended to connect joists (including the rim joist) to the mudsill.

Dust must be carefully blown out of the bolt holes to insert the bolts easily. They should tighten until they crush the wood and should not start spinning. If they will not hold, the concrete may be bad or perhaps the foundation is made of brick. In that case,

more smaller bolts or threaded steel rods must be inserted and then set with epoxy or anchoring cement.

Floor joists should be blocked on the outside edges. In a severe earthquake, only the siding will hold unblocked joists upright, and they can fold over.

### Reinforcing Against Wind

High winds can put severe stress on the connections within a building. Hold-downs, hurricane ties, metal straps, and a host of metal connectors are engineered to strengthen these joints. If you are retrofitting an old structure it is usually worthwhile to have a structural engineer or architect diagnose what is needed.

# FRAMING

*Framing is not necessarily complicated, but it does require a certain amount of heavy labor. This is one of the phases of remodeling that is often done by contractors.*

## Types of Framing

Some homes are framed with heavy timbers, but most wood-frame houses use 2-by lumber. Old houses may have a balloon framing system, in which long studs extend from the foundation to the roof. But by far the most common method is platform framing, which was introduced at the beginning of this century. This system uses short wall studs that extend between floors.

## Framing Floors

Joists are the basic framing member for floors. Joists for the first floor bear on the foundation mudsills or short cripple walls, with large girders or beams supporting them at the midpoint. Joists for upper floors rest on bearing walls. Joists are doubled whenever they carry a concentrated load, such as a bearing wall or bathtub. Joists are set on edge with rim joists (also called band joists) at their ends to prevent them from turning over. They are strengthened by putting a line of blocking or cross-bridging over girders and every 8 feet along spans. Sometimes blocking is used instead of, or in addition to, girders.

## Matching Existing Floor Surfaces

Many materials can be used to make surfaces level. Plywood and particleboard can be purchased in thicknesses from ⅛ inch to ¾ inch. Tapered shims come in bundles. You can also buy plastic shims or you can cut your own. Build the subfloor so that the finish floors align. To end up with matching finish floors, it is almost always best to align the top of the new subfloor with the top of the existing subfloor. That way, if you ever replace the finish floor surface, the subfloors are aligned and it is easy to start over.

## Framing Walls

Stud walls consist of a soleplate nailed to the subfloor, vertical studs, and a double top plate, with extra studs and blocking added where walls intersect. Openings are framed with headers and extra studs. Headers are made of solid 4 by 12 lumber or built up from 2-by lumber and plywood.

The wall is built on the subfloor platform, then raised and braced in position. The process is essentially the same whether or not a section of wall has doors or windows.

Studs are always a standard 92¼ inches long; precut studs come in this length, whereas 8-foot 2 by 4s must be cut to this length. The studs are 92¼ inches long, so when you add the width of the soleplate and the double top plate (the cap plate plus the top plate), the overall height of the wall is 96¾ inches. This allows a ⅜-inch clearance at top and bottom for putting up the interior wallcovering of wallboard or paneling.

After the plates are spaced apart, the next step is to build the corner posts. Both side walls must have these posts at each end. The end walls do not have corner posts. The single stud at each end of the end walls is nailed to the corner posts when the end walls are raised in place.

Corner posts are made by sandwiching three pieces of 2 by 4 scrap, each about

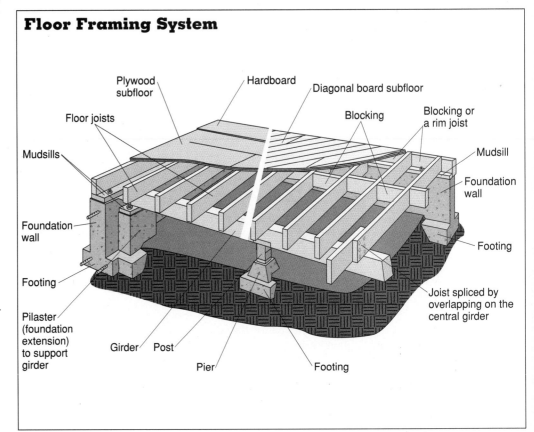

## Floor Framing System

Plywood subfloor
Hardboard
Diagonal board subfloor
Floor joists
Blocking
Blocking or a rim joist
Mudsills
Mudsill
Foundation wall
Foundation wall
Footing
Footing
Pilaster (foundation extension) to support girder
Girder
Post
Pier
Footing
Joist spliced by overlapping on the central girder

## Matching Old and New Subflooring

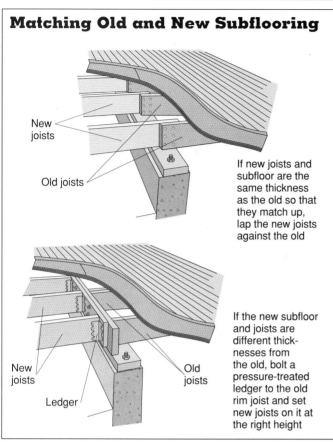

New joists

Old joists

If new joists and subfloor are the same thickness as the old so that they match up, lap the new joists against the old

New joists

Old joists

Ledger

If the new subfloor and joists are different thick-nesses from the old, bolt a pressure-treated ledger to the old rim joist and set new joists on it at the right height

## Hold-downs

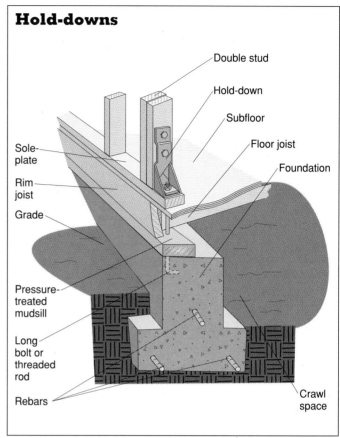

Double stud

Hold-down

Subfloor

Floor joist

Foundation

Sole-plate

Rim joist

Grade

Pressure-treated mudsill

Long bolt or threaded rod

Rebars

Crawl space

## Typical Stud Wall

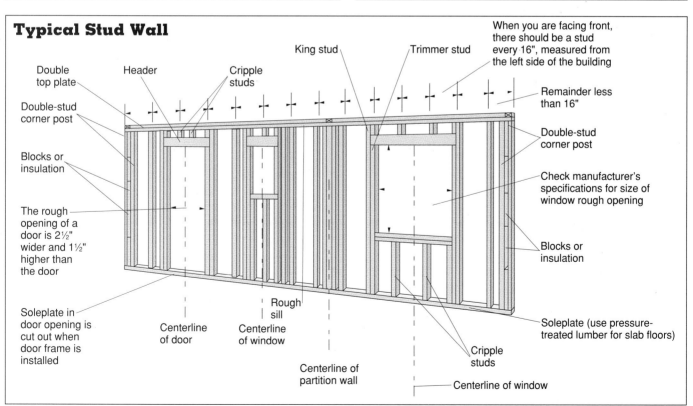

Double top plate

Double-stud corner post

Blocks or insulation

The rough opening of a door is 2½" wider and 1½" higher than the door

Soleplate in door opening is cut out when door frame is installed

Header

Cripple studs

King stud

Trimmer stud

When you are facing front, there should be a stud every 16", measured from the left side of the building

Remainder less than 16"

Double-stud corner post

Check manufacturer's specifications for size of window rough opening

Blocks or insulation

Soleplate (use pressure-treated lumber for slab floors)

Centerline of door

Rough sill

Centerline of window

Centerline of partition wall

Cripple studs

Centerline of window

12 inches long, between two studs. Corner posts and studs are secured to the soleplate with two 16-penny (16d) nails through the soleplate into the bottom of each stud.

## Window Openings

The tops of all windows and doors should be the same height. Standard house construction calls for that height to be 80 inches from the top of the soleplate to the bottom of the header. Therefore, all trimmer studs, which support the headers, should be 80 inches long. The width of the doors and the width and height of the windows are determined by the plans and personal taste.

Rough window openings should be ½ inch larger than the actual window, all around. This allows room to maneuver the window slightly before nailing to ensure that it is square and will not bind when opened. Trim will cover the small spaces between the window, trimmers, and headers.

A header must be placed above this opening for structural support. The trimmer studs on each side frame the rough opening for the window and support the header. Therefore, the header must be 3 inches longer than the rough opening to accommodate the trimmer studs.

It is easiest to make all headers from 4 by 12s. If you are having the framing done by a contractor, this may

also be the least expensive approach, because it requires less labor time than fabricating headers from 2-by lumber and plywood. Discuss this with the contractor during the bidding process and make sure the header material is included in the written job specifications.

If the headers are fabricated from 2-by lumber, there will most likely be a 2- to 6-inch space between the top of the header and the top plate. This space must be supported with short lengths of stud lumber called cripple studs, which are placed where full-length studs would be if there were no window or door opening.

The bottom of the window opening consists of a 2 by 4 sill that fits between the trimmers. Some codes call for double sills.

Cripple studs are also needed beneath windows to support the sill. At the top and bottom, cripple studs should align with each other and be placed every 16 inches on center, just as studs would be placed so that siding and interior panels can be nailed in correctly.

## Door Openings

Door openings are similar to window openings, but you must take into consideration the thickness of the door jamb (the framing around the door itself). The same process is involved in framing the opening, whether or not the door is prehung.

Doors are a standard 80 inches high, so the door opening (measured from the top of the soleplate) is made 80 inches high when it is being framed. After all the walls are

up and the door is ready for installation, the soleplate in the opening is cut out. This additional 1½ inches makes room for the top jamb and the door sill.

Ideally, doors should be placed so that one of the framing studs can also be used as a rough-opening stud. The rough opening formed by the trimmer studs should be ½ inch wider than the door jamb. The additional ¼ inch on each side of the door will be filled with shims when the door is installed.

## Wall Bracing

Buildings with solid sheathing or plywood siding normally do not require bracing, but all others do. The two most widely used types are let-in bracing and metal-strap bracing.

Let-in bracing is made from 1 by 4 stock and runs from the top outside corners of the wall to the bottom center to form a V shape. It is set into notches in the studs and is prepared while the stud wall is still lying on the platform.

Metal-strap bracing is commonly available in 10- and 12-foot lengths and is nailed to the outside of the stud walls after they are up, squared, and plumb. The braces are thin enough not to obstruct the exterior wall sheathing.

Metal-strap braces come with holes for 8d nails drilled every 2 inches. Each brace is nailed at one end to the top plate, and at the other end to the soleplate. Metal bracing must always be put up in crossed pairs, forming an X.

## Matching Existing Wall Surfaces

New wall surfaces should be brought flush with the existing ones when adding to or altering the framing. For example, if an interior doorway is being filled in, the wall must be finished so it doesn't look like a patch and must match the wall surfaces on both sides. For instance, the lath and plaster on one side could be ¾ inch thick and on the other only ⅝ inch thick. Lath and plaster can easily vary by this much on one wall. This could be handled in three ways.

**1.** Demolish all plaster on this wall, fur out the new studs, and cover with new wallboard.

**2.** Fur out the new studs and patch the opening with plaster, matching the texture of the existing wall.

**3.** Fur out the studs and patch with wallboard, matching the existing texture.

The wallboard should be held even with the low part of the wall and filled flush with the existing wall during taping.

## Framing Roofs

Most roofs are framed with ceiling joists, rafters, and a ridge board. Sometimes collar ties connect pairs of rafters near the midpoint (or lower if they take the place of the ceiling joists). The ceiling joists and collar ties prevent the rafters from spreading the walls apart; they should not be removed. The ridge board does not support the rafters. It provides a surface for the ends of the rafters to bear against.

# Foundation and Framing Checklist

## Foundation

Check the following details before pouring concrete.

- Loose dirt and debris should be removed from footings.
- Rebar must be 3 inches from dirt.
- Trenches should be wet down before concrete is poured.
- Dimensions are usually to the face of framing that is the same as the outside face of the concrete. Double-check all measurements against the plans.
- String lines should be level.
- Forms must be strongly braced so they can't spread when filled with concrete. Corners and sides need to be strong and rigid.
- Anchor bolts should be in place or locations marked on the forms so that they can be inserted while the concrete is wet.
- Form boards may run past the ends of the forms. The wood should be oiled to keep the concrete from sticking to it.
- Cold joints should be treated with a latex bonding agent to increase adhesion between old and new concrete.
- Beware of leaving uncovered any open trenches deeper than 2 or 3 feet. If you are working in a trench below the surface, the walls should be shored and you shouldn't work alone.

## Framing

Framing should be level, plumb, and square. Check the following specific points.

## Floors

- Sight across the tops of the joists before installing the subfloor. Look for joists that are high or low. Some joists even take an S shape. A joist that is ¼ inch out of line should be replaced. If it is low, check to see if its crown is reversed. If it is high, it can easily be lowered with a power planer.
- Make sure all joist hangers have nails in all the holes.
- Anchor bolts should be so tight they crush the wood slightly.
- Blocking should be flush with the joists at the top. If this is a second-floor frame, blocking must be flush at the bottom as well.
- The floor frame should be square and level within ¼ inch over 25 feet. To check, measure the room diagonally in two directions. The measurements should be the same. If the frame is out of square, you may be able to rack it before the subfloor is installed, but not afterward. If you decide it is worth making the correction, first be sure the lengths are correct, then cut the toenails holding the rim joist to the girders and kneewall or mudsills. The joist rack can be moved fairly easily once it is loose on three sides.
- A floor frame that is not level can be corrected at this stage. If the framing is done by a contractor, check the frame yourself before the subfloor goes on and insist that it be within the tolerances listed in the contract at no extra cost.

## Walls

- Sight along the wall studs. If any studs are more than ⅛ inch out of line, correct the error. If the stud is vital structurally, at a corner or end of a wall, it should be replaced. If it is nailed into a window or door opening, you can often plane it down flush with its neighbor. Also check to see that the stud is aligned with the plates. It can be driven over with an angled nail and some vigorous hammering.

  Straighten a bowed stud by sawing a kerf. Attach a plywood scab to each side of the stud at the cut with grabber screws.
- Check plumb and square for any walls to be tiled. The allowable margin of error is ⅛ inch over 8 feet for intersecting walls.
- Measure the frame across the top plates from side to side. Starting the roof frame will be much easier if the walls are square at the top.
- Next check walls and rough door openings for plumb. If they are within ¼ inch or so, you can shift the entire wall at the top or bottom by hitting it opposite each nail with a sledgehammer. Don't try to move it more than ¼ inch. If it doesn't move with every blow, pull the nails holding it and tap it into line. One powerful blow causes less damage to the wood fibers than many weaker blows. If the wall bounces back after each blow, find and correct the cause before continuing.

- Check the nailing on top plates, trimmers, and plywood sheathing. There should be a nailing schedule in the specifications, plans, or local building code. If you find a problem at one spot, keep checking until you are sure it is not a general pattern.
- Measure openings, rooms, and halls and compare them with the plans.
- Check locations where switches are specified to make sure there is room in the framing for the outlet boxes.
- Verify that the plumbing wall is framed with 2 by 6 lumber or is large enough to accommodate drain-waste-vent (DWV) lines.
- Check framing for unusual details like passthroughs, recessed medicine cabinets, and soap or shampoo niches.
- Make sure there is blocking or a plywood attaching surface for towel racks and wall hardware.

## Roofs

- Once the roof is framed, check the tightness of the angled cuts. The joints should have wood-to-wood contact from top to bottom.
- Sight along the ridge. It should be straight.
- Sight across the rafters. They should all be crown up. Make sure all collar ties, steel connectors, purlins, and other bracing elements are in place.
- Make sure eave blocks, any other blocking, rafter tails, and all details specified in the plans are in place.

# **R**OOFING

*Roofing work in remodeling involves reroofing, repair, or tying a new roof to an existing one. This section describes how to tie an additional roof to an old one and lists checkpoints for judging the quality of a roofing job.*

## Roof Basics

Roofs consist of framing, decking or spaced sheathing, building paper (except with wood shingles), and the roofing material itself. There are many types of roofing material, each with particular characteristics. Composition shingles and roll roofing are inexpensive, easy to apply, and fire resistant. Wood shingles and shakes are attractive and durable. Tile and slate are highly fire resistant and durable but relatively expensive.

## Tying New and Old Roofs Together

Techniques for tying in new roof framing vary with the design. If the addition is on the gable end of the house, the new rafters will be framed parallel to the old, and the point of connection is simply the first pair of new rafters doubled up against the existing rake rafters on the end of the house.

A more complicated connection occurs when the ridge line of the new roof runs perpendicular to the ridge of the existing house. Then the new roof is tied into the slope of the existing roof, usually some distance below its ridge, creating two new valleys. Frame the new roof by cutting a full

pair of pattern rafters. Temporarily support them on the far end of the addition so that they hold one edge of the ridge board in position. Level the ridge board and mark exactly where it intersects the slope of the existing roof. This point is the apex of the inverted V where the new roof intersects the existing roof slope. Mark this V on the existing roofing material with a nail, and strip away enough roofing so 2 by 4 plates can be nailed directly onto the sheathing along the path of the V. Drive 16d nails through the 2 by 4 plates and sheathing into the rafters below.

Cut an angle on the end of the ridge board so that it will lie on the apex of the 2 by 4 plates. Make sure the ridge board is level. Then use the two pattern rafters at the far end of the addition to mark and cut the rest of the full rafters. Nail the first pair in place, securing one end of the ridge board to them and the other end to the apex of the roof plates. Nail the rest of the full rafters in place, toenailing them to the cap plates with three 16d nails and alternately facenailing and toenailing them to the ridge board with 10d nails. Then cut pairs of progressively shorter jack rafters to fit between the ridge

board and roof plates. Cut and fit each pair carefully so that they maintain the same roof plane established by the full-sized rafters. The best way to check is to lay a long straightedge across their tops.

With the rafters in place, nail down the roof sheathing—either ½-inch plywood for composition and most rigid roofing materials, or 1 by 4 slats for wood shingles.

Where the sheathing intersects the roof, cut and nail it so that its edge fits snugly against the old sheathing to provide a solid nailing surface, without gaps, along the newly created valleys. Lay plywood perpendicular to the rafters.

The roofing for the new addition must be tied carefully into the old. Choose materials that match existing ones, unless you are reroofing the entire house. If the new roof is simply an extension of the old gable roof, tie the new roofing

material to the old by removing one shingle at the end of every other course of old roofing. Then start the new shingles for each course where the old courses end. That way seams between the old and new will be staggered rather than in a straight line from eave to ridge.

For roof intersections with one or two new valleys, apply valley flashing first. If the existing roof is being redone, lay the flashing over the old material. If not, carefully tuck the metal ribbed flashing, or 90-pound roll flashing, under existing shingles all the way up the valley. You will first need to remove individual nails to make sure that the flashing extends the required 8 to 10 inches up under the roofing on each side of the valley. Once the flashing is in place, apply the new roofing over it and the rest of the addition.

## Tying Together New and Old Roofs

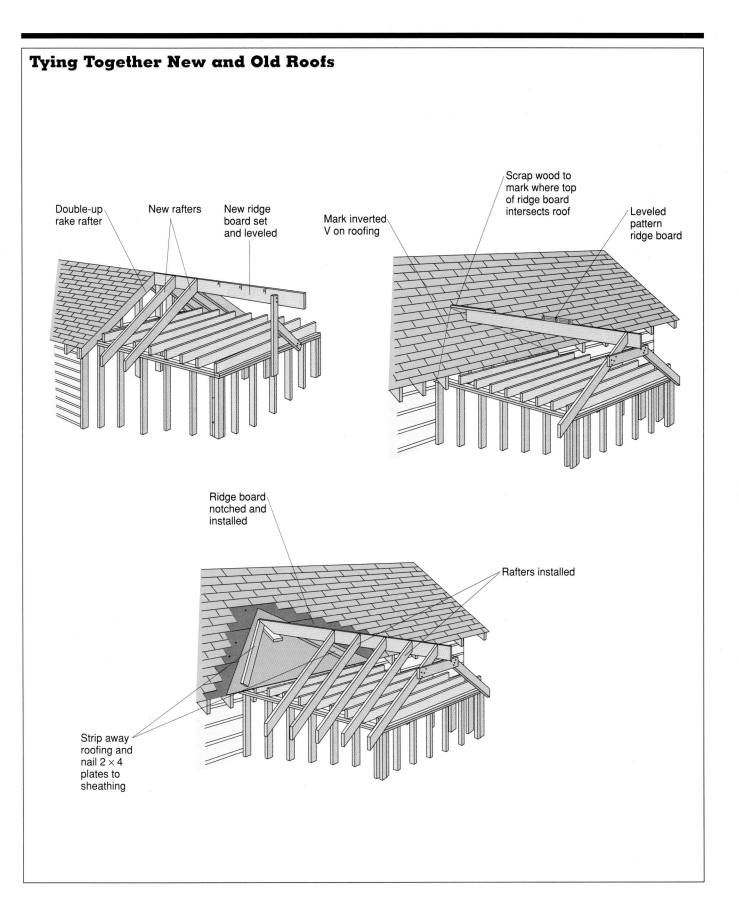

Double-up rake rafter

New rafters

New ridge board set and leveled

Mark inverted V on roofing

Scrap wood to mark where top of ridge board intersects roof

Leveled pattern ridge board

Ridge board notched and installed

Rafters installed

Strip away roofing and nail 2 × 4 plates to sheathing

*Replacing or installing new doors, windows, and skylights is a common remodeling task. Prehung and sliding metal doors, regular and nailing-fin windows, and curb-mounted skylights can all be installed by a homeowner who does careful, precise work.*

## Ordering Doors

To purchase prehung doors (and windows with jambs), you must measure actual wall thicknesses. Take a detailed drawing with you when you order windows and doors, showing a cross section of the existing wall into which they will be installed. Make sure you understand how the opening will be flashed and trimmed.

## Installing a Prehung Door

Prehung doors are available with or without trim (see page 35). To illustrate a typical installation, this section uses the common example of a prehung unit with wood trim. These units are installed by nailing through the face of the trim into the siding and framing around the rough opening.

If you got used to wearing a tool belt when you did the rough framing, a word of caution: Be careful not to get the tool belt between yourself and the door you are carrying, as it can scratch the glass or mar the finish.

In some cases, you will need to install a strip of felt around the door opening before you hang the door.

If the unit is too large and heavy for you to move safely, remove the hinge pins and take the door out of its jamb. Tack the jamb in place in the rough opening. Then reinstall the door and the hinge pins. To ensure that the door unit can't be knocked over by a bump or a gust of wind, brace it securely.

Now shim and adjust the unit so that it is square and opens and closes smoothly. As you look at the door in the opening, pay attention to the small space between the door itself and the jamb. Notice that as the top of the door unit is leaned to the right or the left, this small space will either widen or close up in different spots. Ideally, if the door is perfectly square, the space should be even all the way around. If there isn't enough space in one spot, that is where the door will bind.

Notice the spaces above and below the door. If they are not even all the way across, the subfloor under the door may not be level. Planing or shimming may be necessary. In some cases, the structure beneath the floor may need repair. Once the floor is level, tack the trim lightly (leaving the nail heads exposed in case the nails need to be removed) to the wall near the top of the jamb on the hinge side of the

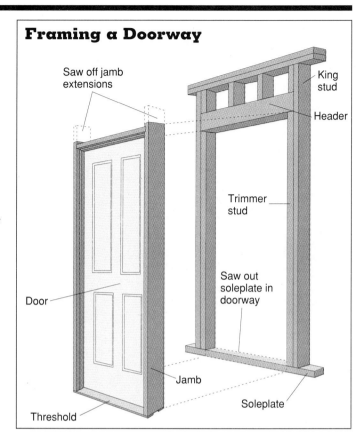

**Framing a Doorway**

- Saw off jamb extensions
- King stud
- Header
- Trimmer stud
- Saw out soleplate in doorway
- Door
- Jamb
- Soleplate
- Threshold

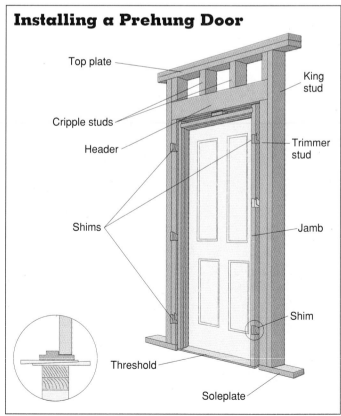

**Installing a Prehung Door**

- Top plate
- King stud
- Cripple studs
- Header
- Trimmer stud
- Shims
- Jamb
- Shim
- Threshold
- Soleplate

door and to the jamb on the strike side of the door. Adjust the space around the door by sliding the bottom of the unit left or right. If it's hard to move, a small crowbar between the rough framing and the jamb will provide plenty of leverage. Once the spacing looks even, open and close the door a few times to make sure that it is operating smoothly. When you are certain that the door fits in the opening properly, either remove the unit or have a helper lean it out so that you can caulk around the opening, beneath where the trim will be. Reinstall and readjust the door, again just tacking it in place. One of the most common mistakes beginners make when installing a door is to pound all of the nails home. Leave the nail heads sticking out until you are absolutely sure that the door is properly adjusted. This will make it much easier to remove the nails if necessary.

It is common for one or more of the jambs to have enough of a bow that the space between the door and the jamb will vary, no matter how you adjust the door from side to side. Adjust the door as well as you can and then work your way down each jamb, shimming it in or out to correct the space as you nail the trim to the wall. Don't drive home the nails until the jambs are fully adjusted and the door operates smoothly.

Attach the trim with hot-dipped galvanized (HDG) nails. Countersink the heads with a hammer and a nail set; then fill the holes with putty and paint the trim. If the door

## Installing Sliding Glass Doors

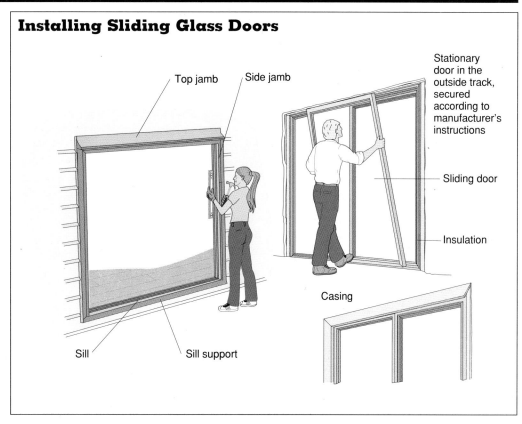

Top jamb · Side jamb

Stationary door in the outside track, secured according to manufacturer's instructions

Sliding door

Insulation

Casing

Sill · Sill support

is already painted and you want to avoid having to touch up the nail holes, use stainless steel ring-shank finishing nails, which are available in many lumberyards. They are expensive, but it takes only a few to install a door. Because they will not rust and streak, you need not countersink them. The heads themselves are fairly small, and the nails often come ready-painted, so you might not even need to touch them up.

Now finish attaching the jambs to the framing. Read the manufacturer's instructions carefully. As a rule, the jambs are shimmed and then nailed through the shims into the framing, particularly at stress points such as the strike and the hinges. However, because designs differ, following the manufacturer's instructions

precisely on this point is imperative. The sill itself is usually screwed to the floor.

The space between the jamb and the framing must be sealed to stop drafts. One product designed for this purpose is a canned pressurized foam that expands to fill the gap and hardens quickly. Be careful with this product, however. The foam expands so vigorously that if you apply too much, it will actually push out the jambs and ruin the fine fit you worked so hard to achieve. Use it sparingly until you get a feel for the right amount. Various solid-foam tubes or rods are also available, which can be stuffed into the space.

## Installing a Sliding Glass Door

Metal sliding doors are installed in much the same way as hinged doors. One difference is that instead of nailing the unit through finished wood trim, you nail through a metal fin that runs all the way around the door. This fin is covered later with trim or siding. Again, do not drive home nails until the unit is adjusted and the doors slide freely.

Metal- and vinyl-clad door-frames resemble metal-framed doors. The cladding itself may include a nailing fin, or there may be a nailing fin that is attached to the door on-site—usually a very simple operation. Again, the fin is covered with trim or siding.

# Removing an Existing Window

It's best to already have the new windows before removing the old ones; however, to order the new window, you need the exact measurements of the rough opening. Therefore, start the process of removing the window by taking off the inside casing. With the rough opening revealed, measure the width (the distance between the inner edges of the trimmer studs) and the height (the distance between the rough sill and the bottom of the header). Because the opening may not be square, take several measurements. The new window must fit within the narrowest measurements. Obtain the new window before you continue removing the old one.

## Removing a Wood-Framed Window

The following instructions, which apply specifically to removing a double-hung window, apply generally to any wood-framed window. Work carefully to protect the wood, particularly any trim that you intend to reuse. A double-hung window can be removed from inside or outside the house, whichever is more convenient.

Start by removing the interior window trim. Carefully tap a broad chisel under one edge and gently pry out the trim. Don't pry the bottom all the way out at first; slowly work your way upward, prying a little at a time, to avoid breaking the trim. If any nails are pulled through the trim and left in the trimmer studs, pull them out with a hammer.

Push both windows down. If the windows are hung by cords, cut them. If there is a spring-loaded balance, twist the metal top to loosen it.

Then use the chisel to pry off the interior stops and lift the interior sash out of the frame.

Working from inside, or outside if convenient, pry off the exterior trim. Again, work carefully if the trim is to be reused. Then remove the exterior stops. On spring-loaded sash balances, twist the metal top, pull it off, and remove the spring. Take the exterior sash out of the frame.

Pry off the apron and the stool. If possible, pry off the jambs. It is sometimes easier to use a nail set to drive the nails through the jambs and sill and then lift the window frame out as a unit.

## Removing a Double-Hung Window

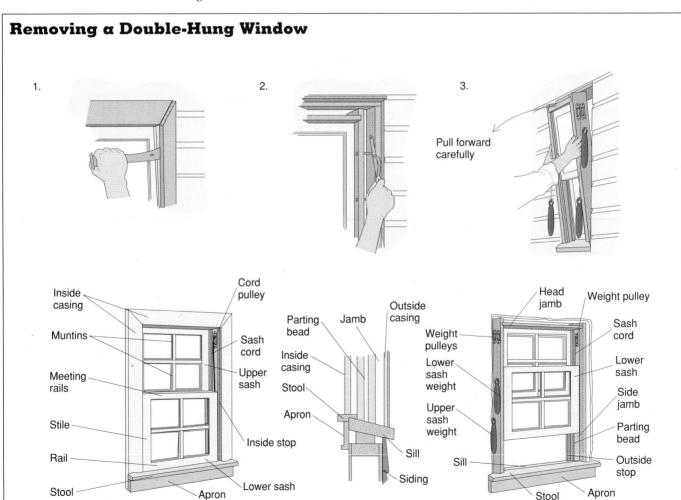

1.

2.

3. Pull forward carefully

Inside casing
Cord pulley
Muntins
Sash cord
Meeting rails
Upper sash
Stile
Rail
Inside stop
Stool
Lower sash
Apron

Parting bead
Jamb
Outside casing
Inside casing
Stool
Apron
Sill
Siding

Head jamb
Weight pulley
Weight pulleys
Sash cord
Lower sash weight
Lower sash
Upper sash weight
Side jamb
Parting bead
Sill
Outside stop
Stool
Apron

## Removing a Nailing-Fin Window

Almost all windows held in a metal frame, including fixed, casement, awning, jalousie, and rotating types, have nailing fins. These surround the exterior part of the frame. The frame is placed in the rough opening and the fins are nailed to the trimmer studs, rough sill, and header. Siding covers the fins. Trim covers the gap between the exterior siding and the window.

Remove nailing-fin windows as follows. Carefully pry off all the exterior trim so it can be reused.

The nailing fin is usually 1½ inches wide, so measure out 1¾ inches from the window frame all around and mark the outline on the siding.

Set the blade on a circular saw to ⅛ inch deeper than the siding thickness. Use a carbide-tipped blade because you may hit some nails. Cut along the lines, then remove and save the siding pieces. Extract the nails from the fins and lift out the window.

## Installing Windows

Modern windows are installed much like doors, one of the main differences being that they have no threshold.

## Installing Regular Windows

Like doors, windows are generally installed by nailing either right through the trim or through nailing fins. Before you start, check that the opening is square.

The illustration on page 33 shows a section cut through the top jamb of a window. Note the metal Z-flashing, which tucks up under the building or flashing paper, then out over the top of the wood trim, then slightly down over the front face of the trim. No caulk is needed to waterproof this system. Because there is no standard thickness for exterior window trim, the Z-flashing over the top of a window is usually custom-made at a sheet-metal shop, typically in 10-foot lengths, out of galvanized material. The basic point is keeping water out of the head jamb by properly overlapping the various materials.

To get the windows into their openings, you will need helpers. Warn them not to scratch the glass or the frames with their tool belts. If a window is awkwardly heavy or large, you can usually remove an operable sash fairly easily. Be extra careful with windows that are high up. It may be wise to build or rent a scaffold to stand on for the installation; don't overestimate what you can do from a ladder. If you will be dealing with a high installation, try to get windows that have folding nailing fins. These fins lie flat against the unit, so you can bring the window to the opening from the inside, place it on the rough sill, slide it out just a bit, and snap the fins into the open position. You can then work from inside, and safely from outside on a ladder.

Once you have the unit placed in the rough opening, slide it to either side as necessary to center it. Tack one of the upper corners in place, but don't drive the nails all the way in. Next, level the sill. Check the manufacturer's instructions to see whether any shimming is recommended at this point. Tack the corner diagonally opposite the upper corner that you tacked first. Now check to see that the window is square and operates smoothly and that operable sashes sit evenly in their openings.

## Removing a Nailing-Fin Window

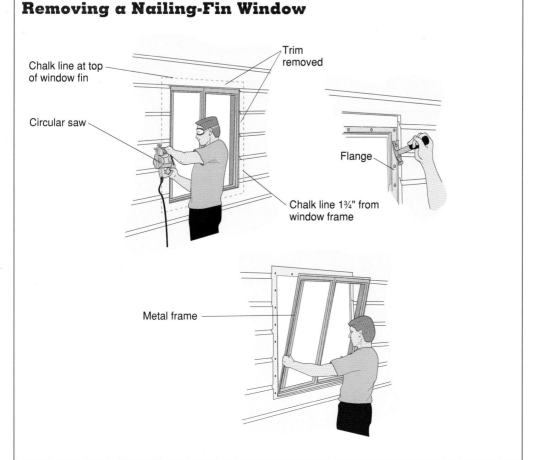

Chalk line at top of window fin

Circular saw

Trim removed

Flange

Chalk line 1¾" from window frame

Metal frame

Tack the other two corners. Shim the unit if further shimming is recommended. Too little shimming may allow parts of the unit to sag; too much can bow the jambs. Either way the window may stick. When you're sure that everything is properly adjusted, drive home all the nails.

Refer to the illustration below to be sure that you have papered and flashed the window properly. After the siding is installed, caulk around the exterior. Remember to insulate the spaces around the window, following the manufacturer's recommendations.

Unlike doors, windows usually come with all of the necessary hardware, including locks. Sometimes the hardware is designed especially for the unit in question, so it may not be easy or advisable to substitute something else. In other cases, the hardware can be replaced with a type of your choosing. It all depends on how the hardware is installed.

## Installing Skylights

This section describes how to install curb-mounted skylights. The installation of roof windows—a type of skylight installed at a near-vertical angle on a steeply pitched roof—varies from manufacturer to manufacturer, and such windows come with instructions that must be followed precisely. Self-flashing skylights, which are difficult to install correctly, should be left to a professional.

### Code Requirements

If you use skylights or roof windows to convert an attic into a usable room, keep in mind that if the room is ever to be used for sleeping, building codes require you to provide a minimum-sized window opening as an emergency exit. It is wise to provide such an exit in any case. As a rule, the exit window must be a minimum of 24 inches high by 20 inches wide, with the sill not more than 44 inches off the floor. Check the local code, however, to see that you have the most up-to-date information. Codes are constantly being revised. It's heartbreaking to be told to remove and replace skylights because they don't satisfy the latest requirements.

Local codes may also specify which types of glazing are permissible in skylights. Laminated safety glass, tempered glass, or some combination of the two is generally required. There may also be restrictions on plastic glazings, though these rarely apply to single-family homes.

Finally, if you want to install a skylight on a part of the roof that is close to a property line, check to see if any restrictions apply. Such regulations are meant to help prevent the rapid spread of fire from house to house.

### Safety Precautions

Start by reviewing the rules of safety. First and foremost, prevent any falls from the roof. Wear shoes with nonskid soles and use safety lines and scaffolding at the eave if necessary. Another unfortunate way to wind up on the ground floor is by falling through the ceiling as you work on the skylight opening or on the light well. Keep your feet on the ceiling joists when you are working in the attic space. You may find it helpful to temporarily place boards or plywood scraps across the ceiling joists to give yourself a place to stand. Finally, cutting roof shingles and decking kicks up a tremendous amount of noxious dust. In addition to safety glasses and ear protection, be sure that

## Installing a Window

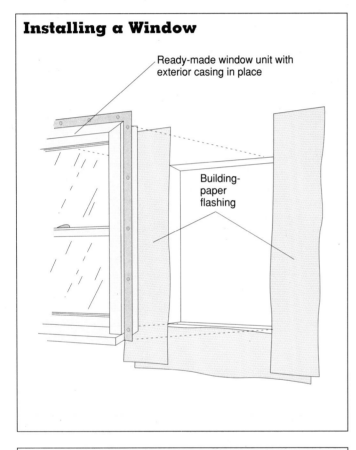

Ready-made window unit with exterior casing in place

Building-paper flashing

## Installing Window Flashing

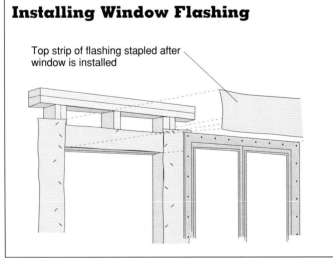

Top strip of flashing stapled after window is installed

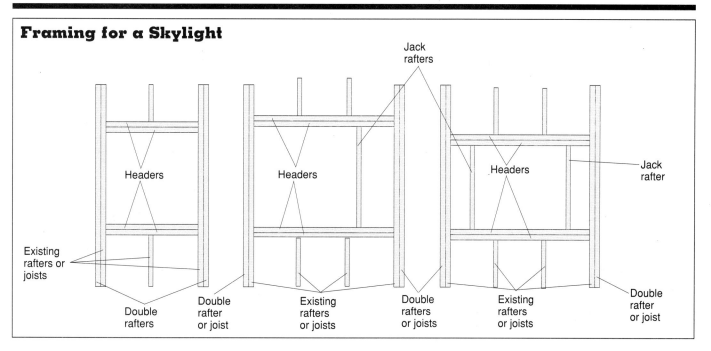

## Framing for a Skylight

Jack rafters

Headers

Headers

Headers

Jack rafter

Existing rafters or joists

Double rafters

Double rafter or joist

Existing rafters or joists

Double rafters or joists

Existing rafters or joists

Double rafter or joist

everyone wears a dust mask. This is essential if a helper is working in the attic while you are cutting from above.

## Constructing the Curb

Start by building a curb on the roof on which the skylight will rest. The flashing pieces will run up this curb, so make sure that the curb is about ¼ inch smaller than the head and base flashings, to allow them to slip easily into place.

The curb is made from 2 by 4 lumber as illustrated on page 32. Measure and cut carefully so that it is ⅜ inch smaller than the interior dimensions of the skylight all around. This allows the skylight to fit over both the curb and its step flashing.

When the curb is nailed together, square it with a framing square. Then tack two lightweight pieces of wood across the diagonal corners to hold its shape.

## Making the Opening

A skylight is normally positioned in the roof so that it and its light well will be centered in the ceiling of the room below. If there is no ceiling, and thus no light well, half of your construction problems are eliminated. If there is a ceiling, decide where you want the center of the light well to be and drive a nail through the ceiling at that point. To find the center of the roof opening, drop a plumb bob from the underside of the roof deck in the attic to the nail in the ceiling. Most skylights are 22 inches wide in order to fit between rafters, so if need be, move the center point a few inches to eliminate unnecessary cutting of rafters or joists. Try to line up one side of the skylight on an existing rafter.

The illustration above shows the different patterns for framing an opening. The simplest way is to use existing rafters rather than building in one or more jack rafters.

Once you have found the center point of the roof deck, mark the inside dimensions of the curb across the rafters and the underside of the roof deck. Do this with a framing square, taking precise measurements. At each corner mark, drive a nail to protrude above the roof.

Now measure down 3 inches below the bottom edge of the curb outline (toward the eaves) and 3 inches above it (toward the ridge). Snap straight chalk lines across the bottoms of the rafters at these marks. The additional 3 inches above and below allows for the double headers that will be installed between the rafters. The intervening rafters will be cut on these lines.

Before you cut, support the rafters by nailing 2 by 4s to them above and below the marks, with the bottoms of the supports resting on ceiling joists and toenailed in place. The opening in the roof can be

cut now, or you can wait until you've finished the interior framing.

When you're ready to cut the opening in the roof, snap chalk lines to connect all the nail points. The inside corners of the curb will be at the points where the nails came through the roof. The outside edge of the curb will be 1½ inches outside the nails. To give yourself a little room to work, snap another chalk line 2 inches outside of the first one. Set the blade of a circular saw to the depth of the roofing shingles and then cut them along this outer line.

Remove the shingles. Snap new lines on the roof deck, using the nail holes as guides. Set the saw blade to ⅛ inch more than the thickness of the roof deck and cut along the lines. You might want to have a friend stationed below to hold onto the cutout piece; remove the decking.

Back in the attic, cut any rafter that crosses the opening

31

you made on the chalk line 3 inches above and below the outline of the curb. Measure the distance at the top and bottom between the two uncut rafters nearest the sides of the opening. Cut four header boards of this length from the same size stock as the rafters. At the top and bottom of the opening, fit a header board between the two existing uncut rafters. Nail through the rafters into the ends of the header with 16d nails. Nail the middle section of the header to the end of the cut rafter. Now nail each second header in place over the first one in the same manner. Install jack rafters as needed. The roof opening is now framed. Remove the braces.

If you planned a light well that is angled or splayed, cut the rafters at the corresponding angle before you install the headers.

## Installing a Curb-Mounted Skylight

Set the curb over the opening; double-check to ensure that it is centered and square; then toenail it from the inside through the roof and deck into the rafters and headers.

Install the roofing and the flashing. Use step flashing on the sides and have collars for the top and bottom custom-made at a local sheet-metal shop. Apply a bead of caulk or some cushioned weather stripping to the top of the curb. Then drop the skylight over the curb and flashing. Nail it to the curb along the upper edge or through the factory-drilled holes. Caulk each nail head.

## Installing a Skylight

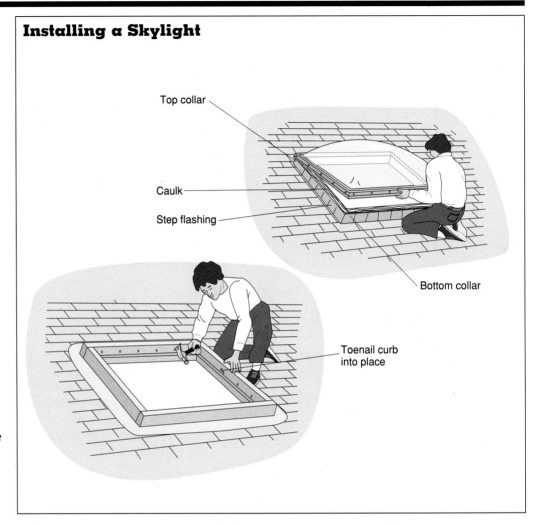

Top collar

Caulk

Step flashing

Bottom collar

Toenail curb into place

## Installation Checklists

Whether you do the installation yourself or have it done, check the following.

### Doors
• Door swings, styles, and hardware should match the specifications and plans.
• Doors should open and close easily.
• Exterior doors should have a suction feel to them if they are weather-stripped, but should not stick.
• The reveal line should be consistent all the way around the top and sides.

• No daylight should be visible at the bottom.

### Windows
• Windows should be level.
• Windows should be weather-stripped and caulked.
• Screens should fit snugly.
• Windows should open and close easily and smoothly; closure should be even and complete.

### Skylights
• No nail heads should be visible to a person looking at

the roof (they should be covered by the roofing material).
• No shingles should be buckled; all should lie flat.
• Headers and trimmers should be installed with the proper number of nails.
• Skylight should be firmly secured.
• Venting or operable skylights should open and close easily.
• Light well should be built to correct measurements.
• Skylight should not leak when sprayed with a hose.

# SIDING AND EXTERIOR TRIM

*Siding and exterior trim are an integral part of any remodeling project. Both decorative and functional, they are readily visible while protecting the building from the elements. Meticulous work and well-chosen materials are essential for positive results.*

## Choosing Siding

Materials for siding are usually selected during the planning phase and specified in the plans. For most room additions it is best to match the existing siding material on the house, but siding on older homes may be difficult to match. Begin your search early so you can make changes, if necessary, before the material is needed.

To match an obsolete or unusual pattern, try suppliers who specialize in recycling building materials, or a lumberyard that does custom milling. Working with new siding that *almost* matches the old is difficult and labor intensive, and you may not be happy with the results.

When removing old siding or trim, consider whether it will serve your patching needs. If possible, plan work that cuts through old siding (such as adding a window) so no patching will be needed, only trim.

If you are unable to duplicate the existing siding, consider the material for the addition carefully. The addition should not look "stuck on," but should harmonize so that it looks like an original part of the house. Newer materials, such as aluminum and vinyl, can match older siding remarkably well if the color is consistent.

There are ways to minimize discrepancies. You can use a similar pattern, paint it to match, and depend on the trim, roof, and window styles to maintain continuity. Or you can plant foliage in front of the seam, where the discrepancy is most obvious. You might also consider re-siding the entire house with the same material as the addition. Or, if

## The Protected Home

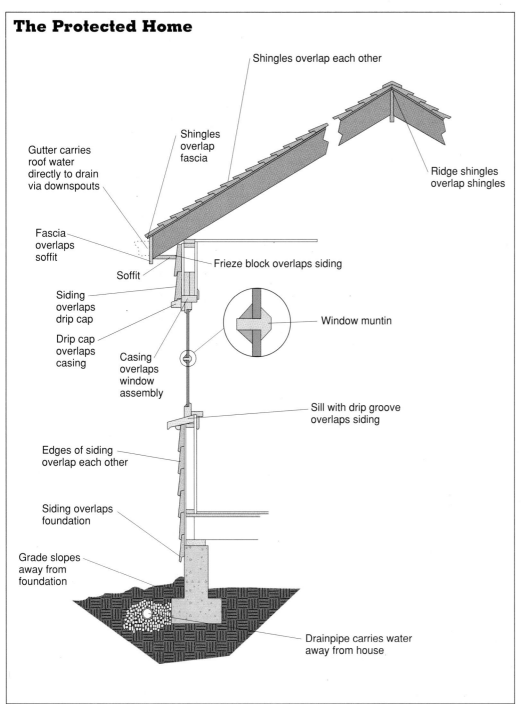

Shingles overlap each other

Shingles overlap fascia

Ridge shingles overlap shingles

Gutter carries roof water directly to drain via downspouts

Fascia overlaps soffit

Soffit

Frieze block overlaps siding

Siding overlaps drip cap

Window muntin

Drip cap overlaps casing

Casing overlaps window assembly

Sill with drip groove overlaps siding

Edges of siding overlap each other

Siding overlaps foundation

Grade slopes away from foundation

Drainpipe carries water away from house

## Sheathing and Siding

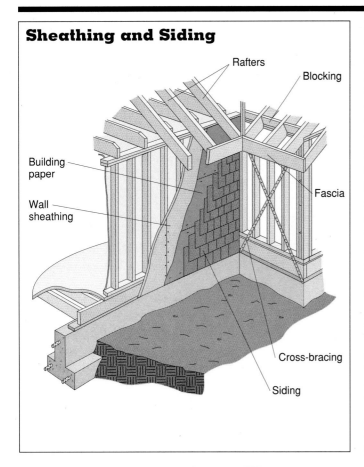

Rafters
Blocking
Building paper
Wall sheathing
Fascia
Cross-bracing
Siding

the proportions of the addition allow it, you could choose a siding that is completely different from the house to effect a complementary contrast. Siding for the top half could be plywood or similar plain material. In some cases, such as a garage conversion, you can remove the old siding from both areas flanking the garage door and redo the entire wall with new siding that doesn't match exactly, especially if there is corner trim. Such mixing of materials can be effective, but it demands skillful and sensitive treatment.

## Installing Siding

Siding for a room addition is applied in the same way as for any new construction, except that care must be taken in joining it to the old siding. If the walls intersect at a corner, most new siding is simply butted up against the old. Careful application of building paper, caulking behind the seam, and tight installation of trim boards prevent leaks.

### Stucco

If the existing siding is stucco, a strip of old stucco must be broken out where the new joins the old. Depending on local code specifications, leave 3 to 6 inches of lath (wire mesh) exposed so that the new

lath can be bent around the corner to lap over the old. Although stucco work will probably be done by professionals, you can cut costs by doing the demolition yourself, under the installer's supervision. Be sure to expose 3 to 6 inches of wire at every seam. To avoid cracks in the rest of the stucco, start with a series of hammer blows along the cut line before you try to break up and remove any stucco. Practice first in an inconspicuous place.

### Wood Shingles

If siding for an addition is wood shingles to match the existing walls, the addition will present a stark contrast to the weathered house shingles. This is only temporary, however, unless the old shingles have been stained or painted. Simply leave the new shingles alone; in a year or two they will weather enough to match the old. If you want the addition to match the house immediately, apply paint or stain to both the new and the old shingles, following the manufacturer's recommendations. Some paints cause shingles to deteriorate by locking in moisture.

The new shingles should be the same size as the old. The most common lengths are 16, 18, and 24 inches. If you are unsure what size is on your house and you cannot measure a full shingle, you can gauge their size by adding ½ inch to the exposure and doubling this number. For example, a 7½-inch exposure would indicate a 16-inch shingle. Use the same shingle exposure for the new walls.

Start the first course at the same level as one of the existing courses. If the house has settled slightly or the original shingles were not applied perfectly level, the first course may not align with the house shingles after wrapping around the addition. In that case, adjust the layout on the least conspicuous wall to match the house shingles.

There are two ways to join new shingles to a house: interweaving the new and old shingles, or butting the new shingles to vertical trim boards. Using a trim board is easier, and works best if the house already has them at the corners. Even if it doesn't, using one at an interior corner will not be conspicuous so long as it is no larger than 2 by 2.

### Wood Siding

Horizontal wood siding—such as shiplap, V-rustic, channel rustic, teardrop, or other patterns—should match the old siding as closely as possible, even if it means having it custom-milled. You may be able to cut costs by using cheaper lumber, such as hemlock or pine instead of redwood or cedar, for the new siding as long as the new siding is carefully painted and well maintained. However, using cheaper siding on north-facing walls or other shady locations is not advisable.

If the original siding is clapboard or shiplap, the boards will have a slanted look because the bottom edge of each course overlaps the top edge of the course below. As a result, the boards do not fully contact the sheathing or studs behind them, making them more prone to crack and splinter. To duplicate this look but with greater durability, choose lap siding that has a rabbeted edge along the bottom. This beveled edge produces a slanted look on the face but allows full contact against the sheathing or studs on the back of each board.

Horizontal wood siding is easy to join to old siding at corners but difficult where a new wall joins an old wall in the same plane. Simply butting the new boards to the old produces an unsightly and potentially leaky seam. Solutions are to interweave the new boards with the old, cover the seam with batten, or hide it with tall plants.

Vertical wood siding is easy to join to the old. To ensure a weathertight seam, remove enough old boards to lap the new paper underlayment about 4 inches over the existing paper. Then replace the old boards and continue installing new boards in the same way. If the vertical siding is tongue-and-groove it can be blind-nailed. Otherwise the boards must be facenailed. Follow the same pattern as the original siding, making sure that horizontal furring strips are nailed across the studs at the nailing line if the addition does not have solid sheathing to nail into.

## Plywood Siding

Existing plywood siding should be easy to match because patterns and thicknesses are fairly standard. You may be able to cut costs

by using a different type of veneer if you plan to paint the siding. If you are staining it, however, use the same species of veneer as on the old. Otherwise it will be difficult to match the stain color.

Where the new panels join the house you can cover the seam with a batten or use trim boards at a corner. Most corners are trimmed with two overlapping 1 by 4s, but the joint will appear more symmetrical if you use a 1 by 3 on one side and overlap it with a 1 by 4 on the other. Inside corners can be done in the same way, or with a single piece of trim such as a 2 by 2 or some cove molding.

## Installing Exterior Trim

Most commonly installed around doors, windows, corners, and roof overhangs, exterior trim may be fashioned from dimension lumber or exterior moldings, which are usually of redwood or other durable species. Don't use finger-jointed moldings outdoors.

Installing trim is fairly straightforward—usually a matter of precise measuring and fitting. However, you must take some extra precautions to ensure a successful, weathertight seal:

• Prime the back sides of all trim pieces.

• When joining pieces of trim end to end—especially vertical members such as battens or corner boards—cut ends on a bevel instead of square. Install so that the face of the upper board slightly overlaps the lower board. That

## Siding Checklists

If you have siding done by professionals, include the following points in the specifications for the job, and check them after the job is done.

Note that hardboard or plywood siding requires nails to be snug to the surface but *not* flush or countersunk.

### Masonry and Stucco
• Mortar joints should be tooled in concave or agreed fashion.

• Walls should be cleaned of mortar stains.

• All window and door openings should have flashing installed in mortar joints.

• Expansion joints should be as indicated in plans (or other agreement).

• Walls should be plumb within ⅛ inch.

• Stucco should be free of large cracks.

• Stucco finish should be consistent. Surfaces should be

smooth. You can sight down a wall from the corner.

### Wood or Vinyl Siding
• All nails should be HDG, aluminum, or stainless steel.

• Nails should be flush or countersunk.

• Joints should be staggered between courses.

• Courses should be parallel and even.

• All openings should be caulked and flashed.

• Any joints in courses should be beveled at a 45-degree angle, so a crack will not open if the siding shrinks slightly.

• Trim should be paint grade or stain grade as specified.

• Siding should be of the quality specified.

• All soffits should be vented (and screened, unless vented from the attic).

way when the boards shrink, the joint will not open up and reveal a gap.

• When covering a horizontal seam of plywood or other material with trim, make sure the seam has a tightly sealed rabbet joint or proper flashing; otherwise the trim will trap water in the seam, making a bad joint worse.

• Apply a bead of caulk to the back before installing each board, and set all nail heads.

• When installing a soffit beneath a roof overhang, make sure each space you are enclosing has ventilation from the attic, or else install soffit vents.

• When trimming windows that do not have integral flashing, such as a nailing flange, install metal flashing or a drip cap over the head casing. The flashing should be tucked under the siding and should overlap the casing. Z-flashing like this is also used to waterproof horizontal joints in plywood siding and places where horizontal members such as deck ledgers are nailed to the side of a building.

# HEATING

*Unlike electrical and plumbing systems, which are essentially the same everywhere, heating systems vary widely in the type of energy they use and the means of distributing it. One of four types of central heating systems is most commonly in use, with solar alternatives and hybrid systems becoming more prevalent.*

## Warm Air

This is the most common central heating system. The ducts can also be used for central air-conditioning. The heat producer is a furnace that burns oil, gas, wood, or coal inside a combustion chamber. Waste gases are vented outside through a metal flue and masonry chimney. When the air surrounding the combustion chamber gets hot, it is distributed through the house via a network of ducts. In a slab foundation the duct work is generally embedded in the concrete. With a crawl space or a full basement, sheet-metal ducts run underneath and between the floor joists. In a two-story house the second-level ducts run up the walls, hidden between studs or inside closets.

The furnace is turned on and off automatically by a thermostat, but the heat supply to each room can also be controlled manually. Dampers inside the ducts and at each register open and close to regulate the incoming warm air.

## Hot Water

In a hot-water (also called hydronic) system, the furnace is a boiler fueled by oil, gas, electricity, or coal. The boiler heats water to about 194° F (90° C), and small pipes (½ to 1 inch) made of galvanized steel or copper distribute the hot water to each room of the house.

If steam and cast-iron radiators are used, the system works with gravity. Pressure from the boiler and lighter density cause the steam to rise naturally in the pipes. Once it circulates through the radiator and condenses, the now-cooled water returns via the same pipe to the boiler, where the cycle begins again.

In a modern hot-water system, water is forced through the pipes by a circulating pump. Like a plumbing system, the hydronic network has a main supply line that branches from the boiler into two or more supply runs, or zones. After serving each room, the cooled water is cycled back into the boiler via a return line. Separate temper-

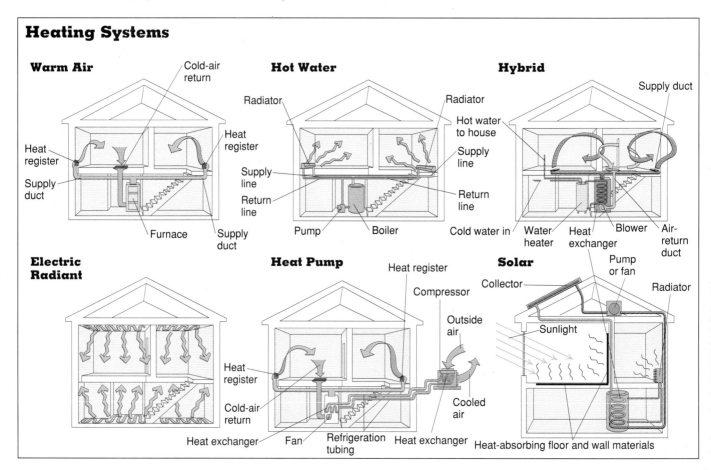

**Heating Systems**

Warm Air — Cold-air return, Heat register, Heat register, Supply duct, Furnace, Supply duct

Hot Water — Radiator, Radiator, Supply line, Return line, Pump, Boiler

Hybrid — Supply duct, Hot water to house, Supply line, Return line, Cold water in, Water heater, Heat exchanger, Blower, Air-return duct, Pump or fan

Electric Radiant

Heat Pump — Heat register, Compressor, Outside air, Cooled air, Heat register, Cold-air return, Heat exchanger, Fan, Refrigeration tubing, Heat exchanger

Solar — Collector, Radiator, Sunlight, Heat-absorbing floor and wall materials

## Central Heating Systems

| System | Heat Source | How Distributed | Comments |
|---|---|---|---|
| Warm Air | Gas, oil, coal, wood | Ducts, vents, and registers | Relatively economical; easy to add air-conditioning, humidifiers, air cleaners; drafty and noisy |
| Hot Water | Gas, oil, coal, electricity | Pipes, radiators, baseboard heaters | Even heat supply; efficient energy conversion; slow to heat up |
| Electric Radiant | Electricity | Wires in walls and floors; radiant panels | Comfortable; efficient energy conversion; expensive to operate |
| Heat Pump | Electricity, atmosphere, or earth | Ducts, vents | Works best in mild climate; needs electric backup system |
| Solar | Sunlight | Ducts, convective air currents | Adds new living space; free heat; must be carefully engineered; requires major construction; needs backup system |

ature controls are provided in different parts of the house.

The heat is distributed by baseboard heaters, which fit unobtrusively along the floor, most often along the outside wall of the house. Generally they are only 8 to 10 inches high and 2 to 3 inches deep.

## Electric Radiant

Homes equipped with electric radiant heat have no furnace, ducts, flue, or chimney. The source of heat is electricity flowing through resistance wiring in wallboard or beneath the plaster.

In regions with a mild climate, the wiring is often located in the floor, embedded in a concrete slab. If the wiring is not in the floor or ceiling, baseboard panels are mounted along the floor. Some electric baseboards use only resistance wiring to heat a room. Others use electricity to heat water permanently sealed in copper tubing. Each heater is a self-contained hydronic system that needs no plumbing or separate water supply. Air drawn from the floor passes over the fins of the tubing and circulates upward to warm the room. The hot water continues to provide heat even after the electricity is turned off by a thermostat.

## Heat Pump

The heat pump is a combination heating and cooling system that operates like a central air conditioner, with a reverse cycle for heating. Electricity is the energy source. In the summer the system withdraws heat from inside the house and dispels it outdoors. In the winter it extracts heat from the outside air or ground and pumps it inside. The air is distributed through the house via sheet-metal ducts just like a warm-air system. If the temperature drops below a certain level, auxiliary electric resistance heaters kick in to provide supplementary heat.

## Solar

The best solar designs tap direct sunlight. The means of collecting it can be as simple as increasing the number of south-facing windows or attaching a hot-air collector to a south wall. Or it can be as complex as a complete re-design of the home to incorporate additional south glazing, heat-absorbing mass, and a floor plan that creates an optimum flow of natural air currents. Solar heating designs require a home with continuous exposure to the sun during cold months for at least the four hours between 10 a.m. and 2 p.m.

## Heating Checklist

If you have subbed out the mechanical work, the ducts, pipes, or other elements of the heating system should be installed and inspected before walls or floors are closed up. This is the last chance to easily and cheaply make any changes in location of registers. Think about furnishings and traffic patterns, and make sure the register won't be located under or behind a large piece of furniture or where foot traffic could damage the register.

Check the system for the following points.

- Flexible ducts that have fiberglass insulation and a plastic wrapper should be well supported, and should have no kinks.
- The connections should have sheet-metal screws (three per joint) and be covered with duct tape, then insulation. The plastic seams should also be taped.
- Insulation and plastic must be added to Y branches and uninsulated parts of the ducts.
- Ends of ducts should be sealed to keep out construction debris.

# ROUGH PLUMBING

*The system of pipes and vents that delivers fresh water and drains waste from the plumbing fixtures constitutes the rough plumbing. It consists of two basic systems: a water supply network and a drain-waste-vent (DWV) system. The supply lines provide water under pressure; the DWV pipes carry away water and wastes by gravity, and gases by convection.*

## Water Supply Lines

A main or service line supplies the house with cold, fresh water. The main normally comes through a basement wall or lower-level utility area. If the house is connected to a municipal water system, the water enters under pressure and travels through a meter. In private supply systems, water is pumped from a well or cistern into a holding tank. Air pressure in the tank creates sufficient water pressure for household use.

Once inside the house the main water line splits into smaller branch lines. One of these goes directly to the water heater. From there hot-water branch lines travel to fixtures that demand hot water, such as the kitchen sink and the bathroom washbasin, tub, and shower.

Cold-water supply lines also split from the main into different branches. One branch, for example, may supply water to the kitchen sink, another may supply water to an upstairs bathroom, and a third may supply an outdoor sprinkler system.

Shutoff valves, an essential part of the water supply system, are quite helpful when remodeling. A main shutoff valve, located where the main line enters the house, turns off the water to the entire house. Each branch run should also have a shutoff valve, as should the inlet line to the water heater. Fixture supply valves beneath washbasins and toilets allow you to turn off the water to a particular fixture whenever necessary.

## The DWV System

The drain-waste-vent system depends on gravity to carry away waste, which means the direction and pitch of the pipes are critical. A drainpipe must slope downward ¼ inch for every foot of horizontal run—otherwise water would stand in the pipes and sludge would build up.

Each fixture or drain in the house must have a trap beneath it, a U-shaped dip in the line that remains filled with water. The trap seals off the waste line and prevents noxious fumes as well as vermin from entering the house.

Cleanout fittings allow access to each drain in case of plugging. Drain lines from each trap carry the waste to a vertical pipe called a soil stack.

The stack connects to the main house drain, which empties into a private septic tank or municipal sewage system.

Vent pipes are an integral part of the DWV system. These pipes rise vertically from the drain lines and connect to one or more vent stacks that exit through the roof of the house. The vents bring fresh air into the waste system and carry away dangerous or unpleasant gases that accumulate.

Both the supply and DWV lines run within the walls and floors of the house. Holes are simply drilled through studs, joists, and plates wherever pipe runs are needed. Code limitations on the size of notches and holes prevent the structural strength of the framework from being weakened. In some instances cuts in the studs and joists must be reinforced with metal plates to protect the integrity of the framing. Where there is a risk that nails will penetrate the pipes, nail guards (small metal plates) are installed on the framing members.

## Gas Lines

Many remodeling projects involve altering gas lines. Although some homeowners, with proper permits, are able to do this work themselves, you will probably need professional help. Among other considerations, gas lines must be sized carefully to ensure a steady flow of gas under pressure to the farthest fixtures. Also, only certain kinds of pipe, fittings, and joint compounds are allowed for use with gas lines.

## Septic Systems

For some remodelers, adding a bathroom or building a room addition may mean enlarging a septic system or even relocating one. This will involve installing a septic tank of the correct size, providing a vent (if needed), and laying an adequate array of leach lines. You should be familiar with the type and age of your system.

## Cross-Connections

A plumbing hazard associated with remodeling often occurs with the reuse of old fixtures, as well as decorative pools, spas, and sprinkler systems. These can cause drinking water to become polluted because of cross-connections.

A cross-connection is a plumbing configuration that connects the potable water supply system to a source of contaminated water. No one would knowingly make such a connection, but it is often done accidentally. The most common cross-connections are made with a hose. If a hose without an air gap is left in a puddle, fish pond, or sink with standing water, it forms a cross-connection. If the pressure in the water supply lines drops below atmospheric pressure (from flushing a toilet, for example), the standing water could be sucked into the supply line if the seal on the hose bibb isn't perfect.

To prevent cross-connections, building codes require that air gaps be installed or created. These may consist of back-flow prevention devices or overflow pipes that prevent cross-connections.

# **R**OUGH WIRING

*The part of the house electrical system that carries electricity from the service entrance to the various locations of fixtures, receptacles, switches, and appliances is the rough wiring. Changes brought about by a remodeling project can range from extending a circuit to replacing the entire system.*

## Sizing Up the System

Before modifying the electrical system, determine first whether the existing system can handle the changes.

Start by looking at the service head (where the wires enter the house). If the house was built before 1940 (or in some cases later) and the wiring system has not been modernized, you will see only two wires leading from an outdoor power pole to the meter box. Each of the two wires carries 120 volts. One is a "hot" wire, which means it is carrying ungrounded electricity. Hot wires are dangerous. The other is a "neutral" wire that completes the electrical circuit. Although technically neutral because it is grounded, a neutral wire still carries current and must be handled carefully.

If you operate many modern appliances with high amperage demands, a two-wire system is probably inadequate for your needs. In modern homes, three wires lead from the pole to the meter, supplying both 120 and 240 volts. Two of the three wires entering the house are hot, and the third is neutral. The two incoming 120-volt wires are combined at one point in the service entrance, or service panel, to produce 240 volts for such major appliances as a range or clothes dryer.

There are two basic types of service panels: one has a circuit breaker and one has fuses. The panel should have room for enough circuits to accommodate the requirements of the household. If not, you'll need a new, higher-capacity service panel.

Wiring in older houses is of the knob-and-tube type (named for the porcelain insulators and wire supports it uses). Sometimes this type of wiring was not grounded. If this is the case, it should all be replaced. Knob and tube circuits should not be extended. If your house has aluminum wiring, the entire system may need to be replaced. Consult an electrician.

## Modernizing the Electrical System

House electrical systems have improved over the years, both for greater safety and to handle the increasing number of modern appliances now in use. Whenever a remodeling job includes wiring, there are several design changes that should (or in some cases must) be incorporated.

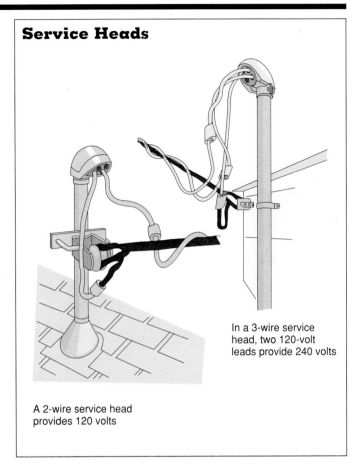

### Service Heads

In a 3-wire service head, two 120-volt leads provide 240 volts

A 2-wire service head provides 120 volts

## Upgrading Fuses

Some building codes require that all old-style fuses be changed to new Type S fuses when remodeling. This is an excellent precaution in any case. Type S or fusestat fuses are designed to prevent the use of fuses with amp ratings higher than the circuit will safely bear. The top of the fuse looks similar to the standard plug type, but the base of the Type S fuse won't fit a standard fuse socket. Instead, the Type S fuse screws into an adapter, which in turn screws into the standard socket. A short piece of steel protruding from the base piece acts like a barb and prevents the base from being extracted after it is screwed in. Type S fuses and bases come in different sizes for each amperage rating and are not interchangeable, so once you install a given base, only the matching Type S fuse will fit into it.

The only trick is selecting the proper size Type S base for the gauge of wire in the circuit. If the wire connected to the existing fuse socket is 14 gauge, the fuse base should be rated at 15 amps. If the wire is 12 gauge, the fuse base can be rated for 20 amps. If you are uncertain, consult a professional to determine what gauge wire you have in each circuit.

## Changing From Fuses to Circuit Breakers

Converting old subpanels from fuses to circuit breakers is a common change when remodeling. The circuit breakers must be sized by their amperage rating to the correct wire gauge. If you are uncertain, check with a licensed electrician. Overloading wires is one of the most frequent causes of electrical fires.

## Maintaining Correct Polarity

Avoid reversing the wires on old electrical systems that had fuses on both hot and neutral wires. When circuit breakers are installed, the polarity of plugs might be reversed, or in the worst case a short circuit could be wired into the system and would have to be fixed.

Before dismantling an old system, label each set of wires. Use white paint, tape, correction fluid, or other easily recognizable marker to identify all neutral wires. In newer systems the insulation is color-coded, but it still pays to test the wires to ensure that they are properly identified. After all, the last person to work on the system may not have had a permit and perhaps didn't know or care about proper color coding. Electric current will flow in copper and isn't influenced at all by the color of the insulation. Don't make assumptions. Test everything.

## Rough-Wiring Checklist

These specific points should be checked, either before final payment if you hire a professional, or before the wiring inspection if you do the electrical work yourself.

• Test all circuits. The ground wire should be continuous back to the subpanel or main panel. Neutral (white) wires also should be continuous, but not connected to the ground wire except at the main service entrance. Hot wires should be provided at each receptacle, but not show any continuity with the neutral and ground wires unless temporarily joined to test the circuit.

• Look at cable where it runs through open framing, particularly at the corners. If the wire is less than 1¼ inches from the face of the wood frame, it must be protected with nail guards.

• Cable must be stapled within 6 inches of any plastic box without a clamp, or within 12 inches of a metal box (all metal boxes should have clamps to hold the wires).

• There should be no loops of cable in the open framing.

The wire should be pulled snug, but not stretched. When wiring is within closed walls, stapling and loops of wire are not so consequential.

• The face of each box should protrude far enough from the framing to be flush with the finish wall surface. Use a plywood template of the proper thickness to test them quickly. Make adjustments as needed.

• Receptacles on any walls that will be covered with wallboard by professionals should have their positions marked on the floor, so if one is accidentally covered by the wallboard you can easily locate it without cutting unnecessary holes.

• Acquaint yourself with the code requirements regarding the number of conductors allowed in each size of box. Check the most crowded boxes to ensure there are not too many conductors.

• Consider whether you may need more circuits in the future and whether it is easier to run them now and leave them stubbed off in an easily accessible box.

• There should be a switch controlling a light or receptacle by each entrance to every room. The switch can't be covered by the door swing.

• If the cable sheathing is scraped through so the conductors are visible, the entire piece of cable must be replaced.

• If you plan to do the finish wiring, do you understand how the electrician left the wires for three-way switches, switch loops, and receptacles? Do all of the outlets have pigtails at least 6 inches long?

• Compare the completed job with the plans and make sure every switch, appliance circuit, receptacle, and light is in place.

• Make sure the wires are folded into the boxes so that no one will be poked. Conductors shouldn't be stripped until after wallboard is taped and textured and any painting is done, so they won't need to be cleaned.

• All new circuits should be labeled.

• The wiring for smoke detectors should be in place.

## Ground Fault Circuit Interrupters

The National Electrical Code® (NEC) now requires that all receptacles located in the kitchen, bathroom, garage, outdoors, or anywhere near water be protected by a ground fault circuit interrupter (GFCI) device. Local electrical codes may require these devices in additional locations as well.

A GFCI protects people from electrical shock. It monitors its corresponding circuit for any voltage leaks and shuts off the outlet or circuit that it is protecting. You can reset the device with a push of a button. There are three ways to protect electrical receptacles: with a portable GFCI device that plugs into an ordinary outlet, with a built-in outlet, and with a circuit breaker that protects the entire circuit.

## Installing Wiring

Rough wiring should be done after the framing is installed. If local code requires that wiring be installed by a professional, this is the time. If you plan to do the wiring yourself, study the local code and a how-to book. Wiring is not terribly difficult, but it must be done correctly to prevent fires and potential injury.

# INSULATION

*New insulation is required for room additions. It should not be installed, however, until after the framing and the rough wiring have been inspected. The plans will specify required R-values and type, usually fiberglass batts or blankets. In attics with insufficient crawl space or with obstructions such as wiring, loose-fill insulation can be blown in.*

## Installing Insulation

Install insulation according to the manufacturer's recommendations. Always wear a dust mask, hat, goggles, and gloves for protection against irritating and potentially harmful fibers. Cut blanket insulation with a utility knife, changing the blade often. Compress thick insulation with a board to make cutting easier.

Make sure insulation fills the entire stud or joist bay, even tiny nooks and crannies. Cut it to fit around electrical boxes, blocking, and other obstructions. Split blankets to fit around both sides of wires rather than compressing the insulation to fit behind them.

Staple the flanges to edges or faces of studs, depending on the manufacturer's recommendation and whether wallboard will be glued to the stud faces. Most insulation includes a vapor barrier, which must face the heated space. If a separate vapor barrier is specified in the plans, stretch 4 mil plastic sheeting over the completed insulation. Staple it to studs and joists. Cut around all electrical fixtures and doors, but wait until plasterwork is completed or wallboard is installed before cutting out windows.

## Supervising a Contractor

If you are contracting the insulation work, make certain the contractor knows the quality you expect. Contractor crews work very quickly, and not all are hired for their skill or attention to detail. Compacted insulation, torn vapor barriers, or many small gaps in the vapor barriers are common. Vapor barriers are critical in climates with cold winters, and poorly installed insulation will not deliver the expected energy savings and may contribute to condensation inside the wall cavity. In general, if the walls to be insulated are open, a contractor can do the job for close to what you would pay for the materials. At that rate, you can hire the contractor and

spend your time improving the installation by stapling small gaps, taping rips, making sure the insulation fits snugly around receptacles, and putting up plastic sheeting for a vapor barrier.

If the remodeling project is a large one, pay attention to the air turnover rate. If you insulate and weather-strip your home and lower the air turnover rates below .5 times per hour, you may need a fresh-air heat exchanger to artificially ventilate the house without losing too much heat.

## Installing a Vapor Barrier

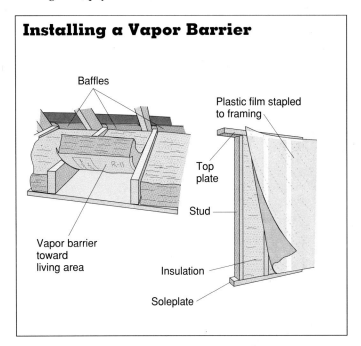

Baffles

Plastic film stapled to framing

Top plate

Stud

Vapor barrier toward living area

Insulation

Soleplate

R-11

## Insulation/Weather Stripping Checklist

• No eave vents may be covered by insulation.

• There must be at least a 3-inch gap between insulation and electrical boxes for lights.

• All open walls must be insulated, including small spaces in the framing around doors, windows, and corners.

• The joint between bottom plate and subfloor should be caulked completely on exterior walls.

• The vapor barrier must always be installed toward the heated side of the wall, floor, or ceiling (facing the living space).

• Duct work and plumbing in the crawl space and attic should be insulated.

• Insulation should be installed tightly between framing members with no gaps or punctures.

• Siding and exterior trim should be caulked.

• All pipe penetrations except heat vents with minimum clearances should be sealed with foam or an appropriate caulk.

# FINISH CARPENTRY

*Your remodeling project begins a dramatic transformation as you start installing the finish surfaces. You have passed the point of maximum chaos, and from now on exciting visual changes occur. From this point the tasks involved in a remodeling project are within the abilities of most homeowners. This chapter tells how to install interior walls, interior trim, and cabinets and countertops.*

*Built-in bookshelves and a window-seat bumpout convert this spare bedroom into a den. Subtle crown molding adds an ornate touch to the simplicity of the room.*

# INTERIOR WALL SURFACES

*This section describes the different types of wallboard and paneling and tells how to install them. Techniques for repairing plaster walls are also included.*

## Wallboard

Wallboard, usually referred to as drywall or by the trade name Sheetrock, is the most common finish wall surface. Almost every remodeling project includes it. The material is inexpensive and easy to install. It covers areas quickly and is forgiving of mistakes. Wallboard is dimensionally stable (it doesn't change size with temperature fluctuations) and is easy to cut without power tools. It can be used as a fireproofing material on interior and exterior walls. Multiple layers provide thermal mass (that is, they absorb heat that is gradually released). Wallboard hung on metal channels dramatically cuts sound transmission between floors, and multiple layers on walls reduce sound transmission between adjacent rooms. Wallboard provides an excellent base for textures, paint, wallpaper, paneling, or tile. It can be used to re-surface old, battered plaster walls and ceilings.

So why do many carpenters groan at the mention of wallboard? It is heavy, messy, and generally requires hand tools for cutting and installation. Also, many carpenters have never learned to install wallboard properly.

## Types of Wallboard

Wallboard is manufactured of gypsum with a layer of paper on both sides. The outside layer is smoother than the inside layer and wraps over the long edges of the panel. Most wallboard is tapered on the long edges to create a depression. This is filled with paper tape and joint compound to hide the seams. When the depression is filled correctly, a smooth surface is the result.

There are five main types of wallboard.

• Regular is used for ceilings and walls where a special fire rating is not required.

• Foil-backed is the same as regular, but with a foil face suitable as a vapor barrier.

• Type W (water-resistant) is also known as MR, WR, greenrock, and blueboard. This type has blue or green paper on the finish side. It is used for bathrooms and other moist areas and as a base for ceramic tiles secured with mastic. It can't be used on horizontal surfaces or on angles greater than 45 degrees from the vertical.

• Type X wallboard has additives to increase fire resistance and is used where building codes specify fire-rated walls with one hour (or more) fire resistance.

• Vinyl-surfaced wallboard is attached with specially made nails and left exposed, without joint treatment.

There are three main types of edging.

• Tapered edging creates a depression so that tape can be bedded, providing a flat surface. It is by far the most common type; it may be the only type available without special-ordering.

• Square edging provides an aesthetically acceptable exposed edge.

• Beveled edging is exposed, like square-edged wallboard. The beveled edge looks like paneling.

## Thicknesses and Sizes

Wallboard comes in various sizes and thicknesses. The standard size available from home-improvement centers is 4 feet by 8 feet. Professional installers use sheets as long as 16 feet, installed horizontally rather than vertically. This reduces the number of joints

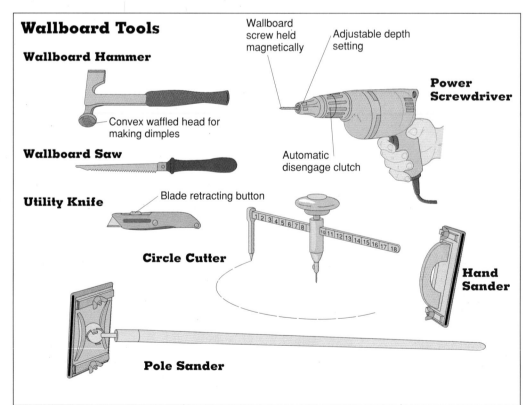

**Wallboard Tools**

**Wallboard Hammer**
— Convex waffled head for making dimples

**Wallboard Saw**

**Utility Knife**
Blade retracting button

**Circle Cutter**

**Pole Sander**

Wallboard screw held magnetically

Adjustable depth setting

**Power Screwdriver**

Automatic disengage clutch

**Hand Sander**

that must be taped. The weight of large sheets can be a problem, however, especially on ceilings. Professionals use wallboard jacks to lift the sheets into position. These jacks can be rented.

Thin wallboard (¼ inch or ⅜ inch) is used to cover old plaster that is sound, but which is cracked or has an undesirable texture. It is also used for curved surfaces and can be applied in several layers. The most common thickness, ½ inch, is used on walls and ceilings that have studs or joists spaced at 16 inches on center.

For certain applications, ⅝-inch wallboard is used. These include framing spaced at 24 inches on center; fire walls (for example, in stairwells and in common walls between a house and garage); where exceptionally smooth walls are required; and where decreased sound transmission is desired. Wallboard is manufactured in thicknesses greater than ⅝ inch, but these are designed for commercial uses, such as in elevator shafts.

## Fasteners

Wallboard is fastened with screws, nails, adhesive, and clips to wood or metal studs and occasionally to a gypsum base. Adhesive reduces the number of fasteners required, but check the local building code to find out whether an inspection is required when you use adhesive.

### Screws

Wallboard screws are the best way to attach wallboard to any base. These Phillips-head drive screws are far superior

in holding power to nails. They are used for many purposes besides installing wallboard and come in a variety of sizes and types. Wallboard screws are recommended for ceilings and are required with metal channel.

Type W screws are used for wood. They should penetrate ⅝ inch into the wood when used with a single layer of wallboard. For a second layer of wallboard, ½ inch is sufficient. Type W screws come in black, hot-dipped galvanized (HDG), and anodized finishes, and lengths up to 6 inches. The black-finished screws are hardened and brittle and shouldn't be used where shear strength is essential (in building scaffolding, for example).

Type S screws are designed for use with metal studs. They are very sharp in order to penetrate without giving the stud a chance to deflect. They need penetrate the metal stud only ⅜ inch.

Type G screws are used to fasten wallboard to gypsum backing, such as double layers of wallboard.

The best way to install wallboard screws is with a screw gun, which can be rented. Screw guns hold the screws with a magnetic tip. They also have a clutch that does not engage to spin the screw until pressure is applied. An adjustable stop sets the screw, pulling the paper under the screw head and the screw below the surface without tearing the paper. Using a screw gun resembles pushing the screw into the stud or joist. Because the gun will not turn the screw unless you apply pressure, you don't

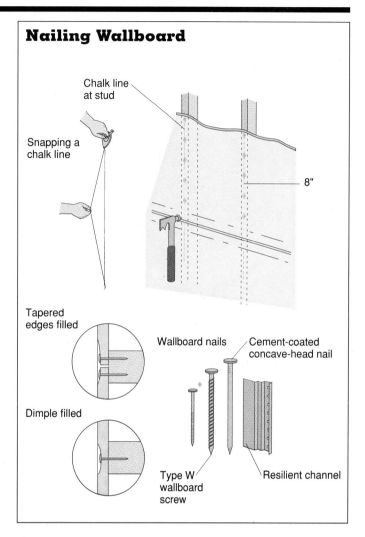

### Nailing Wallboard

Chalk line at stud

Snapping a chalk line

8"

Tapered edges filled

Dimple filled

Wallboard nails

Cement-coated concave-head nail

Type W wallboard screw

Resilient channel

have to adjust its speed. If you can, watch an expert use this tool. It is easy to use properly once you understand how.

You can also install wallboard screws with a cordless screwdriver or an adjustable-speed drill. A magnetic bit holder will make the task easier. Once the bit wears and does not stay in the slot, replace it.

### Nails

Wallboard nails are inexpensive and widely available. They should be HDG; those with ring-shank shafts are less likely to break through the compound that covers them and create nail-pops. Nailing

patterns vary, depending on whether the wallboard is applied on ceilings or walls and on the spacing of the studs or joists. Wallboard nails should penetrate through the wallboard ¾ inch into the underlying wood if they are ring-shank, or 1 inch if they are smooth-shank. Longer nails are not significantly stronger and are more likely to bend during nailing.

Nails should be installed with a wallboard hammer. A standard hammer can be used, but it is much more likely to bend the nail, damage the

## Gluing Wallboard

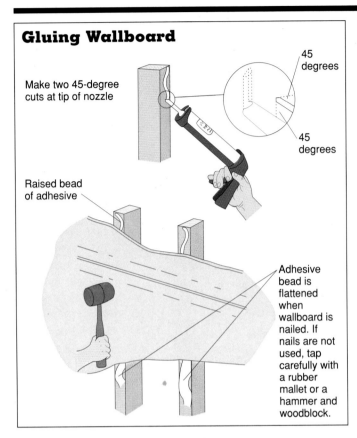

Make two 45-degree cuts at tip of nozzle

45 degrees

45 degrees

Raised bead of adhesive

Adhesive bead is flattened when wallboard is nailed. If nails are not used, tap carefully with a rubber mallet or a hammer and woodblock.

## Wallboard Corner Details

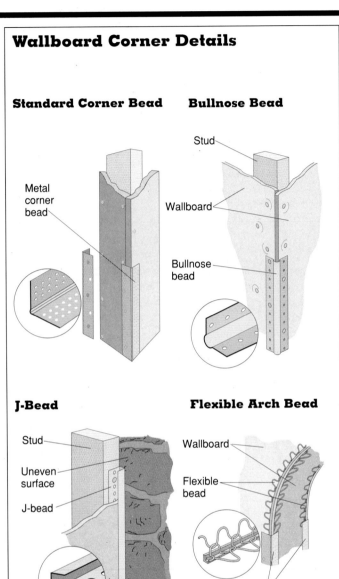

### Standard Corner Bead

Metal corner bead

### Bullnose Bead

Stud

Wallboard

Bullnose bead

### J-Bead

Stud

Uneven surface

J-bead

Wallboard

### Flexible Arch Bead

Wallboard

Flexible bead

Corner bead

---

paper surface of the wallboard, or pulverize the gypsum beneath the paper, decreasing the holding power of the nail. The wallboard hammer is designed so that it is easy to strike the nail properly without striking your knuckles. The curved face of the hammer creates a rounded dimple that normally does not tear the paper. The hammer face also spreads the force of the impact over a wider area, minimizing the tendency of the gypsum to crumble.

### Adhesives

Adhesives are most useful when wallboard extends over a few inches of concrete, and screws or nails can't be used. They are also practical for multiple layers of wallboard, and can help to produce a flat surface on uneven framing.

### Clips

Corner clips are accepted by some building codes. These allow you to skip the corner framing member, which is not structurally necessary and which serves only as a nailer for the wall material.

### Metal Edges

Several types of metal pieces protect wallboard corners. The most common is corner bead, which protects 90-degree corners from damage. It comes in 8- and 10-foot lengths and is either nailed on or crimped on with a corner tool. The corner tool is not required, but it makes the work go quickly and eliminates the need for nails. Screws do not work well with corner bead. Ready-made corners are available for rounded bullnose corners and curved arches.

J- or U-beads and L-beads are used to cover exposed edges of wallboard, such as at an access hatch to plumbing or an attic. These usually have a raised edge that serves as a guide when taping and creates a slight depression that can be filled easily, leaving a smooth transition to the paper.

### Preparing to Install Wallboard

The preparation required for a successful wallboard job is partly determined by the finish wall surface. A smooth wall, covered with high-gloss paint and with skylights and spotlights casting shadows across it, requires excellent handiwork

## Installing Wallboard

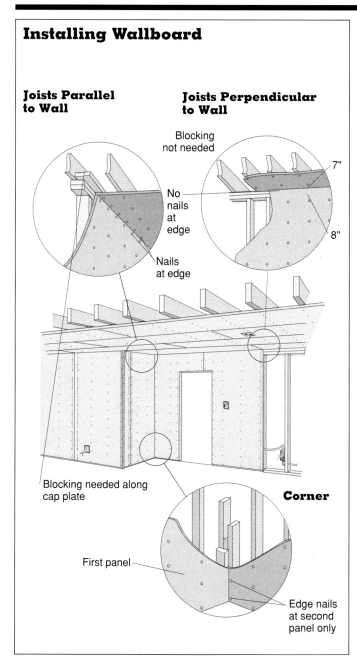

**Joists Parallel to Wall**

**Joists Perpendicular to Wall**

Blocking not needed

No nails at edge

7"

8"

Nails at edge

Blocking needed along cap plate

First panel

**Corner**

Edge nails at second panel only

## Correcting Framing Flaws

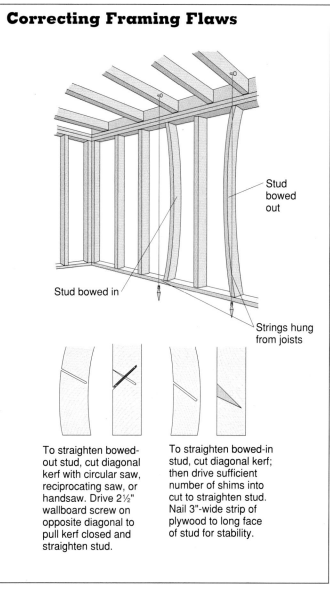

Stud bowed out

Stud bowed in

Strings hung from joists

To straighten bowed-out stud, cut diagonal kerf with circular saw, reciprocating saw, or handsaw. Drive 2½" wallboard screw on opposite diagonal to pull kerf closed and straighten stud.

To straighten bowed-in stud, cut diagonal kerf; then drive sufficient number of shims into cut to straighten stud. Nail 3"-wide strip of plywood to long face of stud for stability.

and the utmost preparation to achieve the desired effect. A wall paneled with resawn boards and battens over a one-hour fire wall requires minimal work, since both the wallcovering and the extrathick wallboard under it will disguise unevenness.

### Evaluating and Correcting Framing

Preparation begins with an evaluation of the frame. Wood framing is the type most commonly encountered in remodeling jobs.

First make sure the framing is on 4-foot centers so that the wallboard joints (which are spaced at 4 feet or multiples of 4 feet) will fall on a stud or joist and not in the spaces between them. Add framing if the existing framing isn't spaced correctly.

Remove any nails from the framing that could obstruct the wallboard screws or nails.

Check the surface for straightness. On ceilings, sight across the joists; use a string or level, or use a long, straight board (an 8-foot edge scrap of plywood works well for this). If the ceiling sags, you can install a strongback, provided

there is access above the ceiling. A strongback also works well when joists are undersized for their span or when a nonbearing wall that was helping to hold up the ceiling has been removed.

Check the walls for crowned or crooked studs. In some cases you can plane down the excess wood or shim a low point until it is level. In other cases, the studs can be cut halfway through, forced into alignment, and locked in place with 18-inch strips of plywood slightly narrower than the studs. Secure the plywood strips to the studs with wallboard screws. If you don't get the stud perfectly straight on the first try, remove the screw partway, push on the stud (or have a helper push) and reinsert the screw.

Check the corners for nailing on both faces unless you are using corner clips.

If wiring, plumbing, or other systems are penetrating the studs or joists, be sure that they are deep enough so that the screws or nails can't hit them. If they are vulnerable they must be protected with nail guards.

### Covering Plaster Walls and Ceilings

Cover plaster walls with ¼-inch or ⅜-inch wallboard, and plaster ceilings with ½-inch or ⅝-inch wallboard.

First remove all baseboards, picture moldings, and interior casing around doors and windows. Remove electrical fixtures and cover plates. Turn off the power and unscrew outlet and switch boxes so that they can be pulled through the new layer of wallboard. Remove any loose plaster or bulges. Shim over areas of missing or removed plaster to bring them up to the level of the remaining plaster, so the wallboard will have continuous backing.

When you apply the wallboard, be careful not to let loose plaster get trapped between the wall surface and the wallboard. Use wallboard screws to prevent this. Pounding nails is likely to break up bits of plaster, which will bow out the new layer of wall-

board. Make sure the screws penetrate ⅝ inch or more through the lath and plaster into the wood frame. Start with the ceiling and keep strong pressure on the wallboard next to each screw as it is installed. On the wall panels, work from the top down so that any plaster crumbs that break loose will fall out and not be trapped behind the wallboard.

### Furring

This is a way to obtain a smooth nailing surface over old framing. Furring is an effective technique for ceilings where the joists are between floors and other methods of straightening the frame are not possible. It is also used over concrete walls, such as in basements. Furring is usually done with 1 by 2 boards, but other sizes will also work. Furring strips over concrete should be approved for contact with concrete. You can also put metal flashing between furring and concrete. Check the local building code for specific requirements.

Furring may produce a slightly uneven nailing surface. The use of ⅝-inch wallboard will help compensate for this, resulting in a flatter wall surface.

First see how flat the wall or ceiling is by stretching strings across the area. Use diagonals and intermediate strings. Long levels or straightedges will also work. Mark low spots on the wall or ceiling, then mark the location of the new furring—usually perpendicular to the existing framing.

Wallboard screws work particularly well to fasten furring because you can easily loosen them to make adjustments. Nails also work. Whether you use screws or nails, the fasteners must penetrate into the studs on a framed wall.

As you tack up the furring, shim it out at each low spot. If you use beveled shims, place one on each side of the furring strip so the strip isn't pushed sideways.

### Soundproofing

One means of soundproofing is resilient channel, which is screwed to ceiling joists to provide attaching points for wallboard. Another method is to build a double stud wall by adding a 1 by 2 or 2 by 2 to the wall plates and interspacing 2 by 3s or 2 by 4s on 16-inch centers (or to match the spacing of the existing framing). Stuffing the wall with insulation or applying one or more extra layers of wallboard will also decrease sound transmission. Each additional layer should be a different thickness and should be installed perpendicular to the layer beneath it.

## Laying Out the Wall

Wallboard can be run parallel or perpendicular to joists or studs. A perpendicular layout will result in a smoother surface, greater shear strength, and a stronger attachment of the wallboard to the wall. For these reasons, a perpendicular layout is usually preferable to a parallel one. Wallboard can be run vertically on 8-foot-high interior walls, which

places all of the end joints at the top or bottom, where they are easy to hide. However, taping the resulting 8-foot vertical joints is no easy task, and makes it difficult to avoid locating joints too close to the ends of headers above doors, windows, and pass-throughs.

The fewer joints in a job, the better. Every joint must be taped, and end joints are difficult to cover smoothly. Because the edges of wallboard are tapered and the ends are not, end joints protrude above the wall surface.

To reduce the number of end joints, use the longest wallboard you can handle (with help, if it's available). On walls, apply it horizontally (perpendicular to the wall framing). Stagger the end joints, since their protrusion makes continuous end joints very hard to hide. If you are not able to span the room without end joints, plan the layout to keep them out of the center of the room.

When you plan the layout, avoid joints within 12 inches of the ends of headers. Shrinkage will crack the new wallboard if you locate a joint near such a large piece of wood, especially with new framing. Even with old framing, stress is concentrated around openings and connections between framing members, so joints located near them are likely to crack.

If the wall is more than 8 feet 1 inch high and you run wallboard horizontally, there will be two horizontal seams. One seam will be approximately in the vertical center of the wall; the other can be hidden behind the baseboard if it extends high enough

## Fitting Panels on Framing

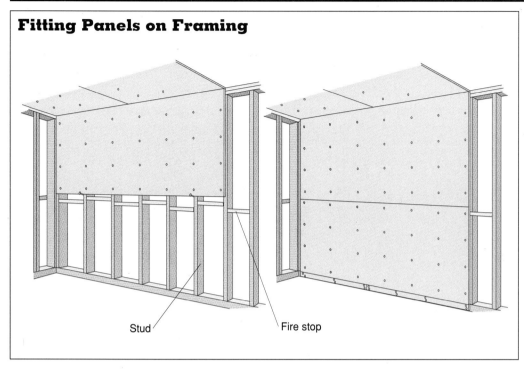

Stud

Fire stop

above the floor. The next-best choice is to place both joints near the vertical center of the wall, with a narrow strip of wallboard between them. This allows you to work at a comfortable height when you tape the seams. Also, both joints can be taped at the same time and both will be below eye level.

If you need an exceptionally smooth wall, place the cut edge of the narrow strip at the top or bottom of the wall, so only tapered edges will be joined where they are visible.

## Estimating Time and Materials

To estimate the amount of wallboard needed, simply calculate the square footage of the area to be covered. Do not deduct material for openings smaller than 50 square feet. This will allow for waste and keep the number of joints to a minimum.

Don't try to use the pieces cut from openings (windows, doorways, and so on) to cover other areas. Wallboard is very inexpensive. Using cut pieces to patch together a section of wallcovering will create many joints. This will be time-consuming (and expensive if you hire a professional taper). The resulting surface will look uneven and will be likely to crack. Also, the building will lose the shear strength that large, uncut pieces of wallboard provide.

For a small job, sketch the layout to calculate how many pieces of wallboard you need. Buy at least one extra piece. Count exterior corners to determine the necessary amount of corner bead.

Check the plans or the local building code for specific requirements, such as moisture-resistant wallboard (which may also require a particular taping compound and certain treatment of cut edges). Other

variables include fire-rated walls and walls in which the wallboard is used to increase the shear strength, thus requiring more closely spaced fasteners.

On large jobs (more than two or three rooms), consider having the job "stocked": Crews of two to four people will deliver the wallboard to each room. Provide them with a list of materials to be placed with it. They will need to see the site in order to plan the delivery and bid the job. When the wallboard is stocked, be sure that all the pieces are separated and left faceup except the last one, which should be turned over to protect its surface until you hang it.

If you have the wallboard delivered, arrange for enough helpers to carefully unload the truck by hand. Don't have wallboard dropped the way lumber is.

## Hanging Wallboard

Always install ceiling panels first. By far the easiest way to do this is with a wallboard jack (also known as a drywall hoist). This device has an H-shaped bar that can be raised or lowered with a crank and locked in place when the wallboard is snug to the ceiling. The jack can be rolled about. With a jack, one person can do a ceiling, although two will work more efficiently. Wallboard jacks can be disassembled for transport and can be rented inexpensively. Other methods of raising wallboard to a ceiling—such as a wood T-brace or scaffolding, a padded hard hat, and brute force—can be used. However, they increase the chance of injury from lifting the heavy, bulky panels.

First mark the wall plates under each ceiling joist so you can find them after you cover them with the panels. Lift the first panel and attach it, following the appropriate nailing pattern. Start from the center and work outward. Stagger any end joints by at least one joist bay (the space between the joists). Any panel cut along its length should have the cut edge against a wall. Leave a slight gap (approximately ⅛ inch) between the panel and the wall.

Install wall panels after the ceiling panels are in place. If you are using long horizontal panels, push the first panel up against the ceiling. Lever the second panel into place with a rolling foot jack, some simple scrap lumber, or a pry bar and piece of wood.

## Tools for Holding Wallboard

### T-Brace

T-brace helps hold a ceiling panel in place for easier nailing

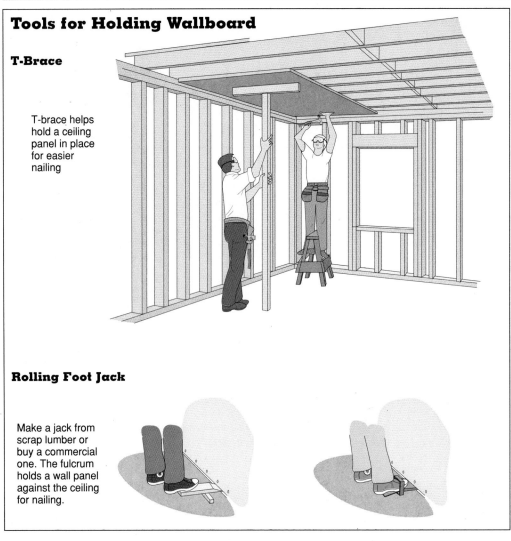

### Rolling Foot Jack

Make a jack from scrap lumber or buy a commercial one. The fulcrum holds a wall panel against the ceiling for nailing.

Be careful not to leave the screws above the surface of the paper. You should be able to slide a 6-inch taping knife over the screws while applying moderate pressure and not hit any screw heads. The screws should not break through the paper.

Nails must be driven below the surface level without tearing the paper. Bent nails should be removed, not hammered flat, because in time they could straighten out and break through the surface. Protect the wallboard with a wood or metal shim while pulling bent nails.

Corner bead must be installed tightly against both sides of the corner. Be sure that it doesn't buckle and leave a raised edge when you fasten it.

### Cutting Tools
The best cutting tool is a utility knife. A sharp blade is essential. Dull blades can tear the paper and are dangerous because they require extra pressure to make the cut. To speed the work, use a knife that has a quick-change feature (but holds the blade securely) or else dress the blade frequently with a sharpening stone.

Wallboard saws, which cut wallboard quickly, come in different sizes. The blades are stiff enough to be driven through the wallboard (before doing this, slide the wallboard panel off the stack or prop it up to provide clearance for the blade). The stiffness of the blade eases the job of cutting out openings for electrical receptacles, switches, and light fixtures.

### Cutting Techniques
It's best to hand-cut wallboard while it is still stacked on top of the other panels. In general, whenever you cut wallboard

subtract ¼ inch from the measured length and width.

For long straight cuts, use a straightedge or large T square to guide the knife. For medium-sized cuts, use a metal tape measure. Extend the tape to the width of the piece to be cut off, then hold the tape-measure case in one hand, gripping the tape tightly between thumb and forefinger. Hold the knife and the end of the tape in your other hand. Slowly slide both hands along the wallboard. The tape guides the knife as it follows the line of the cut.

To make straight cuts in wallboard with a knife, cut just through the paper on the finish side. Snap the panel away from the cut to break the gypsum, then cut the paper on the backside.

L-shaped or U-shaped cuts can also be done with a knife. However, this is a slow process because you must cut all the way through the wallboard on all except the last straight line of the cut. A wallboard saw is much faster.

If you do not have access to a wallboard saw, there is another way to cut small openings. Mark the opening on the wallboard, drive a nail at each corner point, and remove the nail. Use a knife to cut through the paper around the perimeter on both sides of the panel. Cut an X through the center of the cutout piece, then use a hammer to tap the piece out of the panel.

If possible, install wallboard panels uncut over door and window openings, allowing them to extend past the outside corners. Then cut

## Measuring and Marking Cutouts

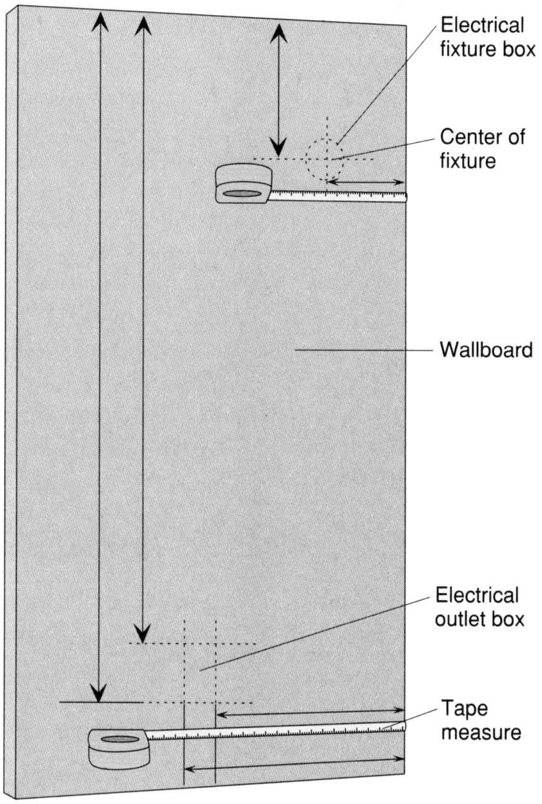

Electrical fixture box

Center of fixture

Wallboard

Electrical outlet box

Tape measure

away the excess with a wallboard saw or knife. This will greatly speed the work and provide more accuracy.

The most difficult measuring task is to position the cutouts for electrical receptacles, switches, and lights without moving the panels or cutting them twice. If the opposite side of the wall is uncovered, you can have a helper trace the openings on the backside of the wallboard while you hold it in place. Professionals often use a router with a particular bit to cut these openings while the panel is in position. Careful measurement, practice, and allowing leeway on the cuts will result in accurately placed holes.

Misplaced cuts can often be repaired in the taping process.

A slow but accurate way to mark wallboard for electrical-box openings requires positioning the wallboard, removing it to make the cut, then repositioning it. To use this method, dust the electrical boxes with colored chalk, position the wallboard, then tap or push the wallboard so that the chalk transfers to the backside.

Wallboard can be scribed in the same manner as paneling, but this is not usually done.

### Common Mistakes

Avoiding these typical mistakes will result in an easier, faster job with a more attractive outcome.

## Cutting Holes in Wallboard

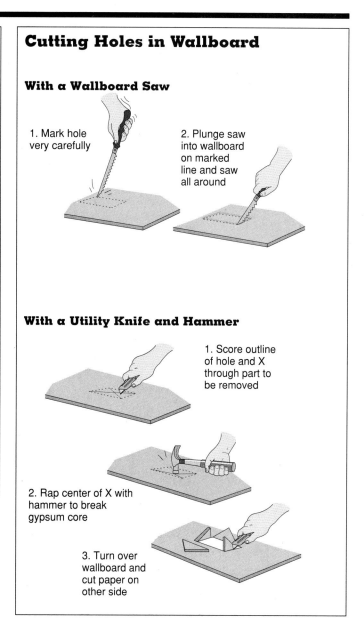

### With a Wallboard Saw

1. Mark hole very carefully

2. Plunge saw into wallboard on marked line and saw all around

### With a Utility Knife and Hammer

1. Score outline of hole and X through part to be removed

2. Rap center of X with hammer to break gypsum core

3. Turn over wallboard and cut paper on other side

• Using too many scraps and small pieces

• Hammering in bent-over nails instead of pulling them

• Tearing the paper and not installing another nail or screw to replace the one that made the tear

• Locating joints too close to the ends of headers

• Not using the proper hammer

• Not setting nails or screws below the surface

• Sanding the paper

• Using improper wallboard in special situations (for example, high moisture or where a fire rating is required)

## Repairs to Wallboard

Small holes 2 to 3 inches across can be patched with wallboard tape and compound. Apply a layer of compound around the hole, press the tape into the compound, and cover it with another layer. When this dries, sand it if necessary and then spread another layer of compound over the patch, feathering the edges. Let this layer dry and then gently sand it.

Large holes can be patched easily. You will need a few Type W wallboard screws.

**1.** Cut a triangular patch and trace the outline onto the wallboard around the hole.

**2.** Cut the wallboard to match the patch.

**3.** Make backing pieces from one or two pieces of plywood or scrap lumber slightly longer than the diameter of the hole. Hold them in place and attach by driving in wallboard screws on opposite sides of the hole through the wallboard into the lumber backing. If necessary, temporarily start a screw in the middle of the scrap to use as a temporary handle.

**4.** Place the patch in the hole and screw it to the backing.

**5.** Tape as you would any other joint.

Holes that span most of a stud bay, usually 14 or 15 inches wide, are best patched by removing a rectangle back to the centers of the studs.

**1.** Use a wallboard saw or utility knife to make the horizontal cuts (be careful not to nick wires or damage the far side of the wall).

**2.** Use a knife to make the vertical cuts. If the hole is close to the floor or if the baseboard can easily be pulled off, cut all the way to the floor.

**3.** Cut the patch and nail it in place.

**4.** Tape and fill the joints.

**5.** When the patch is dry, sand if necessary and texture or feather so the surface matches the existing wall.

# Taping and Texturing

This process is commonly known as taping or mudding. It is done on all wallboard walls, even those that will be covered with paneling or whose appearance is not critical (these require a single layer of tape and compound, a process called fire-taping). Taping and texturing require more skill than attaching wallboard to a wall. Even if you install the wallboard yourself, consider hiring a professional to tape and texture. If you decide to do it yourself, refer to the illustration on page 53. It's advisable to start in an inconspicuous area such as a garage or closet.

### Taping and Texturing Materials

There are three common types of joint tape. Paper tape comes in rolls up to 500 feet long and is creased in the center. It must be bedded in joint compound and covered with one or more layers of compound to produce a smooth, seamless surface.

Self-sticking tape is a loosely woven nylon mesh coated with a tacky adhesive that adheres lightly to the joints without a bedding coat. It is relatively easy to apply over tapered joints, but is difficult to cover on end or cut joints, which have no depression to accept the tape.

Metal-and-paper tape is used mostly for curves or outside corners (other than 90 degrees), where a metal edge serves to protect the vulnerable corner.

Joint compound comes either premixed or as a powder. The premixed kind is much easier to use and is recommended for beginners. Some powdered brands are designed to set up in a short time, from one half to two hours; this can be very helpful when a short drying time is needed. But powdered compounds when dry are much harder than the surrounding wallboard and can be difficult to sand down without damaging the wallboard surface. Premixed compound should be used within the time period recommended by the manufacturer because the compound and water tend to separate. It must also be protected from freezing.

Taping compound comes in different types, which vary according to the additives they contain and the fineness of the clay particles. None contain asbestos.

General-purpose compound can be used for all three layers of taping, as well as for texturing. However, premixed compound tends to be too thick for most people to apply successfully. This type of compound dries slowly, so allow 24 hours between coats.

Taping or bedding compound is stickier and works well for adhering the tape to the wall. It is used for the first and sometimes the second coat. It is effective for nail holes and corners, but it is harder to sand than topping compound.

Topping compound has a finer grain than the other types. It is often a different color, to enable you to see where it has been applied.

Topping compound is easy to sand and shrinks less than general-purpose or taping compound.

Quick-setting compound, commonly known as hot mud, sets up quickly and is used mostly when time constraints require it. It is not recommended for novices. If you do use this type, mix no more than can be used in the time available.

Various textures can be applied with a trowel or sprayer, or can be rolled on like paint. Texture is used for economy and to hide defects in a wall.

### Preparing to Tape and Texture

Find out whether a wallboard nailing inspection is required by the local building code. If so, have it done before taping.

Slide a taping knife over nails and screws to make sure they are below the surface of the paper so that they can be covered. If they are high, drive or screw them in without tearing the paper. If there are loose or bunched paper edges, cut them back. Finally, make sure the metal corner bead is installed.

Before starting the taping, cover anything you don't want to clean. Electrical receptacles and switches should not be installed at this point; they make the taping phase much more difficult and they must be protected from the compound. An inspector can require that switches and receptacles be replaced if compound gets into them.

# Taping and Filling Joints and Dimples

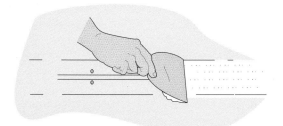

1. With 4" knife fill tapered recess with compound.

2. Lay tape in wet compound and press it flat with 4" knife.

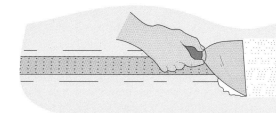

3. With 6" knife cover tape with coat of compound. Let dry thoroughly, then smooth with sandpaper or sponge. Apply second coat in same way and smooth again.

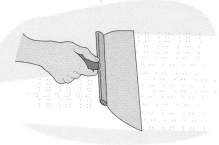

4. With 10" knife apply final thin coat.

5. Sand lightly if necessary between coats after compound is completely dry.

6. With 4" knife fill nail dimples with compound; sand or sponge lightly when completely dry. Two coats are usually sufficient.

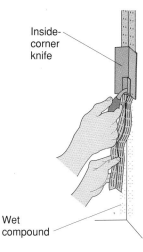

Inside-corner knife

Wet compound

For inside corners, with inside-corner knife fill joint with compound. Fold tape in half and press it into wet compound. Apply one or more coats of compound, letting each coat dry thoroughly and sanding before applying next coat.

## Taping and Texturing Tools

Three tools are essential: a small taping knife, 4 to 6 inches wide; a larger knife, 10 to 12 inches wide; and a tray or hawk so that you can carry a working portion of compound around the room and not have to work from the box or bucket. If you work from a large container you'll quickly contaminate it with grains of hardened compound and other debris that will flaw the finished product. Put compound back into the large container only if you are sure it is uncontaminated.

Many people find inside- and outside-corner knives indispensable. If you are using powdered joint compound, mixing attachments for power drills can speed the process. Another useful tool is a bucket of warm water to clean hands and tools often.

## Time Requirements

With practice a beginner can expect to apply a first coat of compound to an average-sized room in about three hours. Professionals can do a room in about 30 minutes per coat with hand tools and even faster with specialized tools.

If you have to stop during the application of a coat, cover the compound with plastic to keep it from drying out.

## Applying Tape and Compound

Some people prefer to work with dry tape; others like to wet it.

To apply the first coat, thin the compound to about the consistency of mayonnaise. Cover the full length of the joint with a layer of compound. Lay the tape into the wet compound and squeeze out the excess from behind the tape with the taping knife. Be sure to remove any bubbles or wrinkles. Then apply another layer of compound over the tape, feathering the edges carefully. Use as long a stroke as you can. Don't strive for perfection here; the goals are to feather the edges and to cover the tape. As much as possible, work along the joint, not perpendicular to it. Cut or end joints, which are not recessed like edge joints, should be left a little high from the first coat. The center ridge then provides a guide to feather out 6 to 8 inches on either side of the joint during the second coat.

Fill all nail depressions. Wipe them twice at 90-degree angles with heavy pressure so that you leave as little compound as possible. With practice, you can cover three or more nail dimples in one stroke. If you leave ridges around the nails or screws, do not attempt to achieve a smooth wall finish.

Inspect the wall or ceiling between coats. Set up an incandescent lamp so that it directs light at a low angle across the wall. The shadows will highlight areas in need of attention that are invisible in direct light. If you don't do this, you may be in for quite a shock when the wall is painted. Check the work of a professional taper in this manner as well. Once subcontractors are paid and gone, you may be stuck with an unsatisfactory job.

After the first coat dries, scrape off any high points. You can use a sponge or sandpaper to knock down bumps or ridges, but sanding has disadvantages. It will damage the paper surface and it creates a lot of dust. If the first coat is done properly, you can fill any voids or unfeathered edges, so sanding can be avoided. Most professionals sand only a little on the final coat.

The second coat again fills the nail dimples, because the first coat has shrunk. Then the taped joints are recoated. The tapered edges can be filled until they are flush with the surface. Feather the seams. Edge joints should be 7 to 10 inches wide; cut or end joints should be 12 to 14 inches wide. As with the first coat, apply the compound along the entire seam and then smooth it with as long a stroke as possible. Don't keep reworking the same section of compound; move on. If the compound is not too thick, no sanding will be required for the second coat. Just use the knife to scrape off any bumps after the compound has dried.

For the third coat, switch to topping compound or thin the taping compound a bit more. Edge joints should be feathered to about 10 inches wide; cut or end joints should be 20 inches wide or more. Nail depressions will need a third coat if the finished surface must be smooth.

When the compound dries, smooth out as much as possible with the knife. Fill any low spots and use a sanding pole, if necessary.

## Texturing

A smooth wall should be visually flawless. Texturing is much more forgiving. Hand-texturing can be done with sponges, rollers, or trowels. Adding extrafine sand and thinning the compound will give a skip-trowel texture. There are also spray textures. Orange peel is sprayed on and allowed to dry. Knockdown is sprayed on, then the high spots are lightly flattened with an extrawide trowel. These techniques require skill; if you want to try them yourself, experiment in an inconspicuous area first.

# Paneling

Paneling is a wall or ceiling surface that adds warmth and character to a room. Many older houses have paneled or wainscoted walls. Paneling can be equally effective in a contemporary home.

You can choose from a wide range of materials and styles to complement cabinet work, furnishings, or other wood detailing in the house. If you're building an addition, paneling matching that in the existing house can help unify the design.

Paneling provides a distinctive design element anywhere it is used. It is a common choice for family rooms because it requires little maintenance and resists dirt and mild abuse. It is an attractive yet economical solution for covering a wall that needs resurfacing. A disadvantage is, with the exception of minor scratches, paneling is difficult to repair.

Almost anyone can do a good job of paneling. Installation requires few tools and no specific skills. The paneling itself requires little or no finishing and is quite durable. A

## Board Paneling

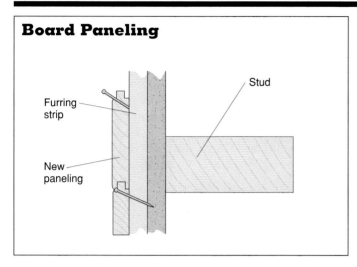

## Extending a Door Jamb

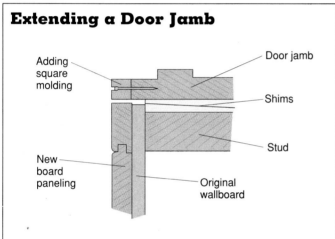

paneling job can turn out badly, however, due to poor workmanship or design. The most difficult part of the job is preparing an irregular wall or ceiling surface. Misaligned joints will look sloppy. In some applications, paneling may be inappropriate or cause the room to be dark and gloomy.

## Types of Paneling

Traditional paneling is made up of individual boards. Board paneling is usually a softwood such as pine, redwood, or cedar. Oak, mahogany, and more exotic woods are also available. The boards vary in thickness from ³⁄₁₆ to

¾ inch and in width from 2 to 12 inches. Many board panels have grooves milled into the surface to give the appearance of two or three narrow boards. Board paneling should be kiln dried to minimize warping and buckling after installation.

In the 1950s, low-relief hardboard paneling became prevalent. Hardboard consists of compressed and heated wood fibers. This type of paneling is almost always ¼ inch thick and comes finished.

In addition to these older styles, numerous types of solid and veneered sheet paneling are available, in hardwood and softwood.

Thicknesses vary from ³⁄₁₆ to ¾ inch. Some of the thicker veneers are grooved to give the look of individual boards at a lower cost. Veneered panels come finished or unfinished.

## Selecting Paneling

Board paneling works better than sheet paneling for long runs (ceilings or two-story walls, for example) because individual boards can be joined randomly whereas 4-foot-wide sheets can be joined only end to end. Board paneling can also be installed diag-onally or in a herring-bone pattern. It is easier to cut than sheet paneling, although more time is required to attach the boards.

Sheet paneling offers the greatest variety and is the most economical in both labor and materials. However, handling the large sheets of paneling without assistance is difficult.

Generally it is better to use expensive paneling to cover a small area than cheap paneling to cover a large area.

Most paneling has grooves, which create a strong linear pattern that can have different effects depending on the application. For example, a short wall seems taller when covered with vertically grooved paneling; horizontal paneling makes a wall seem shorter. If you panel a far wall, perspective lengthens, making the room seem longer.

The color of paneling also yields different effects. A ceiling with light paneling, such as maple or some varieties of oak, appears higher. A room with walls of light paneling

appears larger and brighter. Dark paneling makes a ceiling appear lower and can create either an intimate or a confining feeling.

Always choose a pattern that is consistent with the overall character of the room. Try to match existing wood trim or other details, especially in homes of a distinctive architectural style. Paneling with randomly spaced grooves or a coarse grain that includes wormholes or other markings should be used in casual settings. For a formal look, choose paneling that features a straight, tight grain pattern, narrow boards, and a smooth finish. If you panel a bathroom or other damp area, use real board paneling of a durable species, such as redwood or cedar. Finish it with several coats of a clear sealer.

## Preparation for Paneling

Walls must provide a flat attaching surface for the paneling. If stud walls aren't already flat, they must be furred. All masonry walls must be furred whether they are flat or not.

If moisture is seeping through a masonry wall, be sure to correct the problem before installing paneling. A vapor barrier is required behind the furring, but this doesn't eliminate the need to keep the wall dry.

To prepare an existing surface for paneling, remove all trim, electrical cover plates, picture hooks, and so forth. With the baseboard off, locating the studs should be easy. If they aren't visible, you can find

## Applying Paneling Over Studs

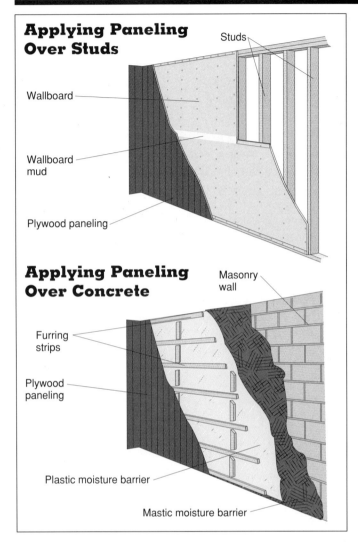

- Studs
- Wallboard
- Wallboard mud
- Plywood paneling

## Applying Paneling Over Concrete

- Masonry wall
- Furring strips
- Plywood paneling
- Plastic moisture barrier
- Mastic moisture barrier

## Fitting an Irregular Edge

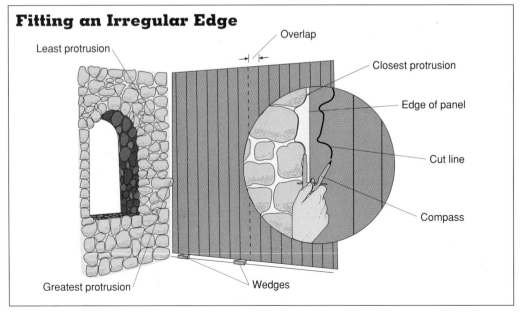

- Least protrusion
- Overlap
- Closest protrusion
- Edge of panel
- Cut line
- Compass
- Greatest protrusion
- Wedges

them with a magnetic or electronic stud finder or by drilling and driving in a nail. Because you will cover the wall with paneling, there is no need to patch the holes. Studs are normally spaced at 16 or 24 inches, so once you find the first two, locating the rest should be easy. If the studs are spaced irregularly, though, you will need to find and mark them all.

Check for high or low spots with a long level or straightedge. If the plane of the wall or ceiling is within ½ inch across the entire surface, you can install paneling directly to the wall after you patch any large holes or cracks. If the wall is irregular, attach 1 by 2 (or larger) furring strips at opposite ends of the wall or ceiling. Stretch strings from end to end and shim out the furring to meet the strings.

If the wall bulges in the center, use thicker furring strips at the ends or thinner furring strips in the center. This applies whether the furring is laid vertically or horizontally.

Furring strips should be located every 16 or 24 inches, as well as anywhere a seam will fall. If the furring is vertical, be sure to use additional horizontal strips at the top and bottom.

If you are attaching paneling to bare studs, install horizontal blocking every 32 inches (or at the top and bottom if you are installing vertical board paneling).

Sheet panels require backing, usually ½-inch wallboard. Building codes usually require wallboard backing for board paneling as a safety measure for fire protection.

Find out whether the floor is level before installing the first sheet in the corner. Take some time to check whether walls, floors, and ceilings are level, plumb, and at right angles, especially in an older house (for best results, use a 4-foot or longer level). If they aren't, plan how to adjust for the variations. This can be done by scribing or by covering gaps with trim.

Scribing the paneling will give a tight fit in irregular corners, but it takes significant time. Tack the piece to be scribed in place so that the edge of the panel touches the point on the adjacent wall that protrudes the farthest. Then, using a compass set to bridge the widest part of the gap, trace the contour of the wall on the panel. Be sure to keep the panel tight to the wall as you scribe the line. Take the panel down and cut along the scribed line with a fine-toothed scroll saw. Cut hardboard or plywood paneling from the backside to avoid splitting pieces out of the finish side. A sharp

56

# Corner Details

### Lapped Corner

Furring strips

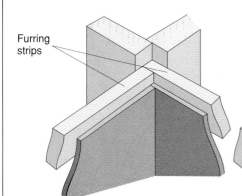

### Overlaid Inside Corner

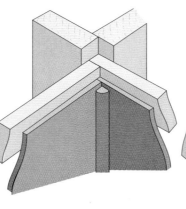

### Inset Corner Molding

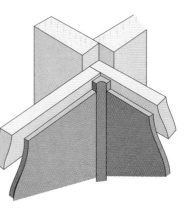

### Inset Corner Molding

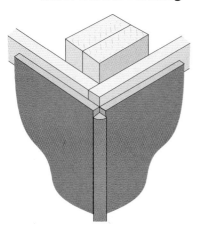

### Mitered Corner

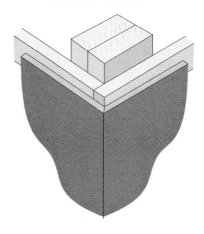

### Overlaid Outside Corner

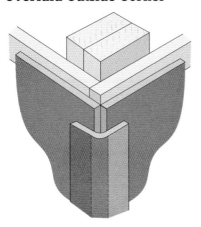

### Ceiling Trim

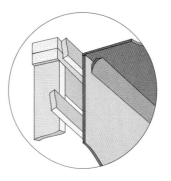

saw blade will help prevent chipping. You can also cut through the surface with a utility knife and then cut just inside the knife line. Bevel the cut edge back slightly with a sharp knife or block plane for an extratight fit. Make sure the edge of the panel is plumb, then scribe the panel along the ceiling if necessary. Cut the panel ¼ inch shorter than the wall height and wedge it tightly against the ceiling.

## Layout and Installation

Sheet panels are laid out and installed much like wallboard (see pages 48 to 51). Panels should fit tightly into the corners and against the ceiling unless you intend to cover these seams with trim.

Interior corners can be handled in three ways: panels or boards can be lapped over each other, the seam can be covered with molding, or corner molding can be inset and the panels butted to it.

To install nailed panels without using a filler piece, position the first one and nail the edges as needed to keep them tight. Nail the seams within the panel if possible. For a thin (¼-inch) panel, it may be necessary to nail every 4 inches on the edges and every 8 inches within the panel. Wire nails or brads should be 1½ inches long for ½-inch or thinner paneling and 2 inches long for thicker paneling. Visible nails in paneling look terrible. Use colored nails to match the paneling or countersink the nails and fill the holes with an appropriately colored putty. Use a nail set smaller than the nail head so that the surface is not marred.

If the first panel is placed correctly and the room is square, each successive panel will butt up to the previous one, fit tightly to the ceiling, and be plumb. Continue until the next-to-last panel is installed. Measure carefully from the top, bottom, and center of the panel to the corner, or rough-cut the last panel and scribe its edge to the wall.

Panels can also be installed with a filler piece. Start with a full sheet on each end of the wall and work toward the center. If the full pieces don't meet, use a filler piece, preferably over a door or window. If the piece is cut and installed well, it will not be noticeable even if it is quite narrow. When the job is complete use appropriately colored caulk to fill any seams or gaps at the edges.

Attaching a panel with adhesive is easy, but the panel can't be removed without destroying it. Installing the first panel when using adhesive takes about the same amount of time as the first nailed panel. Subsequent panels can be installed more quickly. Use a caulking gun to lay a bead of

## Gluing Paneling

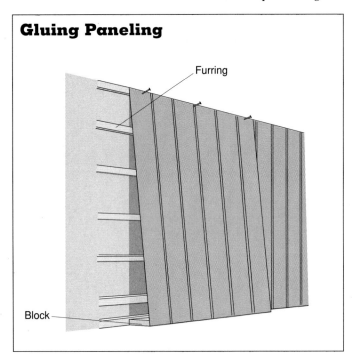

Furring

Block

## Installing a Filler Piece

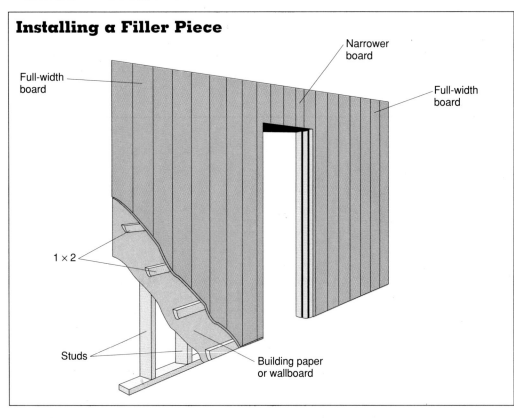

Full-width board

Narrower board

Full-width board

1 × 2

Studs

Building paper or wallboard

adhesive about ½ inch from the edges of the panel and along the studs or furring. Tack the panel at the top with three or four finishing nails. Press the panel into the adhesive to spread it evenly, then pull out the bottom of the panel and slip in a 6-inch woodblock to hold the panel away from the wall while the adhesive cures (follow the manufacturer's recommendations for curing time). While the adhesive cures, you may have time to cut and fit another piece of paneling. You can work on more than one wall at a time.

When the adhesive is cured, remove the block, press the panel against the wall, and nail along the bottom and top.

## Repairing Paneling

Surface flaws can sometimes be disguised, but a badly damaged panel must be replaced. Small scratches can be hidden with shoe polish, wood stain, or commercial scratch remover, but test on a scrap piece first.

If you do replace a panel, salvage as much as possible. Molding can often be removed successfully. A glued panel will come off in pieces. Be careful not to damage any adjoining panels. Scrape off any adhesive remaining on the furring or backing. Board panels vary so greatly in nailing patterns, interlocking design, and even layers of paint that they may be easy or difficult to remove.

Take a sample with you when looking for a replacement. If the exact material can't be found, you will have to stain a panel to match.

## Plaster

Plaster is used to finish interior walls. It is a powder mixed with water and an aggregate to a proper consistency.

Plastering should be done by professionals. Judging proper consistency, knowing when to apply coats, and techniques of application take time to learn.

## Small Plaster Repairs

Cracks in plaster walls are usually caused by settling of the house or by strong vibrations. Small cracks can be patched with spackling compound or flexible vinyl patching compounds. Vinyl materials don't sand well, so don't leave any excess if you use them. Patching plaster sets up quickly, usually within 15 minutes. In many regions the ground swells when wet and shrinks when it dries. This causes walls to move so cracks often reopen after patching. This type of crack can be patched with fiberglass-mesh tape and finished with joint compound.

Larger cracks, where the plaster is still firmly attached to the lath, should be gouged out and widened in the shape of an inverted V (narrower at the surface, wider within the wall). The dried patching material will form a wedge, holding itself in place. Blow out any loose debris, dampen the crack, and force patching plaster into it.

Wider cracks must be opened to about 1½ inches (if the adjoining plaster is firmly attached). If the wall has wood lath, try to expose the spaces between the laths. If

the plaster begins to loosen, use 1¼-inch wallboard screws with 2-inch fender washers to hold it firmly. Install the screws 8 inches from the edge of the crack, spaced 16 inches apart. Try to screw into the framing. Don't overtighten the screws. After the patch is complete, remove the screws and patch the holes.

Use a liquid plaster bonding agent on the lath and on the edge of the plaster in the crack. When it dries, fill the crack with plaster of paris or patching plaster. If you are doing many patches, you can save money by purchasing the plaster in 80-pound bags.

Force the plaster into the crack and between the gaps in the wood lath. Keep the plaster flush with the surface. When it is dry, tape the edge of the crack with paper tape or fiberglass-mesh tape and feather the repair out about 6 inches.

Wood lath cannot be reinstalled but can be patched. Small holes and cracks in the lath can be easily fixed with patching plaster or quick-setting wallboard compound. If the lath is tight, cut back any loose plaster. Gently renail any loose lath or use screws to attach wire mesh over the wood lath.

For best results wet the lath and surrounding plaster and use a bonding agent. Apply the new plaster in two coats, leaving the surface of the first coat rough so that the second coat will bond tightly.

Be sure to scrape down the patch so no excess is left around the edge. Patching plaster and quick-setting wallboard compound dry harder

than regular plaster and are difficult to sand.

If the lath is missing or broken, you will have to provide backing for a base. Cut a piece of expanded wire mesh a little larger than the hole. Hold the mesh in place with a piece of wire while you force the first layer of plaster through the mesh. Secure the wire by twisting around a pencil or stick until the plaster dries. Then cut the wire or push it back into the wall cavity and apply the second coat.

## Large Plaster Repairs

Plaster may fall off the wall, or may stay on the wall but separate from the lath. Check suspect plaster for looseness by tapping on the wall. Loose plaster will give a little and will sound different than securely attached plaster. Loose plaster must be removed and the area resurfaced. In severe cases, it is best to resurface the whole wall, or ceiling, or even the entire room.

The easiest way to patch a large hole is to install a piece of wallboard slightly thinner than the plaster, secure it with screws, and apply a thin coat of plaster over it. The edges can be taped. Sand and touch up with topping compound.

To match the texture of old plaster walls you may need to thin some topping compound and roll it on the wall with a stippled paint roller to match the existing layers of paint. Some surfaces are nearly impossible to match exactly, because everything from sponges to grapefruits to newspapers has been used to texture plaster walls. Be inventive.

# INTERIOR TRIM

*Interior trim, or molding, is ornamental and serves to conceal the joints between finish materials. Trim allows a reasonable margin of error in the installation of major building components such as doors, windows, and wallboard. Many of the tools and techniques used for interior trim are used throughout finish work.*

## Trim Materials and Styles

Trim materials come in two main categories: stain grade and paint grade. Paint-grade molding may be solid or finger jointed. Finger-jointed molding is suitable for interior trim only. Paint-grade trim should be smooth, close grained, and free of pitch pockets. The color and grain of stain-grade molding should be as consistent as possible. Trim should be kiln dried (5 to 12 percent moisture content) and protected from moisture and high humidity to reduce the chance of shrinkage after installation.

If you are remodeling only part of a house, try to match the existing trim styles. Custom trim can be fabricated if what you have isn't available ready-made. Most of the cost is in setup, so be sure to order plenty of molding if you choose this approach. An alternative is to transfer trim from an inconspicuous room to the remodeled area, then trim the room with molding that looks as much like the original as possible.

## Types of Trim

Types of molding used for different applications have standard names.

- Base or baseboard: Used where walls meet floors, and sometimes for window and door casings.
- Base shoe or shoe: Small trim used to cover the gap between the baseboard and the floor.
- Cap: Added to baseboard and over windows, doors, and wainscots.
- Casing: Used to trim windows and doors at the side (side casing) and at the top (head casing).
- Chair rail: Used to protect wall surfaces from the backs of chairs.
- Cove: Used on inside surfaces that meet at right angles.
- Crown: Used at the junction of walls and ceilings, at the tops of cabinets, and below mantels.
- Dowel: Used for closet poles and handrails.
- Half-round: Used to conceal joints in surfaces. Rarely used as casing.
- Picture rail: Supports picture hooks and adds an emphasis line to the upper part of the wall.

- Quarter-round: Used as base shoe, stop, and general all-purpose molding to cover corner joints.
- Screen bead: Covers the edge of the screen material on wood window and door screens. Used where small, flat trim is needed.
- Shelf cleat: Used for supporting closet shelves.
- Sill: Bottom trim of window. Slopes downward to shed water.
- Stool: Interior trim at the bottom of a window.
- Stop (also called glass bead): Used as a guide for windows, to lock fixed windows in place, and to seal doors to jambs.
- Threshold: Used at the bottoms of doorways. Covers the seams of floor-covering materials between rooms, and seals door bottoms.

## Tools and Tips

The carpenter's tool belt for trim work should hold the following tools.

- 16- to 20-ounce smooth-faced hammer
- Sharp block plane
- Tape measure (a 1-inch-wide retractable tape is best)
- Nail set (smaller than the smallest finishing nail you use)
- Combination square
- Bevel gauge
- Utility knife with extra blades
- Hard-lead pencil
- Level (a plumb bob is also helpful)
- Coping saw
- ¼-inch chisel
- ¾-inch chisel
- Rasping plane (for shaving wallboard)

A power miter box, table saw, or manual miter box is necessary to cut trim accurately. The power miter box (also called a chop saw) is best because of its speed, accuracy, and ability to make paper-thin adjustment cuts. If you use prefinished trim, inspect the saw blade periodically for built-up finish. Clean it off with solvent.

A pneumatic nailer is helpful if you plan to install a lot of trim. These tools are light and drive nails so quickly that you can hold the work with one hand while nailing with the other. They reduce the risk of splitting the wood when nailing near the end. Be sure to use safety goggles and follow the manufacturer's instructions if you use a pneumatic nailer.

## Preparing to Install Trim

Check that door and window jambs are level, plumb, and square. If they are seriously off, there is little that can be done but to remove and rebuild them. Jambs that are more than ⅟₁₆ inch below the finish wall can be brought flush by gluing and nailing wood strips to them. If the jambs are only ⅟₁₆ inch or less below the finish wall, plane the wallboard or plaster with a rasping plane. Mark the outside edge of the molding and be sure not to trim too much. This is practical only with molding that is relieved on the back.

If jambs project more than ¹⁄₁₆ inch above the wall, plane them down. Before you start, step back and look at the junction of wall and jamb. Trim any shims and remove any protruding lumps of joint compound.

If you plan to stain the trim, paint the walls first and stain the trim before you install it. If you will paint the trim, install it first. Paint both trim and walls with wall paint, letting the wall paint prime the trim. Then mask off the trim and spray or brush it with trim paint.

Before you start cutting, test the saw for accurate square and 45-degree cuts. If you have a trued framing square or a mechanic's square, make a sample cut and check it. Then cut a piece of straight square scrap at 45 degrees, reverse one piece, and butt them together. They should form a perfect right angle.

## Making Joints

Well-made joints give trim a professionally installed appearance. Before installing trim, study different types of joints. Figure out which ones you'll need, and practice making them on pieces of scrap molding.

## Types of Trim

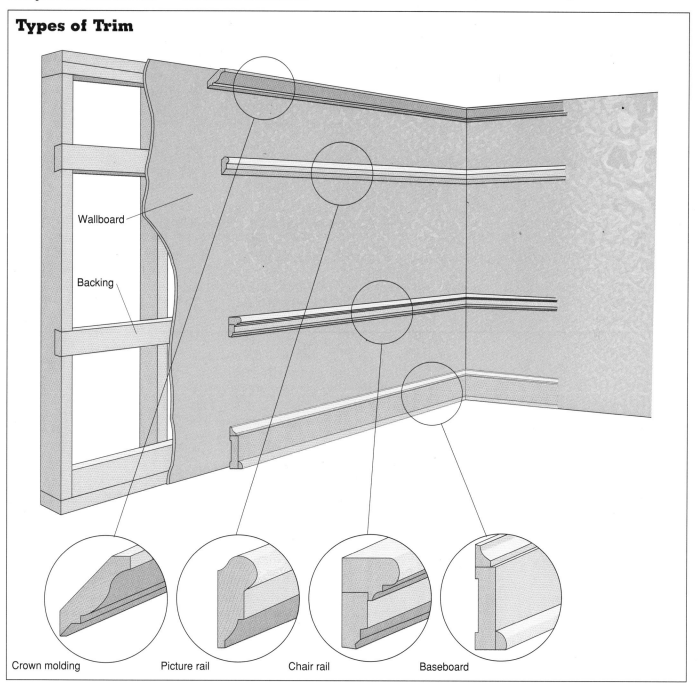

Wallboard

Backing

Crown molding          Picture rail          Chair rail          Baseboard

## Butt Joints

This is the easiest joint; the trim is simply cut square and butted where the pieces meet. A variation uses head blocks and occasionally a base block. Casing with curved edges cannot be butted to itself, only to casing with square edges. Butt joints are used with caps or corner blocks.

Head casing butted to the side casings either extends past the side casings or is flush with them. If corner blocks that are thicker than the casing are used, they should be wide enough to extend slightly beyond the casing.

## Miter Joints

These joints are used for door and window casings. They are also used on outside corners of walls (but not on inside corners). The ends of the molding are cut at 45 degrees for square corners, with variations as necessary to compensate for corners that are out of square.

Mitered corners can be measured long to long (outside measurement) or short to short (the length from corner to corner along the reveal line). For long to long, measure the same as for a flush butt joint. For short to short, start at the 1-inch mark on the tape measure and measure to the length you want plus 1 inch.

## Coped Joints

This type of joint is generally used only on inside corners of baseboard or crown molding. It is a variation of the butt joint. Most trim shrinks or shifts a little with time. This is most noticeable at inside corners because you can see directly into the gap. A coped joint overlaps the corner, concealing any separation. It also helps disguise corners that are out of square.

Cut the first piece of molding square and install it. Cut the second piece at a 45-degree angle with the molded face the short side of the cut. Then cut with a coping saw along the edge of the cut, following the profile of the molding. Back-cut the profiles lightly or dress the cut with a rasp, knife, or sandpaper to get a tight fit. Butt the coped piece against the first piece. Once it fits correctly, cut the other end of the coped piece to the required length.

## Scarf Joints

A scarf joint connects pieces in a straight line. The joint is similar to a butt joint, but with the pieces bevel-cut at 45-degree angles, so any shrinkage won't show as a gap. Use these joints with restraint and in inconspicuous locations, such as inside closets.

## Installing Trim

Before you start, make sure you have all the necessary tools. Select the best pieces of trim for the most conspicuous locations. Check your miter saw and square for accuracy.

Trim should be installed in a specific order. Start with the window stools and aprons. Then do all door and window casings. It's best to install the finish floor before installing door casings, but if this isn't possible, shim up the door casing with a sample piece of floor covering. Next, install specialty moldings such as chair rail. Finally, install crown and cornice molding. For best results, do all of one type of trim throughout the house, then do the next type. Start in inconspicuous areas and work toward the more visible areas. Do fine work while you are fresh. If you make several mistakes, take a break or switch to a simple job, such as cleaning up the job site or finding your missing tools. If it's late, it may be best to leave the job overnight and start again in the morning.

Step back occasionally and look at the work from a few feet away. It is easy to become too critical. Look at other trim work to give yourself a standard for comparison.

## Window Stools and Aprons

Stools and aprons are commonly used as part of window trim (although some windows have only wallboard jambs and no trim at all). The stool is the piece at the bottom of the window; the apron fits directly beneath the stool to support and finish it. Trim styles vary; select one that complements the rest of the house.

First cut the stool to length. It should be equal to the length between the jambs plus twice the width that the stool projects out from the casing. Mark the centerline and align it with the center of the window. Place a combination square against the jamb and extend the line across the stool on each side.

Next determine the cut for the horns. Measure the distance from the stool to the window frame to each corner and in the middle. If the points form a straight line, mark the horn over the cut area and cut it out. If the line is not straight, scribe the horns. Set the compass to the greatest distance between the jamb sill and the stool held against the wall. Scribe the inside of the stool and the horns. Place the cut edge until the fit is tight. If the stool butts to the window, leave a ½-inch to ¹⁄₁₆-inch gap to allow the window to open and close after painting or finishing. Before you nail the stool, consider the ends of the horn. They can be rounded or mitered and returned. Nail 8-penny (8d) finishing nails into the sill, shimming it up as required. Set the nails.

Line up the apron with the edge of the casing. Miter and return the edges of the apron. Simple square or beveled stock can be rounded over by sanding or routing. Use 6d finishing nails to nail the stool into the apron and the apron into the framing. Use a spring stick or hold the apron tightly against the stool while nailing.

## Door and Window Casings

Door and window casings are installed with mitered or butted joints. Mitered casings are the most common for interior work, especially with simple moldings. Butt joints are used with more ornate trim.

# Window Trim Options

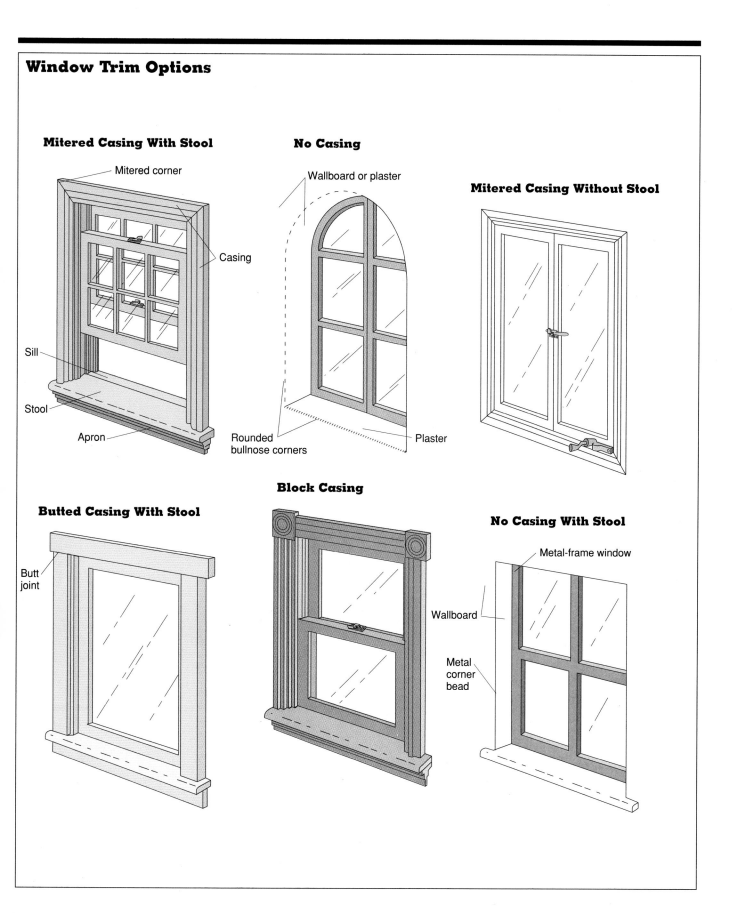

**Mitered Casing With Stool**

Mitered corner

Casing

Sill

Stool

Apron

**No Casing**

Wallboard or plaster

Rounded
bullnose corners

Plaster

**Mitered Casing Without Stool**

**Butted Casing With Stool**

Butt
joint

**Block Casing**

**No Casing With Stool**

Metal-frame window

Wallboard

Metal
corner
bead

## Mitered Casings

Ideally the casing should be set back from the inner edges of the jamb at least 3/16 inch but not more than 1/4 inch. Put a guideline on the side jamb to mark where the edge of the casing should go. To do this, adjust a combination square so that 3/16 inch protrudes, and then slide the square along the jamb with a pencil tip following the edge of the blade. Mark the head jamb in the same way.

Once the jambs are marked, cut the base of one side casing at a 90-degree angle. Place the side casing along the guideline on the side jamb. Mark the top of the casing at the point where the lines on the side jamb and head jamb meet. From that point make a 45-degree cut on the casing. Use a miter and backsaw or a power miter saw. The work must be precise.

Nail the side casing in place. Then make a 45-degree cut on one end of the head casing and fit it to the side casing. Mark the other end at the point where the guidelines on the side and head jambs meet. From that point cut the head casing at a 45-degree angle. Nail up the head casing.

Finally, cut the bottom end of the other side casing at a 90-degree angle and put it in place. Mark where it meets the head casing, cut it, and nail it.

**An alternate method** The foregoing description gives the textbook method of putting up trim in cases where the door is square. Unfortunately, doors often aren't. As a result the 45-degree cuts will not match up. Some pros do the job in the following way.

Mark the edges of the jambs 3/16 inch back, as previously described. Cut the bottoms of the two side casings square and fit them against the side jambs. Note where the top ends meet the right angle of the guidelines on the head jamb. Mark the side casings at these two points. Cut a 45-degree angle in each one. Nail the side casings in place.

Next take a length of trim for the head casing that is 4 inches longer on each side than the outer edges of the side casings. Cut 45-degree angles at both ends of the head casing. Now fit the left end of the head casing to the left side casing and position it precisely on the guideline. Let the other end overlap the casing on the other side. Check how the joint fits. If there is a gap and all three casings are positioned exactly, then that side of the door is out of square. Check the other side in the same manner. If one side fits, put it in place. Then mark the top and bottom edges of the head casing to match the mitered cut on the other side casing. Adjust the miter saw to correspond and cut—*but* cut the head casing 1/16 inch longer than the space in which it will fit. This helps to ensure a tight joint. Wedge it into position and nail. If a small gap still exists, it can be tightened by lock-nailing.

## Corner Techniques

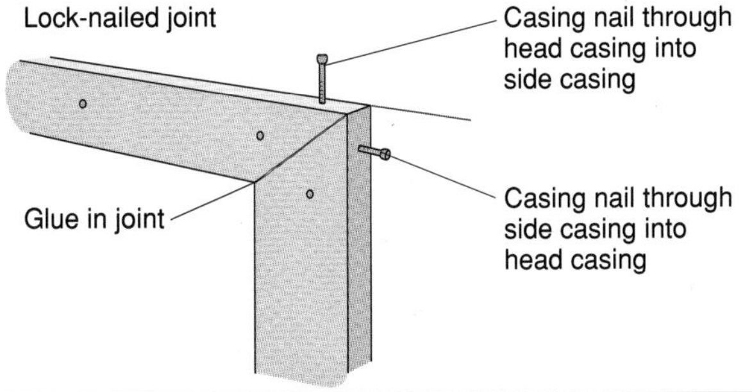

Lock-nailed joint

Casing nail through head casing into side casing

Glue in joint

Casing nail through side casing into head casing

**Lock-nailing** When a mitered joint is slightly off, this method can often be used to close the gap; it works because the trim wood is usually flexible. First squeeze some glue into the crack. Then drive a casing nail through the head casing into the side casing, and another nail through the side casing into the head casing, as shown above. Wipe away any excess glue immediately and sand lightly when dry. The trim wood is flexible enough that lock-nailing will often close a gap in a mitered joint.

## Butt-Jointed Casings

Before cutting the tops of the side casings, check that the head jamb is level. If it slopes slightly, adjust the cuts at the tops of the side casings. Use a long level to mark the cuts, cut the head casing, put it in place, and nail.

## Baseboard

Baseboards can consist of one, two, or three pieces of molding. One-piece molded baseboard is the most common. Base cap dresses the top of the baseboard. Base shoe protects the baseboard from vacuum cleaners and hides the gap

between a sloping floor (common in remodeling) and the baseboard.

Older homes may use wood siding capped with molding as the baseboard. In this case, use butt joints for the baseboard. Cope and miter the cap molding joints.

Baseboard should be level. If the floor slopes, carpet or base shoe can be used to conceal the uneven joint. Another option is to scribe the baseboard in the same manner as for paneling (see page 56).

Prepare a plan view sketch of the room and determine the installation sequence. Arrange the cuts so that the joints are out of the direct line of sight as you enter the room.

Install the first section of baseboard along the longest wall. Cut the ends square and nail it. Nail baseboard more than 3 inches high into the studs and base plate at top and bottom. If you're using base shoe to compensate for a sloping floor, nail it to the floor, not the baseboard.

Cope inside corner joints. Mitered joints will show a gap if the baseboard shrinks. It is advisable to glue all joints. Wipe away excess glue immediately with a damp rag.

# Installing Baseboard

## Measuring for Baseboard

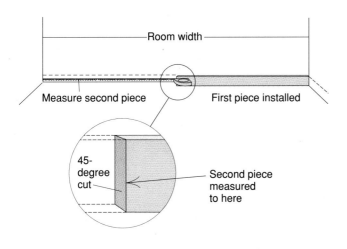

Room width

Measure second piece

First piece installed

45-degree cut

Second piece measured to here

## Butting Baseboard Against Casing

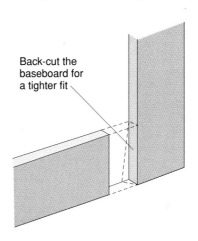

Back-cut the baseboard for a tighter fit

## Marking a Mitered End Cut

Mark intersection by scribing along scrap

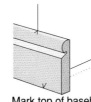

Mark top of baseboard at wall, and bottom at intersection marks

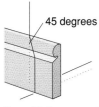

45 degrees

Draw 45-degree angles and connect all marks for cutting

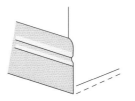

Finished cut

## Attaching Baseboard

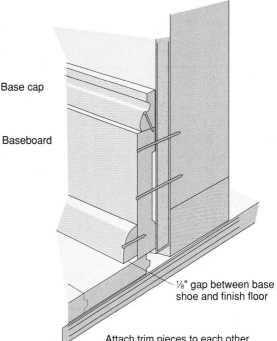

Base cap

Baseboard

⅛" gap between base shoe and finish floor

Attach trim pieces to each other and nail baseboard assembly through wall into studs. Do not nail to floor.

Beveled end

Coped end

Mitered and returned end

Miter outside corner joints. It's easiest to mark the miter from the corner directly to the inside face of the molding. Leave all of the pencil line when you cut. If the saw tears chips out of the surface, mark the corners from the outside (see page 65). Cutting from the outer surface of the molding will minimize chipping.

If baseboard butts to a cabinet or deep casing that is out of square, determine the correct angle with a bevel gauge or by scribing, then cut the end of the baseboard accordingly. If the baseboard will be painted, small gaps at these locations can be caulked.

## Picture Rail

Picture rail is generally positioned 6 to 12 inches down from the ceiling. Since it is intended to carry considerable weight, nail it or screw it securely into the studs. To install the picture rail, snap a chalk line on each wall at the desired height. The line must be level, even if the ceiling is not. The bottom edge of the rail will be on this line and will cover it after installation. As with the other types of horizontal trim, prepare a plan view sketch of the room and determine the sequence for installing each piece. Miter outside corners and cope or miter inside corners.

Nail or screw the rail into the studs, using the same installation sequence as for baseboard. Because the outside miters may project some distance from the wall, nail them in place. Glue all joints and wipe them clean with a damp cloth.

## Chair Rail

Position the molding according to the height of the chairs you intend to use in the room. Chair rail is usually installed about one third of the way between the floor and ceiling, although if you use it as a cap for wainscoting or wall-covering, you can adjust the height accordingly. Follow the same procedure as for other horizontal trim. Plan the installation sequence. Miter and cope the corners. Nail to the studs, following the rules for baseboard. Glue all joints and wipe away excess glue with a damp cloth.

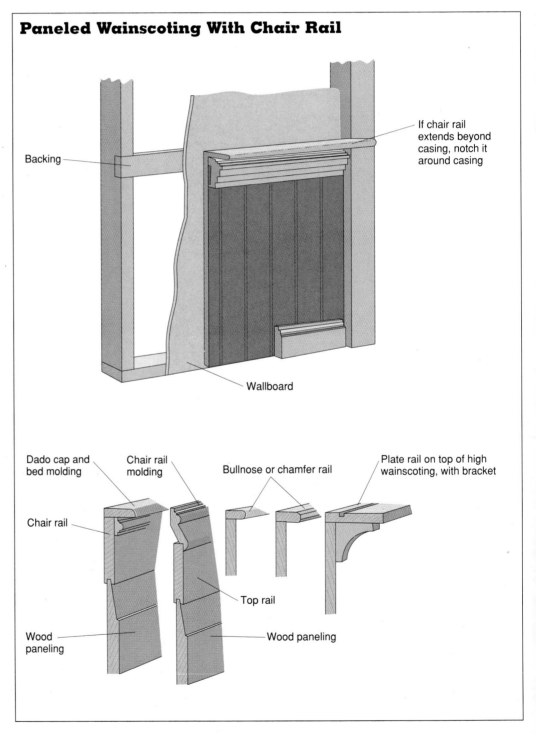

### Paneled Wainscoting With Chair Rail

Backing

If chair rail extends beyond casing, notch it around casing

Wallboard

Dado cap and bed molding

Chair rail molding

Bullnose or chamfer rail

Plate rail on top of high wainscoting, with bracket

Chair rail

Top rail

Wood paneling

Wood paneling

# Crown Molding

Crown molding does not lie flat against the ceiling or wall; rather, it spans the angle between them. Therefore you must provide backing wherever fastening is necessary. You can install backing before or after the wallcovering is applied.

To ensure that the installation is done correctly, make a template with a scrap of the molding. Hold it in position and with a pencil lightly mark where its edges meet the ceiling and wall.

If the ceiling sags, use a carpenter's level to determine the low point of the ceiling. Then measure down from that point the height of the molding and make another mark. Snap a horizontal chalk line from the lower mark around the room. The bottom edge of the molding will be placed along the line during installation. This will leave gaps between the ceiling and the molding; these must be shimmed, and the top edge of the molding nailed through the shims. If the gaps are quite small, they can be caulked. For larger gaps, hire a professional wallboard taper to float the edge of the ceiling with wallboard tape and compound so that it is parallel to the upper edge of the molding.

Don't worry about placing joint cuts out of the direct line of sight; the profile of crown molding makes it too difficult to fit complex cuts at both ends. For crown molding, outside corners should be cut and installed first; each piece has a square cut at the opposite end from the miter. You may have to install a long piece with a coped end cut that is more visible than you would like, but the trade-off in difficulty, and perhaps in wasted material, will be worth it.

Nail crown molding through the flats (near the edges) into the back (see illustration at right). The nails must penetrate the backing or framing by ¾ inch or more. It is also advisable to nail outside miters after they have been installed; predrill the holes.

## Ceiling Trim Sequence

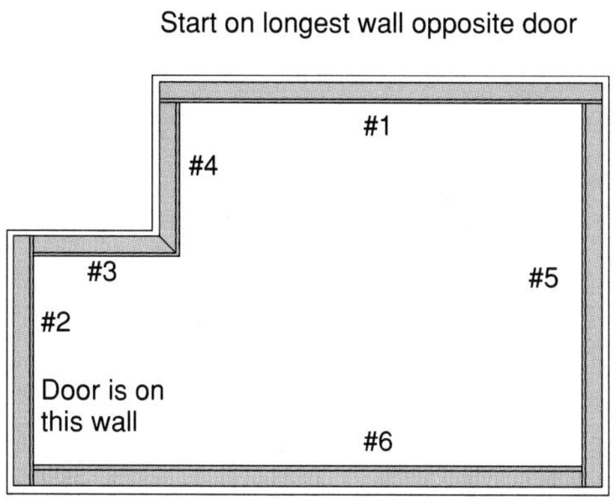

Start on longest wall opposite door

#1
#4
#3
#2
#5
#6
Door is on this wall

## Ceiling Trim

### Flat Ceiling Trim With Wood Paneling

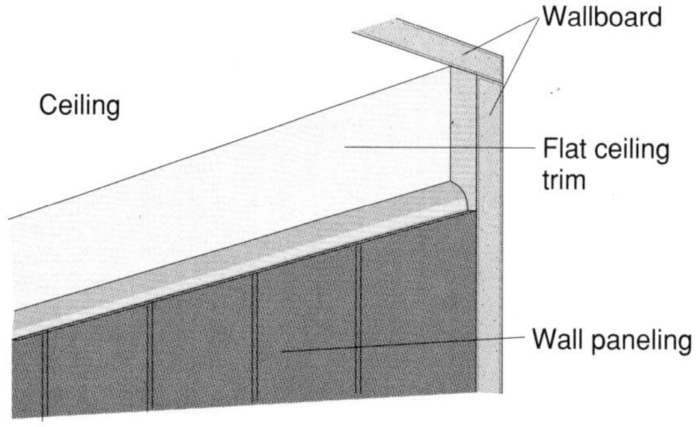

Ceiling
Wallboard
Flat ceiling trim
Wall paneling

### Crown Molding WIth Plain Edges of Backing Exposed

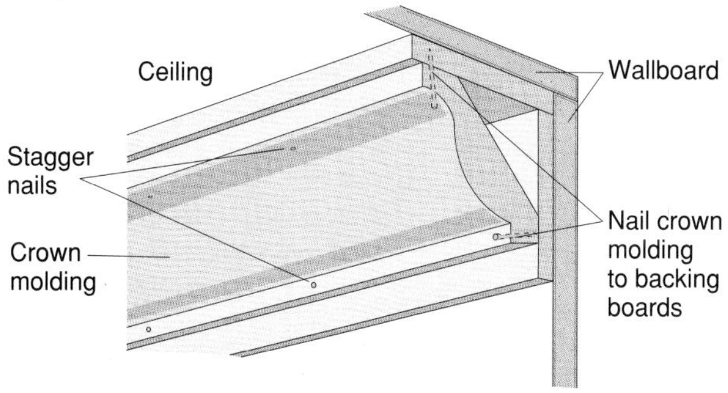

Ceiling
Wallboard
Stagger nails
Crown molding
Nail crown molding to backing boards

### Crown Molding With Concealed Backing

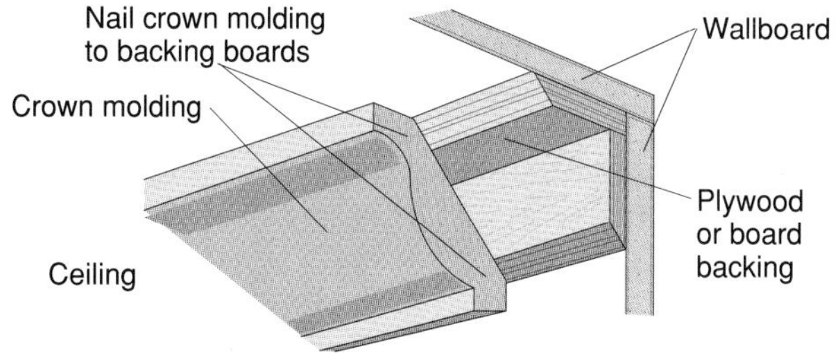

Nail crown molding to backing boards
Wallboard
Crown molding
Ceiling
Plywood or board backing

### Crown Molding Mitered at Outside Corner

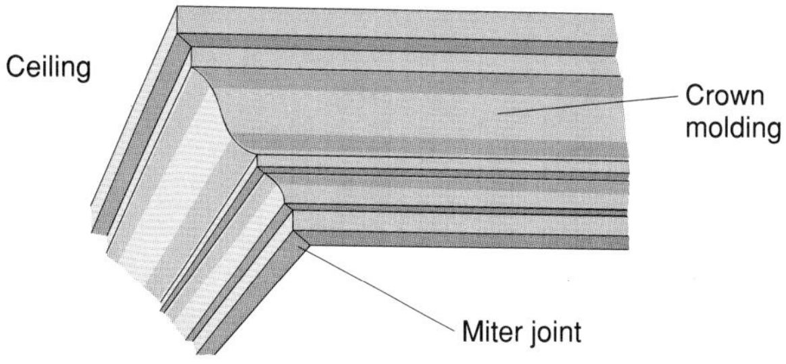

Ceiling
Crown molding
Miter joint

67

# CABINETS AND COUNTERTOPS

*Installing cabinets marks the transition to the final construction phase. The finish surfaces must be protected, and the work must be done conscientiously and correctly. Every stage of the remaining work will have a visual impact.*

## Successful Installation

Successful cabinet installations are level, plumb, and square. Cabinets should be tightly joined to each other and to the walls. In addition to achieving an attractive appearance, this allows easy installation of appliances. Doors and drawers won't open mysteriously or continually stick or bind. Counters should have the correct slope so that water doesn't run off one end or collect in one corner.

If you are painting or refacing old built-in cabinets, hinge styles and drawer slides of an appropriate type can compensate for some settling and other unfavorable conditions of age. Often the old countertop can be removed and a new one installed level, even though the old cabinets may be out of plumb.

## Sequence of Installation

Professionals dispute the proper sequence for cabinet installation and painting. If you paint the walls first, you avoid the need to mask the cabinets. However, the paint will probably need touching up and the texture may be difficult to match. If you install the cabinets first, painting will

take longer and you must protect the cabinets.

Floors present the same dilemma. If you install floor covering first, protect it from damage with cardboard or drop cloths. Secure the edges to ensure that debris such as nails and grit doesn't get underneath. Floor covering should be installed before cabinets in two cases: where the floors are not level and the veneered end panel of the cabinets must be scribed to them; and when the floors are made of hardwood. Resilient floor coverings are more forgiving and can be installed after cabinets.

If cabinets are installed first, consider whether the thickness of the floor covering will cause problems for such factors as toe-kick space, installation of a dishwasher, counter height, or the edge detail of the floor material. Compensate for the height of the floor covering by shimming up the cabinets. Determine the amount of shimming needed during layout. Remember that most vinyl floors will need a ¼-inch or ⅜-inch underlayment. Protect the underlayment from dirt and damage as you would a finish floor surface.

## Refacing Cabinets and Countertops

If your budget is limited, replacing doors or the entire face frame will create a dramatic change. Repainting cabinets, changing pulls and hinges, and installing a new countertop will also provide a significant improvement at a relatively low cost.

Adding molding to a flat door will create the look of a recessed panel door. This works best on painted cabinets.

Stripping the finish or paint from cabinets will not leave a stainable surface in most cases; stripping fuzzes and bleaches the wood. If you want to stain wood cabinets, strip and test a sample first. It may be easier and cheaper to start with new cabinets. If you remove the cabinet doors to strip and paint them, carefully note the location of each. Cabinet doors aren't necessarily interchangeable and may not fit correctly if they are installed other than in their original locations.

## Cabinet Dimensions

Except for specific situations that require a custom design, cabinet dimensions are standard throughout the industry. Base cabinets are always 24 inches deep (the countertop is usually 25½ inches) and 34½ inches high, so that by adding a 1½-inch countertop the total will be the normal 36 inches above the floor. Upper cabinets are 12 inches deep and from 12 to 48 inches wide. Most are 30 inches high; when they are

installed 18 inches above the countertop, the tops are 7 feet above the floor. Upper cabinets are also available in 12-, 15-, 18-, and 24-inch heights for installation over sinks, ranges, refrigerators, and windows. Allow for at least 30 inches of clearance above a cooktop, even when a range hood is under a cabinet. A bar counter is generally 42 inches high, and built-in desks are usually 29 or 30 inches high.

## Preparing to Install Cabinets

When you begin installing cabinets, the walls should be clear of all baseboard, trim, old cabinets, and electrical cover plates. Patch holes behind the cabinets. Test any electrical wiring or plumbing that will be behind the cabinets before you install them (test again after the cabinets are installed).

Check that the corners are square and the walls are plumb. Always check in several places because proportions may be correct in one area but not in others. If you install the cabinets without compensating for existing variations, the cabinets will twist and distort. Doors and drawers will not open and shut properly, and the cabinet seams could split under the tension. A commendable job of cabinet installation can be done in a house with walls and floors that are not plumb or level. The secret is to compensate with shimming, scribing, visual tricks, and molding.

Use a 6-foot to 8-foot piece of lumber as a straightedge (or a carpenter's level of the same length) to check the walls for straightness vertically and horizontally. Note high points and leans; if you intend to cover or repaint the walls, mark directly on them. Occasionally a high point can be sanded down, but shimming the cabinets is more common. Also check floors and mark the highest point that will be covered by cabinets.

Try to arrange for help, at least with the upper cabinets. You will have to predrill the uppers and hold them in place while screwing them to the wall. If you must install upper cabinets by yourself, use a temporary ledger screwed into the wall at the height of the bottom of the upper cabinets. A simple T-brace works adequately with this arrangement. A more elaborate version that will work without a ledger is shown in the illustration on page 70. Another approach to working alone is to install the base cabinets first, then build a frame to hold the uppers at the correct height. You can use a padded jack on top of the base cabinets. Because frameless cabinets in particular are very heavy, some people prefer to install the base cabinets first, cover them for protection, and then jack up the upper cabinets one at a time.

## Tools and Fasteners

It's best to use Phillips-head screws and a variable-speed or cordless drill with a Phillips-head bit. Self-guiding screws with a length of 2½ to 3 inches are the most convenient. If the

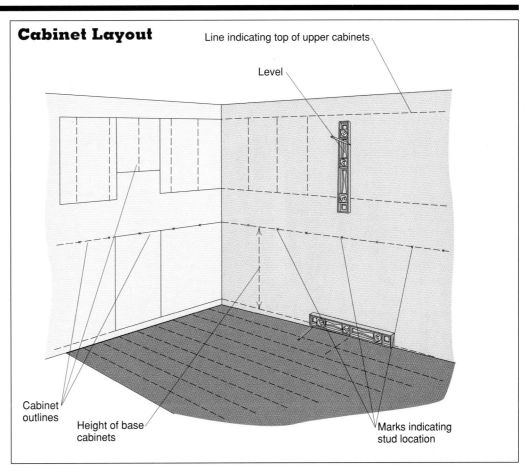

**Cabinet Layout**

Line indicating top of upper cabinets

Level

Cabinet outlines

Height of base cabinets

Marks indicating stud location

cabinets have particleboard backs, use large washers with the screws. Frameless cabinets come with specially designed fasteners that fit into each other like a nut and bolt, leaving only a smooth plastic face exposed.

A magnetic bit holder simplifies the job by holding the screws. With practice, you can pick up a screw with the drill. If you must drive screws by hand, predrill the holes, lift the cabinets into place, and mark through the holes. Check that the marks are on the studs, and predrill those holes about half the diameter of the screw shafts.

## Plumbing and Electrical Preparations

Double-check all wiring and plumbing before installing the cabinets. Make sure the appropriate plumbing and electrical connections are in place for each appliance. The literature accompanying most new appliances specifies the exact height and horizontal placement of necessary receptacles and plumbing connections. Ventilation ducts for hood or fan units must be in place and correctly sized. Vents for clothes dryers should also be in position.

## Laying Out Cabinets

Begin the layout at the high point of the floor (if the floors are level, start by marking the walls as shown in the illustration above). Mark a horizontal line on the wall level with the high point. All the base cabinets will be shimmed up to that line. If the floors are badly out of level, it may be necessary to raise the cabinets. Measure up from the line the distance to the bottom of the upper cabinets. Allow for the thickness of the countertop in your calculations, including shims and base material. Measure the height of the upper cabinets. Using a level, draw horizontal lines along the wall at the top and bottom of the upper cabinets.

Locate and mark the studs behind the cabinets: tap the walls, use a stud finder, or drive a nail (the cabinets will cover the holes). If the walls are newly painted, use tape or some other temporary marker. All wall marks should be measured from the horizontal line to the high point, not from the floor. Draw and label the cabinet plans directly on the wall.

If upper and base cabinets are to line up, measure and plan the layout for the base cabinets and adjust it so that they line up with the upper cabinets.

Install the stove hood, if there is one, to its cabinet while it is on the floor. If a stove duct passes through a cabinet, make a cutout on the bottom of the cabinet and where the duct will penetrate the side or back. Fashion a paper template of the cabinet and place it on the wall where the cabinet will be installed. Locate the duct hole and trace it on the pattern. Transfer the template to the cabinet and mark the hole. Start the cutout by drilling one or more holes, then finish with a jigsaw.

Keep the cabinets boxed if you are storing them on-site. If you are installing custom-made cabinets, have them delivered just before installation and protect them from damage.

## Installing Upper Cabinets

Most cabinet boxes have a piece of 1 by 3 or larger board across the upper back of the

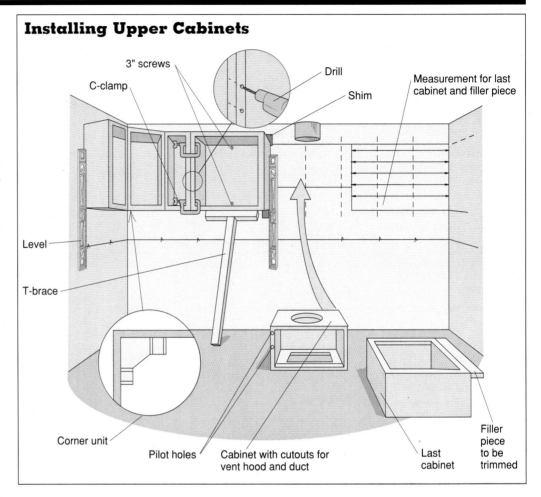

**Installing Upper Cabinets**

3" screws
C-clamp
Drill
Shim
Measurement for last cabinet and filler piece
Level
T-brace
Corner unit
Pilot holes
Cabinet with cutouts for vent hood and duct
Last cabinet
Filler piece to be trimmed

carcass or box. Some also have a lower mounting rail. Predrill them both so that screws will penetrate into the studs. Transfer the marks by measuring or by lifting the cabinets into place, marking the positions of the holes, and setting the cabinets back down.

Even though self-guiding screws will easily penetrate the mounting rail, predrilling the rail is better (especially if you are working alone). This makes it much easier to start the screw and pulls the cabinet more securely to the wall. Frameless cabinets come with partly drilled side holes about 3 inches from the front, bottom, and top. Complete the holes.

If you have installed continuous blocking, you can predrill for screws through the mounting rail about 3 inches from each upper corner. If there is no rail, drill through the top of the cabinet frame. Remove the shelves. Most professionals remove the doors as well; if you do, label them so they can be reinstalled in their original positions.

Start with a corner cabinet or two cabinets that form a corner. First set the corner cabinet by itself. This cabinet sets the level line for both walls, so it must be plumb and level. If two cabinets form a corner, position either one first but leave a ⅛-inch gap from the

corner wall (if this wall is perfectly plumb and square with the adjacent wall, the gap isn't necessary).

If the cabinets don't form a corner, start at either end of the run. If a filler strip is needed to match the dimensions of the cabinets with those of the room, plan for an identical gap at each end and use two filler strips of the same width for a symmetrical appearance. The gaps may vary in width; scribe the fillers to achieve a friction fit, then screw them into place through the front rail or carcass edge of the adjoining cabinet.

Lift the cabinet into place and install the screws tightly enough to hold it while you check its fit to the wall. Leave a little play in the screws; if you fasten them too tightly you can twist the cabinet or tear the back of it loose. Don't fasten the bottom of the cabinet yet. Is its back flush with the wall? Is it plumb and level? If so, there's no need for shimming.

Make any necessary adjustments to set the first cabinet plumb and level. If you need to shim out the top, remove the screw nearest to the shim location, insert a shim, and drive the screw through it.

Position the adjoining cabinet. Clamp it to the first cabinet along the front rail, using blocks or pads to protect the frame. Screw it to the wall just as you did the first cabinet.

The ends of some cabinets are exposed (finished ends); others are concealed by walls or other cabinets (wall ends). Finished ends are either finished directly on the surface or covered with a veneer piece that is scribed to the wall and glued to the end of the cabinet. Prefinished ends may extend past the back of the cabinet ⅛ to ⅜ inch. The extra material can be scribed to the wall. If there is no means of scribing the cabinets to the wall, cover any gaps with molding. A gap at the bottom of the cabinets should also be covered. If it is small enough, it can be caulked.

Being very careful to line up the stiles, or front frame edges, flush at bottom and front, drill holes about 6 inches from the top and bottom of one stile. As with the mounting screws, make the hole through the first stile

the same size as or slightly larger than the screw. Use a countersink bit to place the screw head below the surface. The hole can be filled with putty or left as is.

If you drill the second stile, use a drill bit about half the diameter of the screw shaft. Fasten the two stiles at top and bottom. If there is a gap in the center, use an additional screw. If you predrill the holes correctly and clamp the faces flush beforehand, there will be no visible gap. Two or more cabinets can be assembled in this way and then lifted into position. Such preassembling ensures that the face frames will line up at the bottom.

When a run of cabinets or complete section of uppers is connected together, check them for level and plumb. Adjust the tightness of the screws and shims at the top and bottom until the whole unit is plumb, then tighten all screws.

The frames of most upper cabinets are designed to hang from a wall. Cabinets mounted over an island must be designed for attachment through the top or to a soffit or the ceiling, unless some way of attaching them by their backs is provided. For a soffit mount, screw through the top of the cabinet into the front frame of the soffit. Shim any gaps; do not distort the cabinet by overtightening without a shim.

Hide any gaps with molding attached to the cabinets, unless the cabinets butt the ceiling. In this case, attach the molding to the ceiling framing so the gap will still be covered if the cabinet sags a little.

Once the cabinets are attached to the walls, install the shelves. If they must be cut to fit, leave a gap of 1/16 to 1/8 inch at the sides and ⅛ inch in front. Don't leave any gap at the back.

Hang and align the doors. Even though doors are attached by the manufacturer, they will need some adjustment after the cabinets are installed. Lightly mark where the bottoms of the doors should align, and clamp a straight piece of wood on the line. This will greatly speed the process. Flush-face, frameless cabinets have two-piece concealed cup hinges. These hinges are hidden when the doors are closed and are easily adjusted. Knife hinges are partly hidden and are adjusted by loosening the screws and sliding the hinges on the enlarged mounting holes. Barrel hinges are adjusted in the same manner.

Drilling for and setting the pulls must be done carefully. Do it when you are fresh, and set aside a full day to do an entire kitchen or roomful of cabinets. Positioning the pulls is a matter of taste, but a common location for the bottom (or only) holes for the pulls is 3 inches from the bottom of the door. Some people prefer to set the pull along a line drawn at 45 degrees from the corner. To align the pulls, either snap a chalk line or build a simple jig. Start the drill bit with an awl or use a vix bit or bullet bit to prevent the drill bit from traveling off the mark. Drill from the front of the door to prevent splintering the front face.

## Installing Base Cabinets

If the cabinets have attached platform frames (plinths), set the base cabinets in place, starting with the corner unit if there is one. If separate plinths are supplied with the cabinets or must be built on-site, set them in place. The cabinets or the plinths must be shimmed level and secured to the floor with angle brackets, screws, toenails, or cleats. Drive through shims in the same manner as for upper cabinets. Be sure to shim under the points where the cabinets join.

Separate plinths can be ripped down to adjust their height, but be careful not to end up with less than 3 inches of room from the cabinet face to the finish floor. A toe kick of less than 3 inches can catch a foot as you turn to walk away, presenting a safety hazard. Include in the measurements any lip hanging down from the face frame and the thickness of the finish floor if it isn't yet installed. Once the plinths are adjusted, set the base cabinets in position. Shim all the base cabinets level and attach them through the plinth.

Screw the cabinets together through the face frame or cabinet walls in the same manner as for upper cabinets. Then attach the backs of the cabinets to the wall in the same way as uppers, into studs or framed-in blocking. Be sure to shim any gaps between the backs of the cabinets and the wall to prevent the cabinets from being distorted.

Be sure the tops are level and the faces are flush. Make

## Cabinet Finish Panels

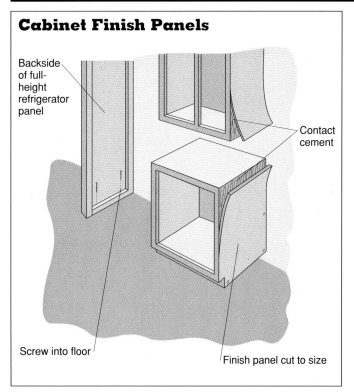

Backside of full-height refrigerator panel

Contact cement

Screw into floor

Finish panel cut to size

## Measuring for a Countertop

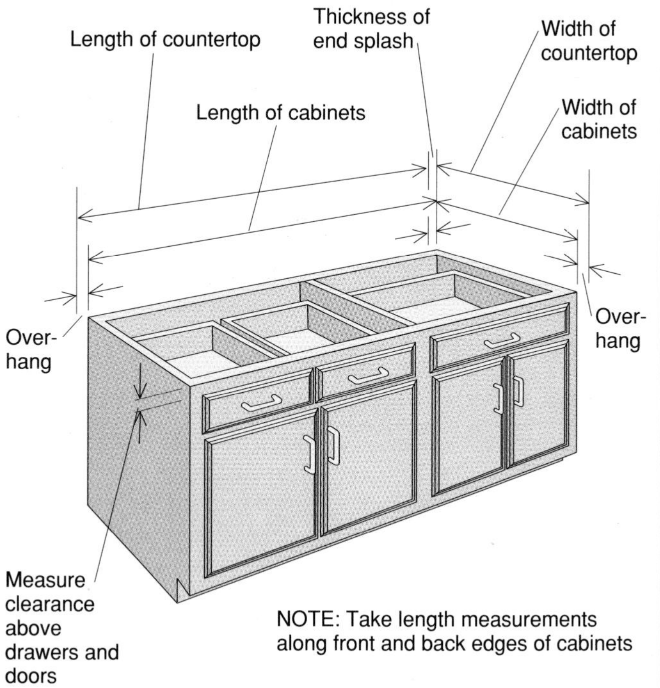

Length of countertop

Thickness of end splash

Width of countertop

Length of cabinets

Width of cabinets

Over-hang

Over-hang

Measure clearance above drawers and doors

NOTE: Take length measurements along front and back edges of cabinets

any adjustment and tighten the screws. Cut the shims flush and attach the toe-kick facing. If the floors were so badly out of level that you had to raise the cabinets, cover the resulting gap with molding or extend the baseboard onto the cabinet face. If the end cabinet has an unattached finish panel, scribe it to the floor and wall. Glue on the panel with contact adhesive, using small brads if necessary. Set the brads and hide the holes with wax sticks (if the cabinets are finished) or putty (if they are unfinished).

Some sink bases come without backs to ease plumbing connections. If your sink base does have a back, mark it and cut it out for the pipes.

Run any needed wiring through the cabinets before installing shelves, hinges, and doors. These are installed in the same way as for upper cabinets.

The location of drawers should be marked on their underside. When you reinstall them, pull them in and out to be sure they travel freely. Drawers that stick can usually be fixed by realigning the guide rails.

Leave ¼ inch of clearance for appliances to be installed. Double-check plumbing and electrical connections.

## Installing Bathroom Vanities

Bathroom vanities are like base cabinets with veneered ends. They often come finished. Scribe the back edge of the cabinet to the wall and the bottom to the floor. Cut the bottom first, then scribe the wall ends. You will also have to cut out the back for plumbing connections. If the

cabinet fits between two walls, it will have side rails that were meant to be scribed to the walls. If not, filler pieces should be supplied. Attach the vanity to the wall just as for base cabinets. The water supply pipes and drains should all be protected at the studs with nail guards.

## Installing Countertops

This section deals with countertops of wood, stone, plastic laminate, solid-surface material, and synthetic marble. Tile counters are covered on pages 87 to 89.

### Countertop Dimensions

Countertops are usually between 33 and 36 inches high and are at least 24 inches deep. A standard backsplash is 4

inches high. The front edge of a countertop should clear the top of any drawer or door by a minimum of ¼ inch and normally overhangs the front face by ¾ inch to 1 inch. Where the countertop terminates at an appliance, a ⅛- to ¼-inch overhang is standard.

Thickness varies from as little as ½ inch for natural stone or solid-surface material to as much as 2 inches for tile with plywood and a mortar bed. The substrate or core is usually exterior-grade particleboard for plastic laminate and ¾-inch plywood for tile, stone, or solid-surface material. Stone and solid-surface material don't require a core, but usually have one to prevent the counter from cracking at the narrow points around sink cutouts. Wood counters such as butcher block can be connected directly to the base cabinets.

## Preparing to Install Countertops

If the cabinets are level and accurately aligned, little shimming should be necessary. The back wall can create difficulties if it is wavy or out of plumb because the backsplash must conform to it. Small gaps can be filled with caulk or the wallboard can be carved out at a high point. Shave down the backsplash of a laminate countertop. If there is protective paper on the countertop, don't remove it.

Attach the counter substrate with screws through the top or the bottom, depending on the material. Any substrate not intended for laminate can be screwed through the top into the base-cabinet frame. When screwing into the face frame, predrill the hole to prevent splitting the wood. A suitable place to attach the substrate is the corner blocks found in many cabinets. You can add your own cleats if there is room above the top drawers. A substrate that will be covered with laminate should be attached from the bottom. Screw through the cleats or use metal brackets. Small L brackets will work, or use figure-eight finish washers.

Whenever possible, use a single piece of particleboard or plywood. If joints are needed, fasten them with drawbolts rabbeted into the base or cleats. Lining up the joint with the side frame of the base cabinets also provides adequate support. Plan laminate countertops so that the joints in the laminate don't align with the joints in the substrate.

## Postformed Laminate Countertops

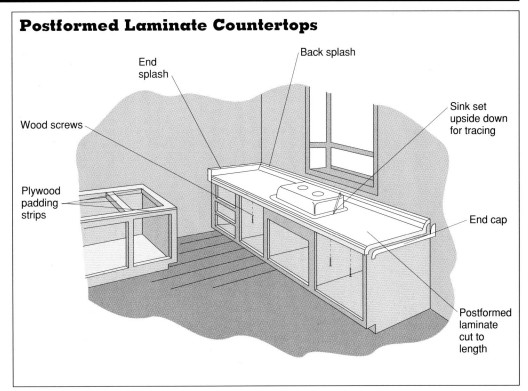

End splash

Back splash

Wood screws

Sink set upside down for tracing

Plywood padding strips

End cap

Postformed laminate cut to length

After the cabinets are installed but before the countertops, take measurements for the sink, cooktop, and built-in appliances. Keep these measurements available. Decisions about backsplashes, corners, and seams need to be made or verified. Professional builders of countertops usually take their own measurements. If you are responsible for the measurements, make a sketch and label it clearly. Take all measurements in inches only. Attach a copy to your order. Be sure to measure the longest distances. Sometimes when a counter ends at a wall, the distance against the wall is different from that at the face of the cabinet. If the countertop has a lip, calculate whether it will block drawers, the dishwasher, or the cutting board. If so, nail plywood strips over the leveling shims or have the cabinet fabricator pad the countertop.

## Installing Laminate Countertops

Start by examining the backsplash. Postformed counters usually have a backsplash integral with the countertop. Ready-made counters have a backsplash that must be attached to the counter. If your countertop is ready-made, note whether it butts into the backsplash or whether the backsplash rests on the countertop. If the countertop is L-shaped, you'll need end caps and mitered ends.

First check the corner with a framing square. Mark the approximate line with masking tape and draw the exact line over the tape. The tape will help to prevent the laminate from chipping when you cut it. The laminate is about $\frac{1}{16}$ inch thick and is very hard and brittle.

Cut the countertop with a sharp saw. If you cut by hand, use a crosscut saw with at least 10 teeth to the inch. If you use a circular saw, cut from the underside of the counter to prevent chipping the surface.

Test-fit the end splash (if there is one) against the cut. Sand, file, or plane the end until the fit is tight. Glue and screw the end cap to the counter. Predrill the screw holes, slightly larger than the screw shaft through the first piece and about half the diameter of the shaft through the countertop.

If there is no end splash, glue or screw supplied ½- by ½-inch wood strips to the bottom and back of the countertop flush with the end. Use contact cement to glue on the end cap. If it is slightly large, glue it on and trim it in place. Trim the edge at a 45-degree angle. A fine file will work, but a router with a bevel bit or belt sander with fine sandpaper will produce a more uniform edge. Use a mask if you sand; the dust is very irritating.

Set the countertop in place and inspect the joint at the wall. If there is a molded backsplash, it will have a thin top that can be planed or sanded down with a belt sander (use medium-grit paper for this). Carefully shave down the back a little at a time, and test it for fit. You can also scribe this edge simply by sliding a pencil against the wall and marking a line on the top edge of the counter.

Once the countertop fits, position any cutouts for sinks or cooktops. Read any instructions supplied by the manufacturer. A sink cutout should be at least 1¾ inches back from the front edge if there is a 1-inch overhang and a ¾-inch face frame.

The cut can be marked from a paper or cardboard template or by laying the sink upside down on the countertop and tracing around it. If the sink has its own rim, draw another line about ½ inch in from the traced line. If it has a separate rim, use the rim to trace the cutout and reduce it by ½ inch in the same way. Step back and take a broad look at the countertop and at the marked cutout. Look for obvious mistakes in locating the cutouts, such as not centering the sink on a window or not placing the cooktop under the hood.

Check the measurements again. Make sure the bowl of the sink will clear the cabinets.

Drill out the corners with a sharp ⅜-inch or larger bit. Rounded corners will help prevent stress cracks. Cut with a fine-toothed jigsaw or saber saw. Support the panel as you cut; it is quite heavy and can tear out near the end. You can support the cutout by screwing small plywood panels under each side after you've made a cut. A quicker method is to cut most of two sides and the front, lift the center cutout piece, and drive a 4d finishing nail in about ¾ inch at a slight downward angle at the center of each cut side. Another method of supporting the cutout piece is to take a scrap of lumber or plywood longer than the cutout and attach it to the cutout with one screw in the center so that you can rotate it out of the way of the saw blade as you cut.

The back cut may be too close to the backsplash for the jigsaw or saber saw to fit. You can flip the countertop over (note that the cutout support braces won't work if you do this) and cut from the back, or cut out the last part with a handsaw. You can also make the cutout in small pieces and remove them as you go.

Double-check that everything fits and is level. Seal the bottom and cut edges of the countertop with silicone, especially near the sink or other potentially wet areas.

Assemble L- or U-shaped countertops before you attach them to the cabinets. The joints are often accessible if you slide the counters out from the wall. If you can't get to the joints any other way, take off the countertops and assemble them upside down.

Apply waterproof glue or silicone to the edges to be joined. The countertop should include routed cavities and drawbolts. Tighten the drawbolt with an open-end wrench. Check the top of the joint to be sure it is flush as you tighten the bolts. If there will not be access to retighten the drawbolts after the counter is installed, screw and glue a plywood reinforcement into the countertop under each joint. The reinforcement should be about 8 inches wider than the joint. This can prevent the particleboard from compressing under the drawbolts, which would allow the miter joints to eventually separate.

Carefully place the countertops and attach them from below. Use screws that can penetrate the counter only ½ inch. Do not overtighten the screws. Countertops can also be glued down with silicone caulk or an adhesive recommended by the countertop manufacturer. Carefully caulk between the counter and the wall.

## Installing Site-Built Counters

The simplest method is to apply new laminate directly to the old. Check the manufacturer of the new material to make sure it is compatible with the old. The substrate should be new or in like-new condition. For curved areas, ready-made thin laminate is available. You can also thin regular laminate by sanding the backside with a belt sander.

Remove sinks, cooktops, the edge trim, and removable backsplashes. Sand the old

laminate with 120-grit sandpaper. Don't skip any areas; this is likely to cause delamination of the new layer. Fill all joints and sand them smooth. Make sure all edges are clean, smooth, dry, and shaped.

There are two ways to cut laminate. It can be scored with a laminate cutter and then snapped along the score mark, or it can be cut with a saw. The saw must be sharp to lessen chipping (beware: blades dull quickly). Fine-toothed blades, such as laminate (for jigsaws) or plywood, should be used.

The teeth of the saw blade should cut into the surface of the laminate. If you use a circular saw, the laminate should be facedown; with a handsaw or table saw, the laminate should be faceup. If you cut from the face, protect the laminate from scratches by taping over the bottom plate of the saw. Cut the laminate pieces ¼ inch oversized. This protects the finish surface from small chips and allows a margin for installing the laminate.

Keep all seams away from cutouts and major work areas on the counter. If possible, leave factory edges at the seams; if not, cut the pieces to be seamed together with a router and a carbide cutting bit. Guide the router with a straightedge clamped along both sides.

Test-fit the pieces. Vacuum the entire area and double-check the surfaces that will be bonded for debris. Even a speck of grit can cause a bubble, and trying to flatten it could crack the laminate. Once large surfaces are bonded with contact cement, they can't be

# Fabricating a Site-Built Countertop

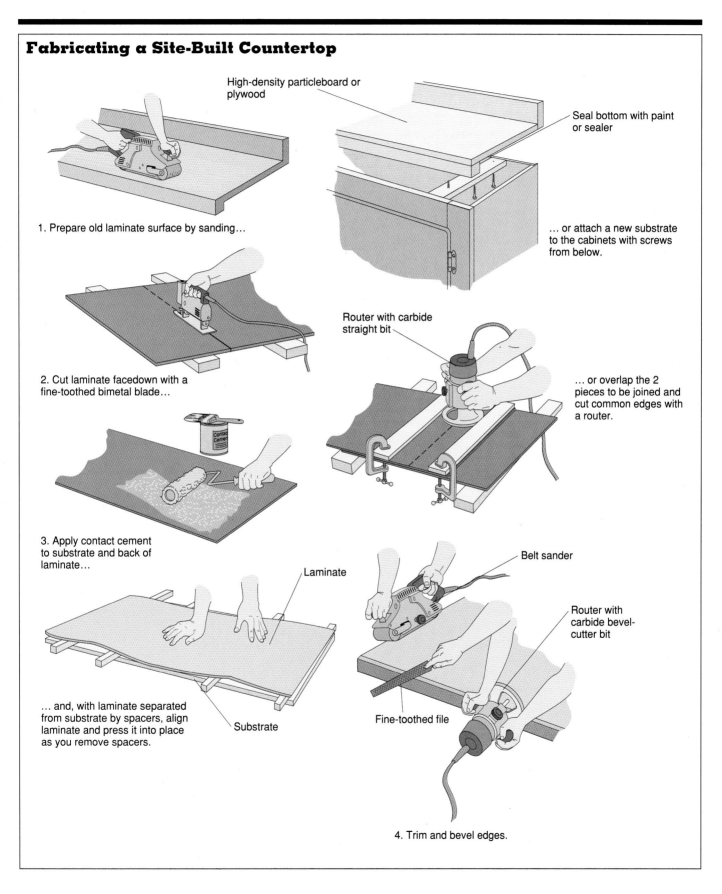

High-density particleboard or plywood

1. Prepare old laminate surface by sanding...

Seal bottom with paint or sealer

... or attach a new substrate to the cabinets with screws from below.

2. Cut laminate facedown with a fine-toothed bimetal blade...

Router with carbide straight bit

... or overlap the 2 pieces to be joined and cut common edges with a router.

3. Apply contact cement to substrate and back of laminate...

Laminate

... and, with laminate separated from substrate by spacers, align laminate and press it into place as you remove spacers.

Substrate

Belt sander

Router with carbide bevel-cutter bit

Fine-toothed file

4. Trim and bevel edges.

separated without destroying one of them.

Apply contact cement evenly to both surfaces. Use a smooth, short-napped roller or an animal-hair brush. Follow directions and use caution. These cements are volatile and the fumes are toxic. Use a chemical-filter respirator and make sure there is sufficient ventilation. Turn off the electricity and all pilot lights in the area.

Install the edge strips first. For curved countertop edges, heat the laminate with a hair dryer or heat gun to soften it. Precisely position the material before making contact. When the cement is dry enough that a piece of paper won't stick to it, it is ready for bonding. Lay ¾-inch spacers on top of the substrate, about 12 inches apart, from the back wall past the front edge. Place the laminate onto the spacers, being careful not to let the cemented surfaces touch. When the laminate is aligned, start at the middle and pull the spacers out one at a time, pressing, rolling, or hammering the laminate as you go. Work the entire surface, squeezing out any air bubbles. Pay particular attention to the edges. Bevel the edges with a router and a carbide bevel bit with a ball-bearing tip. Use a fine file at inside corners where the router won't fit.

Make any cutouts after laminating the countertop.

## Installing Stone Countertops

Because stone is expensive and easily damaged, it should be installed by professionals. The supplier should cut and edge the pieces (including cutouts) and polish the stone. Be sure to tell the supplier not to leave sharp exposed corners; they are dangerous. Do not have the countertop delivered until it is time to install it. When it arrives, check for scratches or flaws. Shine a bright light onto the surface from one side to make any defects stand out.

A ½-inch-thick stone slab should have support every 16 inches. A substrate is not absolutely necessary but is recommended to protect the stone from cracking in narrow areas around cutouts. Use plywood.

Stone is secured to cabinets with adhesive. If you want the extra security of screws, have the supplier drill the slab for screw anchors. Before attaching a stone counter, position it on top of the base cabinets and check the fit. Make sure it is level and that any backsplashes and end pieces fit properly. Shim any low spots.

Remove the countertop and spread thick beads of the adhesive recommended by the supplier along the tops of the cabinet frames. If you are also using screws, thread them into their anchors. Snug the screws only until the countertop is firmly held.

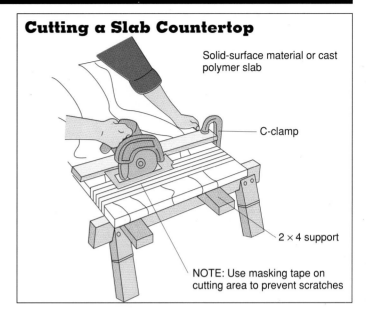

## Cutting a Slab Countertop

Solid-surface material or cast polymer slab

C-clamp

2 × 4 support

NOTE: Use masking tape on cutting area to prevent scratches

## Installing a Solid-Surface–Material Countertop

Large countertops or complicated installations with laminated edges, joints, and inlays should be left to the professionals. A simple slab, however, is fairly easy to install.

Sheets in ½-inch and ¾-inch thicknesses are used for countertops, which can have sinks molded into them. Ready-made 5-inch-wide strips are available for backsplashes.

Start by measuring the length and width of the countertop area. Allow about 1 inch for each overhang. Install a ¾-inch plywood base over the cabinets on which to mount the countertop. Shim, if necessary, to make it level. For a recessed sink, cut out the opening and then rout a groove around the edge so that the sink rim rests flush with the top of the plywood. Provide extra support for the sink by attaching cleats under the edges of the opening.

Cut the countertop and the backsplashes to size. Use a circular power saw with a carbide-tipped blade and cut from the backside of the slab, or according to the manufacturer's instructions. Wear goggles. Clamp a straightedge to the countertop to guide the saw. (Protect the finish surface with masking tape.) For sink openings, cut the straight lines with a circular saw and the corners with a saber saw or router. Set the top in place to check for fit.

To create a thicker edge, turn the top over and attach pieces of trim along the edge, using an adhesive recommended by the manufacturer. Clamp the joints and let them dry overnight. You can do the same for the backsplash, or you can attach it after the top is in place.

Fasten the countertop to the plywood base, using a mastic recommended by the manufacturer. Attach the backsplash and seal all joints with silicone. Wipe away the excess and smooth the sealant with a damp rag.

## Supporting a Slab Countertop

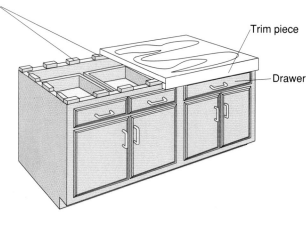

Wood shims

Trim piece

Drawer

1. Self edge

2. Rounded edge

3. Pinstripe

4. Wood chamfer

5. Wood ogee

## Installing a Cast Polymer Countertop

Measure the countertop, leaving 1-inch overhangs at the front and sides and 1 inch to cover any end panels. Remember to plan for the edges of the slab. You can leave these edges plain, cut a decorative groove in them with a router, or attach trim pieces by butt-joining them around the bottom of the edge. Making miter joints is difficult and not recommended.

Cut both the countertop and backsplash pieces according to your measurements. Use a blade with carbide teeth and wear goggles and a dust mask. Make sink cutouts by tracing the outline of the sink onto the slab, sawing the straight lines with a circular saw, and cutting around the combers with a saber saw. Set the countertop in place and check both level and plumb. Make sure that front trim pieces do not catch when you open doors or drawers. If they do, pad the cabinet tops with shims. Replace the countertop, check for level, and add more shims wherever necessary.

Turn the top over and attach the trim pieces by gluing them to the underside of the edge, using a recommended adhesive. Clamp, and let the joints dry overnight. Scrape off any residue or wipe it off with a drop of acetone on a rag. Apply silicone or other mastic to the top edges of the cabinet or shims. Place the countertop in position, press down firmly, and let the glue dry. Finally, attach the backsplash to the counter with the recommended adhesive, fitting it snugly against the wall. Seal all joints and seams with silicone, wiping away the excess and smoothing the seams with a wet rag wrapped around your finger.

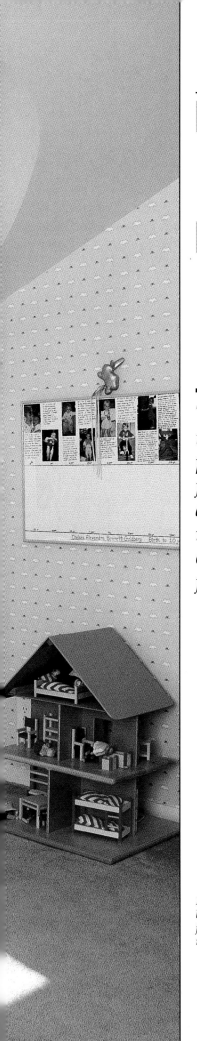

# FINISHING THE JOB

*This chapter deals with the tasks that complete your project: tile, paint, floors, wallcoverings, finish electrical work, plumbing fixtures, and appliances. All are realistic projects for a homeowner and can be done individually or as part of a larger project. All will produce visible improvements at relatively little cost and effort. For these reasons, the areas covered in this chapter provide excellent starter projects for beginning remodelers.*

*Placing the bed in a bumpout increased the usable floor area in this small bedroom. The arch over the bed gives a spacious feeling; the uninterrupted flow of the ceiling color down the walls of the alcove integrate it into the room. Drawers below the bed provide hidden storage.*

# TILE

*Tile is suitable for most surfaces in a house. Styles and colors are available to match nearly any decor. Installing tile with thin-set techniques is within the capabilities of most homeowners.*

## Types of Tile

There are many ways to classify ceramic tile, but common designations are glazed wall tile, mosaic tile, quarry tile, and pavers.

### Glazed Wall Tiles

Glazed wall tiles are the standard type used for walls, tubs, showers, vanities, and kitchen countertops. Glazing makes most tiles waterproof, although the actual clay bodies vary from nonvitreous (highly absorbent) to vitreous (low absorption) to impervious (won't even absorb dye). Some handmade types have soft glazing, which is not suitable for tubs, showers, or countertops. Sizes of imported tile vary, as they are in metric measurements; standard domestic sizes are 4½ inches and 6 inches square.

### Mosaic Tile

Mosaic tiles are small, usually 1 to 2 inches across, although some are as small as ⅜ inch square. Tiles are assembled into sheets, usually 1 foot square. They are held together by sheets of paper on the face or mesh on the back. Some are bonded together with rubber-like elastomeric grout, and the joints between the sheets are grouted with the same material applied with a caulking gun. Mosaic tile comes glazed or unglazed and is ideal for

curved or intricate surfaces. Elastomeric-grout mosaic tile is excellent for tub and shower enclosures, but should not be used for surfaces where food is prepared.

### Quarry Tile

Quarry tile is intended for floors and hearths. It usually comes unglazed and is vitreous to semivitreous. Because most kinds of quarry tile are manufactured by an extrusion process that is not as precise as the dust-press method used for most wall and mosaic tiles, it lends itself to more informal installations.

### Pavers

Pavers are quarry tiles made by the dust-press method. They can be found either glazed or unglazed and are quite durable. They are generally 12 inches square and tend to be quite thick. Pavers are intended for patios and floors. If used indoors, they should be sealed. Beware of using them outside in areas with severe winters; expansion and contraction due to freezing and thawing can cause them to crack.

## Trim Tile

Trim tile comes in a number of shapes, such as surface bullnose, radius bullnose, and down-angle versions of these. Surface bullnose is flat with rounded edges and is designed to fit flush with adjoining surfaces. Radius bullnose is applied over a built-up bed or substrate and curves back to the adjoining surface, concealing the substrate. Down-angle versions of both types of trim tile are available for the outside corners of countertops.

## Words of Caution

You may be tempted by sales on manufacturer's seconds. These can be warped or of varying thickness. Such tiles are difficult to use—and expensive if you hire a profes-

sional tilesetter. Use a straight-edge to check seconds for warpage. Don't buy warped tiles unless you plan to cut them for edge pieces.

Trim tile may not be available for seconds, handmade tiles, and odd lots. Although it is possible to make countertop edges of wood or complementary tile, you should be aware of the problem and make plans to deal with it.

## Preparation

A successful tile installation depends on a smooth, firm base that will not shift and settle. In addition, installations in wet areas need a backing that will not deteriorate if moisture seeps through the tile or grout. Common backing materials are a bed of mortar, wallboard, plywood, and tile backing board (panels of cement material sandwiched between two layers of fiberglass mesh).

Do not try to tile over wallpaper, lumber subflooring (even tongue and groove), particleboard, paneling (except dimensioned lumber), or multiple layers of resilient flooring.

---

**Tile Trim Pieces**

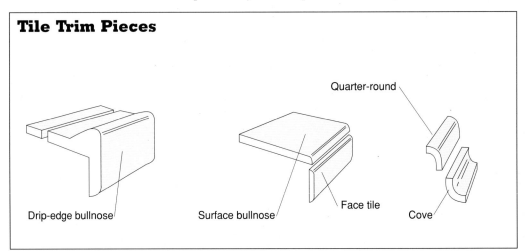

Drip-edge bullnose

Surface bullnose — Face tile

Quarter-round

Cove

On a countertop, any slope within ¼ inch over 8 feet is acceptable. Old counters were often sloped to drain water back to the sink. Except for this, counters should be level. Check to make sure that the top drawers will still open after the edge material is installed.

Check the surfaces to be tiled for straightness, using the longest straightedge that will fit. Mark any bows, dips, or high spots with a pencil or crayon. If the irregularities are small, plywood or tile backing board may be adequate to correct the surface. If the area is out of level or very irregular, installing a mortar bed or reframing the area is the best solution. If walls are so far out of square that a mortar bed cannot create plumb and level surfaces, consult a professional. The only solution may be to reframe the walls, which may be too expensive.

If two or more tiled surfaces intersect, plumb and square measurements should be within ⅛ inch over 8 feet.

Whenever laminating materials such as plywood and tile backing board to other layers, glue with construction adhesive and screw the layers together. Attach the additional layers through to the framing. Stagger the joints between layers. The screws or nails must penetrate at least 1 inch into the framing every 6 inches. Elsewhere, nail or screw into the center unless local code requires closer spacing. Predrill the screw holes. The holes should be the same diameter as the screw threads through the top layer of substrate. The hole through the remaining substrate and into the framing should be slightly smaller than the screw shaft.

Leave 1/16-inch gaps between pieces of plywood substrate to allow for expansion. Cover the plywood with 30-pound felt and seal the seams.

Before installing the substrate and tile, remove anything that projects above the surface if possible. Repair any deterioration exposed when you remove fixtures (such as water damage around a toilet). Lights and electrical receptacles should be removed. First, though, turn off the power to the area and make sure it is off. Protect or remove chrome pipes or other hardware so the chrome won't be damaged by the tile adhesive.

Electrical boxes can be elongated with extension rings to bring them flush with the new surface. Valve stems can be replaced with longer ones in some cases. Check this before you install the tile.

If you are tiling the floor around a toilet, do not raise the floor surface more than ¼ inch above the flange. If the substrate raises the floor more than this, the flange must also be raised. Plastic pipe can easily be changed by a homeowner. However, cast-iron or lead pipes require a professional plumber.

## Preparing to Tile Walls

In areas that are dry or exposed to a limited amount of moisture, tile can be installed over any smooth wall surface with thin-set organic adhesives. Some surfaces, such as new wallboard, should first be sealed with a primer that is compatible with the adhesive to be used. Existing wall surfaces must be free of wax, grease, efflorescence, or other residue, and should be roughened by sanding if they are glossy or painted. Install a new backing material, such as wallboard, over walls with cracks or irregularities.

Wet locations, such as tub and shower enclosures, require a waterproof backing. The most reliable is a professionally installed mortar bed; but if the tiles and grout are properly sealed, you can expect satisfactory results with moisture-resistant wallboard or tile backing board. Check the local building code to see if any particular backing material is specified. If you use wallboard, tape and fill the joints with an appropriate waterproof compound, coating all cut edges and nail heads. Some adhesives may require that you seal the entire surface. If you install tile backing board, tape the joints with fiberglass-mesh tape, fill them with compound, and use dry-set or latex-portland mortar.

## Preparing to Tile Floors

Tiles can be installed over concrete or wood, but the floor must be prepared properly. For new construction over wood framing, install a subfloor of ⅝-inch CDX or better plywood and put an underlayment of ⅜-inch plywood over it (⅝ inch for epoxy adhesives). For existing floors, a traditional portland-cement mortar bed will level irregularities. For heavy materials, such as thick pavers, or for any installations over a mortar bed, add extra joists, making sure that the surface of the finished tile floor will be flush with the other floors.

Before installing tile in an existing room, it is best to remove the finish floor to reduce thickness, and then nail ⅜- or ⅝-inch plywood over the subfloor. If the existing floor surface is noncushioned vinyl laid over plywood (not particleboard), you can leave it on if you remove all wax and roughen the surface so that the adhesive will bond. Tile can also be installed over old tile if the floor is solid and you are able to roughen the surface for adequate bonding. Applying a liquid underlayment (if you are using mastic) or epoxy mortar will level off any irregularities.

Concrete floors make an excellent base as long as they are dry, smooth, and level. Remove any old flooring material first and roughen the surface to facilitate adhesion. If the floor is cracked, damp, or otherwise unstable, repair it before installing tile.

Concrete slabs should be sound, well cured, and free of any wax, oil, or curing compound. Tile will adhere directly to a steel-troweled slab with the use of organic adhesives or dry-set mortar. Rougher surfaces call for epoxy or portland-cement mortar.

## Preparing to Tile Countertops

For thin-set organic and epoxy adhesives, use plywood at least ¾ inch thick. However, it may deteriorate in wet locations if the tile is not well sealed. A better backing for dry-set and latex-portland

## Marking for a Cut

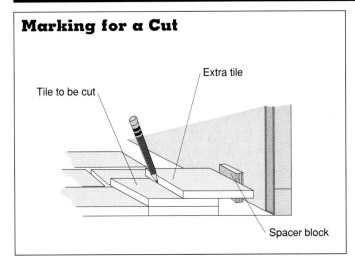

Tile to be cut

Extra tile

Spacer block

## Cutting Tile

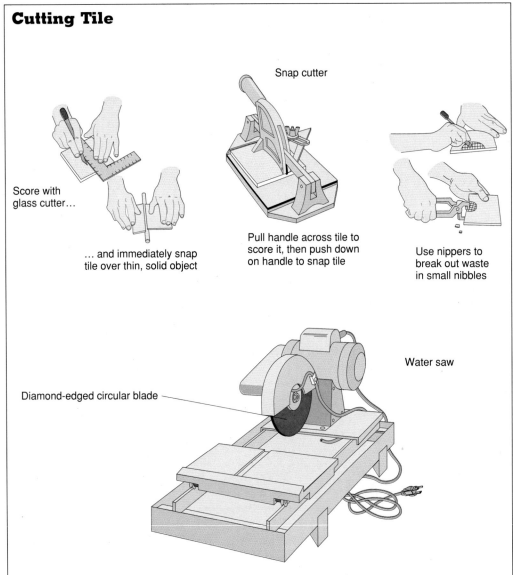

Snap cutter

Score with glass cutter...

... and immediately snap tile over thin, solid object

Pull handle across tile to score it, then push down on handle to snap tile

Use nippers to break out waste in small nibbles

Diamond-edged circular blade

Water saw

mortars is glass-mesh mortarboard installed over plywood. The best installation is a reinforced mortar bed floated over plywood or 1-inch boards.

## Cutting Tile

Whether you have just a few or a great many cuts, it is easiest to pay the extra charge and have the tile supplier make perfectly smooth cuts with a water-cooled cutoff saw. You can also rent a diamond wet saw, or use one of the following techniques if the tile is soft enough.

## Cutting With a Tile Cutter

This tool, which can be rented, makes straight cuts easily and accurately. The handle has a small cutting wheel that scores the tile as you pull it across the surface. An extension arm on the handle forces the sides of the tile down to snap it in two.

## Round Cut

Mark the diameter of the circle to be cut out, then score and cut the tile along this line. On each half tile, score around the half circle. Also make crosshatch scores all over the area to be cut away.

Using pliers or nippers, break out waste in small chips.

## Marking for Cutting

When laying out a tile installation, strive for the fewest cuts. Try to adjust the layout so that rows end with full tiles. However, short rows look better if they are equal on both sides of the centerline. When a row must be ended with a cut tile, use the method shown here to mark the tile for an accurate cut. Mark individually each tile to be cut in case there are variations in the wall. The spacer accounts for grout lines on both sides of the tile.

## Setting Tile

Spread adhesive over an area approximately 3 feet square, using a notched trowel. If the floor tends to get damp, apply a preliminary coat of adhesive over the entire surface with a smooth trowel, let it dry, then apply a second coat. Set tiles into the wet adhesive with a firm, twisting motion. Insert spacers between the tiles and wipe off excess adhesive immediately.

## Applying Grout

Remove spacers and let the adhesive dry, after checking that it does not fill any of the grout spaces. Mix cement-based grout according to the type of tile: stiff for mosaic tile, loose for most white-bodied tiles, and runny for red-bodied tiles. Force grout into the cracks by spreading it diagonally across the tiles with a rubber float or squeegee. Work it into joints. A toothbrush handle is an effective tool for this purpose.

Remove as much excess as possible, and wipe off the remainder with a wet sponge. Wait 30 minutes, let a haze form, and polish the surface with a soft cloth. To cure, keep the grout moist by covering the tiled area with plastic sheeting or spraying it at regular intervals for two or three days. Seal after two weeks.

## Tiling Floors: Method 1

This method is effective for rooms with large doorways that make the floor clearly visible from other parts of the house. With this method you establish tile locations from preliminary lines drawn through the middle of the room.

### Starting the Layout

Snap a chalk line down the center of the room, perpendicular to the doorway (see page 84). Snap another chalk line perpendicular to the first. Then, starting with a full tile at the doorway, lay a dry run of tiles along the first line. Use spacers between tiles for uniform grout lines. If you do not have enough space for a full tile at the end, decide whether to have a cut tile at one end or at both ends; another solution is to widen the grout spaces. Repeat the process along the second chalk line, readjusting both lines so that they intersect at a tile corner.

### Installing Temporary Straightedges

Draw a line on the floor to mark the edge of the last full tile at the doorway. This line must be perpendicular to the first chalk line and perfectly straight, even if the wall is not.

Extend the line along the length of the wall. Repeat this process for the other walls. Set long boards on the outside of each line and nail them to the floor. Use 1 by 2s or 1 by 3s so that you can straighten them as you nail. Use a 3-4-5 triangle to square the boards: Measure 3 feet out from the corner along one board and 4 feet along the other. If the two points are exactly 5 feet apart, the boards are square.

### Setting the Tiles

Starting in the corner where the boards intersect, spread a small area of adhesive with a notched trowel. Follow the manufacturer's instructions, and be sure to wear gloves if you are working with epoxy. Then gently press the corner tile into place with a slight twisting motion. Continue setting tiles in the order shown on page 84, inserting spacers between them to keep the alignment straight. Use molded plastic tees, scraps of plywood, or similar material for spacers. Tamp down uneven tiles with a rubber mallet or beat on a cushioned 2 by 4 with a hammer. Wipe off any excess adhesive from the tile surface immediately. Allow the tile to set, remove the straightedges, and install cut tiles along the edges, leaving a ⅛-inch gap along the wall.

## Tiling Floors: Method 2

Use this method if you want a border of contrasting tiles or if cut tiles will not be too noticeable. Begin the layout along a prominent wall and establish perimeter lines.

## Setting Tile

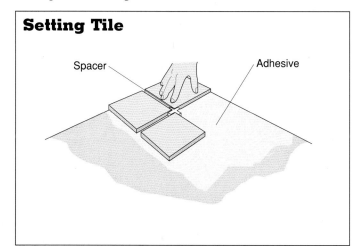

Spacer

Adhesive

## Applying Grout

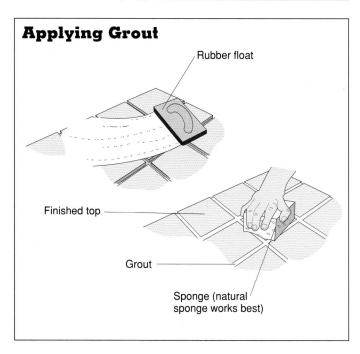

Rubber float

Finished top

Grout

Sponge (natural sponge works best)

## Tiling Floors: Method 1

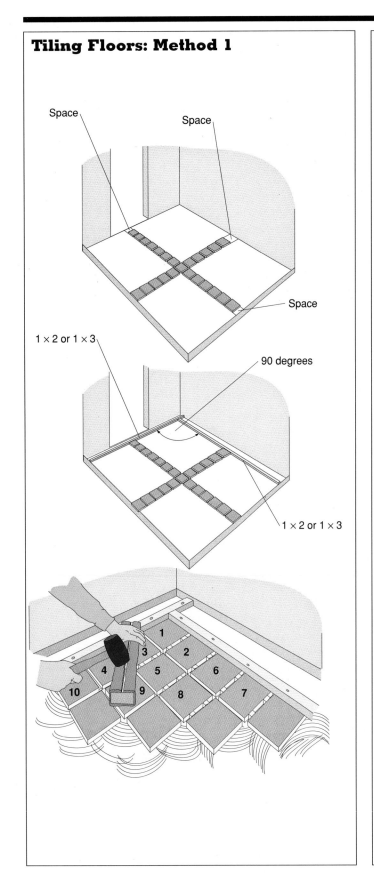

Space

Space

Space

1 × 2 or 1 × 3

90 degrees

1 × 2 or 1 × 3

## Tiling Floors: Method 2

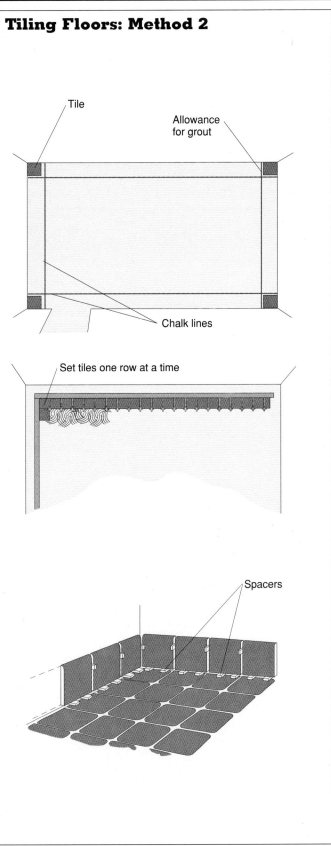

Tile

Allowance for grout

Chalk lines

Set tiles one row at a time

Spacers

## Starting the Layout

Decide which is the most prominent wall—the one along which full tiles are most crucial. Lay two tiles, one in each corner of the chosen wall, allowing for grout. Snap a chalk line between the tiles. Repeat this process for the other three walls, using a framing square or a 3-4-5 triangle at each corner to keep the lines perpendicular. Double-check for square by measuring both diagonals to be sure they are equal. Then make a dry run, as described in method 1, to decide where any cut tiles should go. You may want to have full tiles on the prominent wall and finish with cut tiles on the wall opposite.

## Setting the Tiles

Nail straightedges along two intersecting chalk lines. Spread a small amount of adhesive according to the manufacturer's instructions. Be sure to wear gloves if you are working with epoxy. Spread adhesive right up to the boards, but not over the working lines.

Set the first tile in the corner, abutting it to both straightedges. Complete the starter row, inserting spacers as you go. Then start the second row from the same end and complete all subsequent rows in the same order. If the spacing is regular, you can prepare in advance the cut tiles needed to finish the rows. After the last row, wait for the adhesive to set, remove the straightedges, and set the remaining tiles.

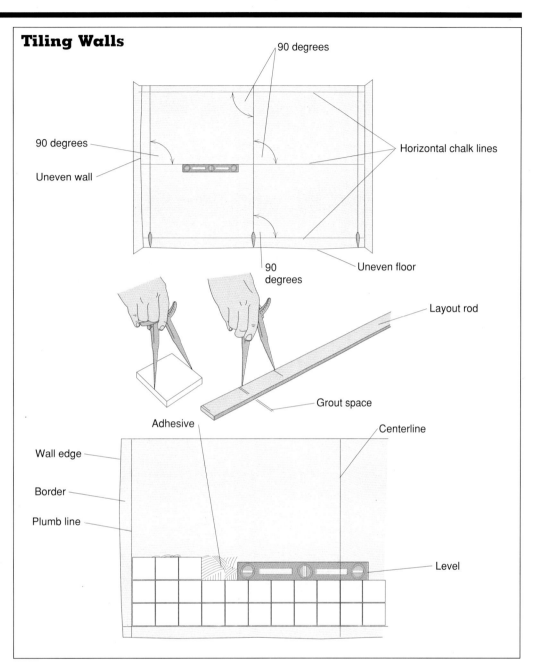

**Tiling Walls**

90 degrees

90 degrees

Uneven wall

Horizontal chalk lines

90 degrees

Uneven floor

Layout rod

Grout space

Adhesive

Centerline

Wall edge

Border

Plumb line

Level

## Tile Base Trim

Instead of a wood baseboard, you may wish to use tile that matches or coordinates with the floor. If you do, use bullnose trim tiles so that the visible edge (the top of the tile) is a finished one. After the floor has been installed, cut and fit the first border piece so that the rest will align with the existing grout lines of the floor. Set each tile by applying adhesive on the back. Use spacers between and under border tiles.

## Tiling Walls

Before you start, check the walls for plumb. First, find the center point of the wall and snap a plumb line from the ceiling to the floor. Snap two more plumb lines close to the edges of the wall. Then snap an exact horizontal chalk line across the center of the wall. If the walls are more than ⅛ inch out, the tapering cuts needed to fit the corner tiles will be noticeable. This can be corrected by installing a mortar bed or by reframing the walls.

## Laying Out Walls

In order to do a layout for a wall installation you will have to simulate a dry run on a stick known as a layout rod. Cut two 1 by 2s to the height and width of the wall. Mark a tile layout along each rod, adjusting grout spacing and the location of cut tiles until you are satisfied that the layout will look right. If you need to start over again, turn the rod around. If you are using trim pieces or contrasting tiles as a border, be sure they are included in the proper ends of the rods. Transfer the marks from each layout rod to the wall by holding the rod against two of the plumb lines or horizontal lines. These marks will guide the installation.

If the gap at the edge of the wall is too small for cut tiles, you can change the width of the spaces between the tiles. If two tiled walls form a corner, you can lap the tiles on one wall over those on the other.

## Setting Wall Tiles

Begin the installation on the bottom row, starting at the centerline. Apply enough adhesive for the first few tiles, but leave the baseline and centerline visible for accurate alignment. Set the first tiles in place and insert spacers between them. For a thinner grout line than the one allowed by a spacer, use matchsticks, toothpicks, or any other suitable material.

When the tiles are set, let the adhesive dry for a day or two before grouting the joints. For wide joints, use cement-based grout with sand added for bulk. Grout narrow joints

### Installing Mosaic Tile

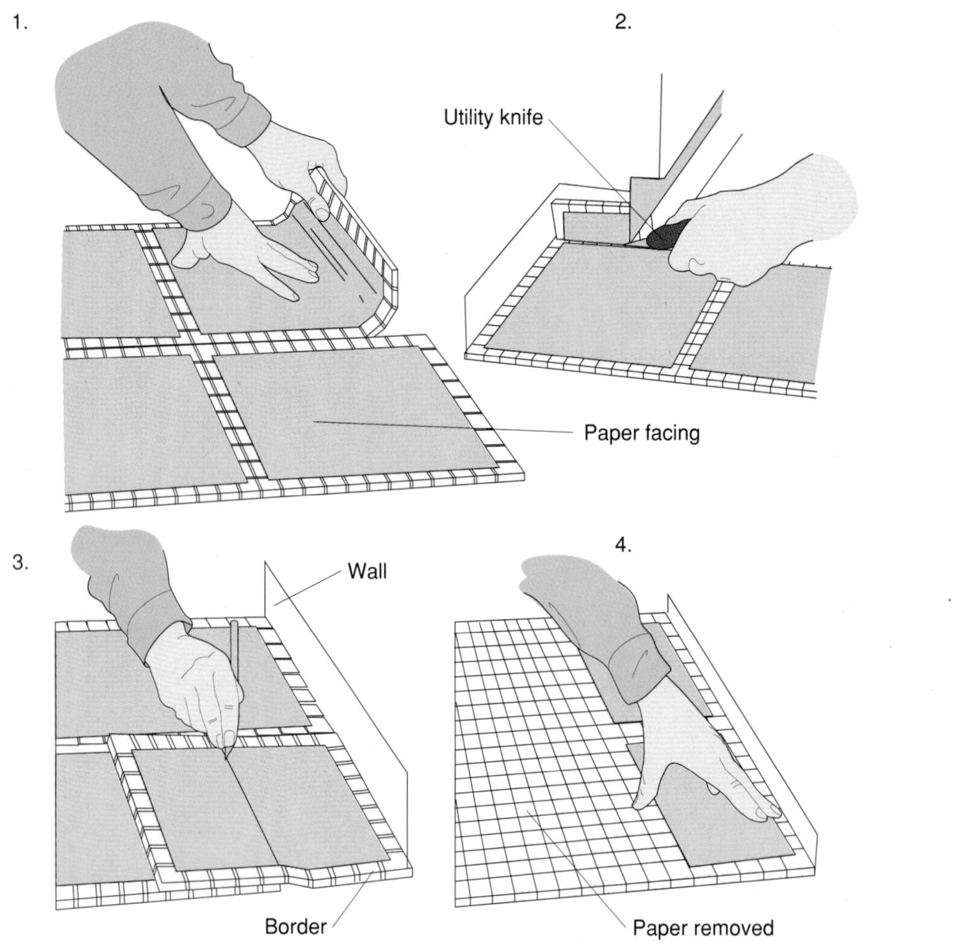

1.

2.

Utility knife

Paper facing

3.

Wall

4.

Border

Paper removed

with cement, epoxy, or elastomeric grout. Use a toothbrush handle to pack it in tightly. If you are grouting a bathtub or shower, plug the drain with a rag to keep grout out of the plumbing. To cure the grout, keep it damp for at least 72 hours by covering it with plastic sheeting or spraying it periodically.

## Installing Mosaic Tile

Use the same subsurface preparation techniques and layout guidelines as described for floor and wall tile installations.

Check the layout by setting sheets of tile in place. Avoid tugging on corners and distorting the spacing. Instead, set down one edge of the sheet and unroll the rest. The space between each sheet edge should equal the space between each tile.

When you fit a sheet of mosaic tile around an obstruction, use a utility knife to cut the paper or mesh and to remove full tiles. Cut individual tiles to fit any remaining spaces, using nippers to notch out corners.

To fill border spaces, turn over the sheet, slide it into the space, and mark it, allowing for an expansion gap. Cut along the line with a mechanical tile cutter, or cut single tiles with nippers or a hand cutter.

Spread adhesive with a notched trowel, embedding sheets of tile in it. Unroll the sheets to prevent sliding them around in the adhesive. Press them into place. If the tiles are attached with paper glued to the top surface, soak the paper with warm water and gently peel it off.

After the adhesive dries, grout mosaic tile the same way you would other kinds of tile. Force it into the cracks with a rubber float or squeegee, working on the diagonal. Bear in mind that you'll need a lot more grout to fill the joints around mosaic tile than you would for an equivalent area of larger tiles.

## Installing Tile Countertops

This always involves these same basic steps: Prepare the backing, perform a dry tile layout, draw the working lines, apply the adhesive, set the full tiles, set the cut tiles, grout, caulk, and seal. All but the first two steps are the same as those for installing ceramic tile on floors. Both jobs also require the same tools.

## Tile Backings

An existing tile countertop can be used as a backing if the tiles are securely attached. The edges may present problems, however; old edge tiles may have to be removed, and it may be difficult to find new edge tiles in the correct size. Using hardwood edge trim flush with the countertop may help in such situations. Sand the old tile to break the glaze.

If you install a new backing, start by installing a ⅜-inch or ¾-inch plywood substrate over the base cabinets. Cover this with a mortar bed or tile backing board. Cut backing-board sheets by scoring and snapping, using a utility knife or a saw. Work on the coated side of the material. Precut each piece and make any necessary cutouts prior to instal-

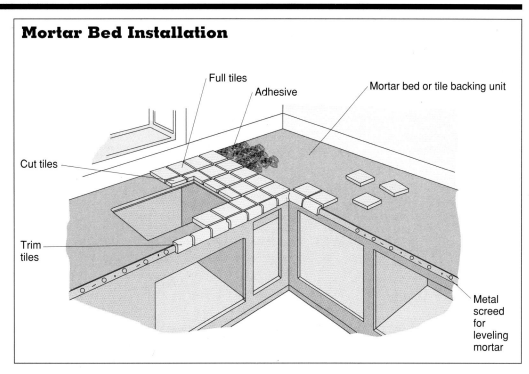

**Mortar Bed Installation**

Full tiles

Adhesive

Mortar bed or tile backing unit

Cut tiles

Trim tiles

Metal screed for leveling mortar

lation. Position the backing board over the plywood with the coated side up. Secure each piece with 1¼-inch hot-dipped galvanized (HDG) coarse-thread sharp-point screws. Predrill the screw holes through the backing board the same diameter as the screw shafts. Install the screws flush with the coated surface but do not countersink them. Tape all seams in the backing board with fiberglass-mesh tape, cover the tape with the setting adhesive, and allow it to dry before installing the tiles.

Tile can also be attached directly to a plywood backing, but this method requires sealing the plywood carefully, using epoxy-based mastic, and adding latex or epoxy modifiers to the grout mix.

If you are not adding a mortar bed or tile backing board to the countertop, raise the plywood by attaching 1 by

3 strips to the bottom along the edges. This provides a backing for the tiles along the front edge and keeps them from interfering with the drawers. Screw in the top from below to make future removal easier. Use shims as necessary to make it level.

Cut out openings for the sink and cooktop (see page 73). If you are installing a recessed sink, set it in place now. Surface-mounted sinks are installed after tiling.

## Dry Tile Layout

A dry tile layout (see page 89) allows you to position the tiles in their exact location before a single tile is stuck in place. It is practical only for small installations, such as a countertop.

First tape any trim tiles along the edge, then start taping the field tiles. If the counter is L-shaped, start the layout at the inside corner and work outward. The inside-corner

piece should be a full tile. For straight counters, start with full tiles at the front and work toward the back. On islands and peninsulas without sinks or other inserts, begin setting full tiles at the measured center point of the field and work out toward the trim in all directions. Use tile spacers to maintain uniform grout lines. All of the trim pieces should be laid out so that their grout lines match up with those of the field tiles.

Because they tend to be less stable, avoid setting very small cut tiles at the counter back and around the sink and other inserts. If the sink is surface-mounted, mark tiles for cutting by laying them in place and scribing them from beneath. Cut them with a tile cutter or nippers. The sink rim will cover the raw edges. If the sink is recessed, fit the trim pieces around it and cut the field tiles where they abut the trim pieces, allowing for the grout line. These cuts must be smooth and accurate because they will not be covered by a sink rim, so it is best to make them as you set the tile.

Once you are satisfied with the design, mark working lines on the setting bed so that you can reproduce it when you install the tiles. For a countertop with a sink or a range insert, mark working lines around the cutout to position the trim tiles around the fixture. Extend the working lines up the backsplash to keep the tiles aligned.

## Installing Tiles

Spread the adhesive and set the tiles exactly as for floor tiles (see page 82). Finish the last row of countertop tiles, then work up the backsplash wall. As soon as you have finished, remove the excess adhesive. Then let the work dry for a day or two. You may need to tape the backsplash and trim tiles in place while the adhesive dries.

After about 24 hours grout the joints as described on page 83. Then cover the countertop with plastic sheeting or spray it periodically to keep the grout damp for at least 72 hours.

## Repairing Tile

Before you begin tearing up tiles, be sure to mask any nearby drain holes to prevent debris from clogging pipes. Cover surrounding surfaces before installing new adhesive, tile, and grout. Always wear safety goggles and heavy gloves when removing tiles. Tile demolition is unpredictable; pieces can fly up, and broken edges are sharp.

## Tiling Around a Sink

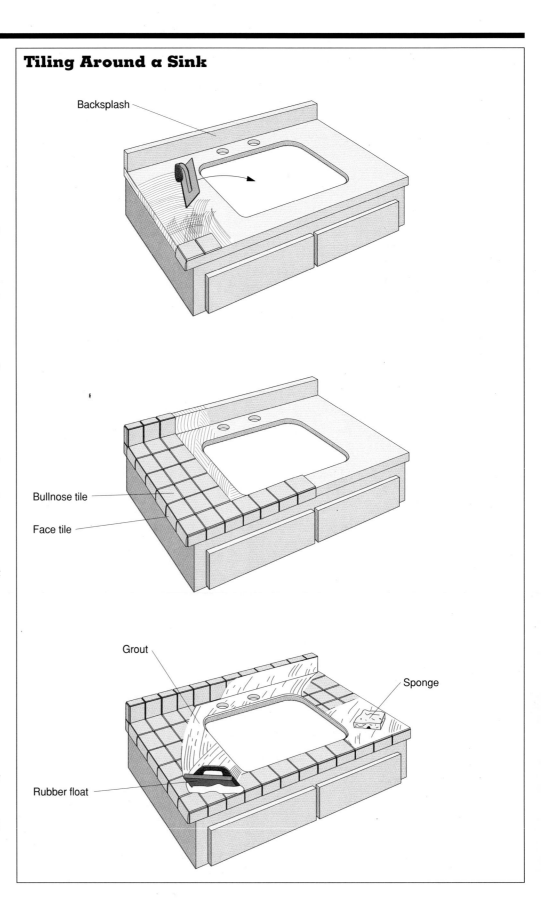

Backsplash

Bullnose tile

Face tile

Grout

Sponge

Rubber float

## Dry Layout

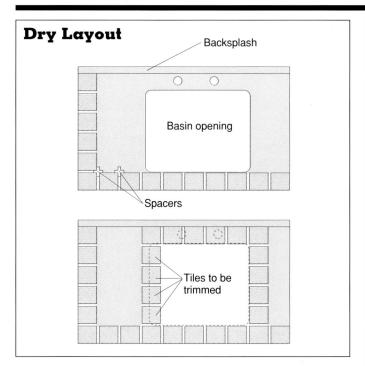

Backsplash

Basin opening

Spacers

Tiles to be trimmed

## Replacing Tiles

If you can't match the existing tile, consider replacing it with a complementary accent tile. You could also remove several tiles and install a pattern or contrasting strip that will make the additions look like a renovation rather than a repair.

First remove the grout so that blows do not break tiles in the surrounding area. Use a grout knife, a utility knife, a small hacksaw blade, or the pointed end of a can opener to scrape out the grout.

Once the grout has been removed, use a hammer to break up the tile to be replaced. Tap gingerly with short, sharp blows. Carefully dig out and discard all pieces.

Use a putty knife, utility knife, or margin trowel to scrape off the exposed adhesive. If you don't remove all traces of adhesive, the replacements may not set flush with the existing tiles. Avoid using chemicals to eliminate the

adhesive residue because they can interfere with the bonding ability of the new adhesive. Scrape off any grout remaining around the edges, and vacuum the area to remove all dust.

When replacing tile, it is best to use the same adhesive as for the original installation. If you don't know exactly what product was used, try to use the same general type (either a thin-set adhesive, which resembles mortar, or an organic mastic, which resembles hardened rubber).

Start the installation by spreading a thin coat of adhesive on the back of the tile, making sure it is completely covered. Then apply more adhesive to the tile to cushion the installation. Set the tile in place, use a mallet to bed it, and clean off excess adhesive. To hold the tile in place while the adhesive cures, insert finishing nails or toothpicks into the grout joints or tape the tile in position.

## Replacing Tile

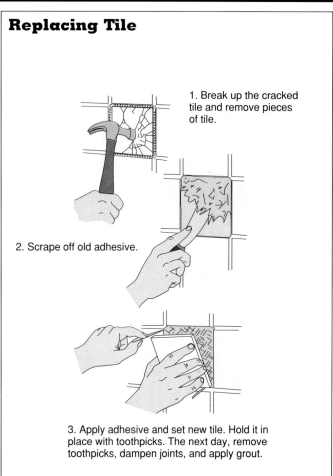

1. Break up the cracked tile and remove pieces of tile.

2. Scrape off old adhesive.

3. Apply adhesive and set new tile. Hold it in place with toothpicks. The next day, remove toothpicks, dampen joints, and apply grout.

## Replacing Grout

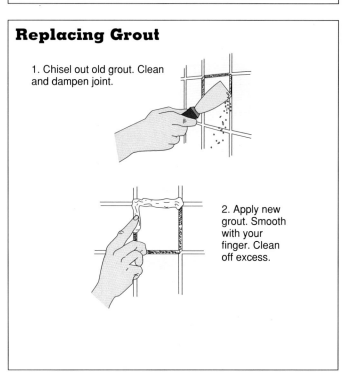

1. Chisel out old grout. Clean and dampen joint.

2. Apply new grout. Smooth with your finger. Clean off excess.

# PAINTING

*Painting is the most common remodeling job. It is easily done by homeowners, is inexpensive, and quickly effects a dramatic change. This section outlines the three keys to a successful paint job: high-quality paint and tools, complete preparation, and proper painting techniques.*

## Types of Paint

Consider the quality and the application when selecting paint. Top-of-the-line paint or stain may cost more, but it will save time, and possibly money, by requiring fewer coats and by lasting longer. Types of paint have different characteristics; many are intended for specific purposes.

## Latex Paint

Latex is the best paint for most situations. It is thinned with water and easily cleaned up. Latex dries quickly, is durable, and comes in finishes from flat to high gloss. It adheres well to wood, stucco, wallboard, plaster, and most other surfaces commonly painted in residences.

Latex paint contains lower percentages of solvents than oil-based or alkyd paints, so its fumes tend to be less irritating. Even so, provide plenty of ventilation, and don't remain in a room that has been freshly painted.

Latex enamel comes in semigloss and high-gloss finishes. It is not as hard as alkyd paints, and it has a greater tendency to show brush marks. Don't use latex enamel in direct sunlight or in extremely hot, dry weather. It's very hard to spread under these conditions, and the paint will dry before any brush marks disappear.

## Alkyd Enamel or Oil-Based Paint

The old standby is still the best for wood, especially if it is aged and dry. These paints are thinned with petroleum-based solvents, which carry pigment and oils deeper into the wood than latex, providing better adhesion and surface protection. Some localities require low concentrations of solvent in alkyd or oil-based enamels. These paints are more difficult to use and dry more slowly than the older formulations.

Alkyd paints are more durable and washable than latex. They adhere to most surfaces, although they are not suitable for fresh plaster or masonry.

Local regulations may require certain methods of disposal for containers of oil-based paint. Check this before deciding which type of paint to buy.

## Stains

Stain formulas are changing rapidly. There are now water-based stains and full-bodied stains that cover painted surfaces. Because stains penetrate wood rather than coat it, they do not chip or flake.

## Primers

Primers can have an oil or a latex base. Choose a primer with the same basic formulation as the topcoat to be used. Always heed the manufacturer's recommendations; primers are formulated to adhere to a specific surface and to provide a base for a particular type of topcoat. In some cases, primers penetrate the surface and change composition of old paint to provide better "tooth," or adhesion. In other cases they stick tenaciously to old paint. Special stain-locking primers are available for surfaces such as redwood that tend to bleed through paint.

## Specialty Paints

There are paints and primers for specific applications. These include metal, concrete block, new masonry with a high alkali content, nonporous surfaces (such as glass or ceramic tile), and appliances subject to high temperatures (such as flue pipes or radiators). Certain paints can be used to seal cracks, stop moisture penetration through masonry, and even recoat enamel bathtubs and sinks.

## Estimating Time and Materials

Measure the square footage of the area to be painted. Disregard door and window openings unless they total more than 50 square feet for a given wall. Have the dealer convert square footage to gallons. Coverage varies according to paint formulation.

To estimate time, prepare and paint a small surface area (50 square feet, for example). Keep track of the time this takes. Use this figure to calculate the time per square foot of surface area, and multiply that by the total square footage to be painted. Next, prepare and paint a door or window, again keeping track of the time. Multiply this figure by the total number of doors and windows, and add it to the total time for painting the surface areas. This will yield a viable time estimate for the job.

## Buying Paint

Always buy a high-quality paint. There are no standard terms for paint quality, although the better paints sometimes bear the designation "premium." Avoid discount brands, which sometimes bear the designation "professional"; they are the lowest in price and quality.

Buy paint in 5-gallon cans if you can use that much. Get enough to do the entire job, plus some extra for touch-up or unexpected needs. If you must buy in 1-gallon cans, mix them together in a spare 5-gallon bucket to make sure the color doesn't vary. If you are using a custom color, write down the color and its formula, then file it where you can find it later, when you need to match the color.

## Stirring Paint

1. Pour off thin paint

2. Stir thick paint in bottom of can

3. Pour thin paint back into can and stir

## Painting Tools

First-rate tools will save time and money. With proper care, they will last longer and do a better job. A cheap roller may shed nap into the paint or even delaminate; an inferior brush holds little paint, loses bristles, and doesn't make clean edges. A badly designed sprayer may apply paint inconsistently, break down, or be difficult to use.

### Brushes

Brushes with flagged bristles (split ends) hold paint better and produce a finer stroke. Use natural bristles with oil-based paints, varnishes, polyurethane, and most chemical strippers. Use synthetic bristles for latex. A 4-inch, a 3-inch, and a 2-inch brush will serve most purposes. Tapered or sash brushes are excellent for trim work, where you must control the edges precisely. Square-cut brushes are used for larger areas.

## Rollers

The most common roller is 9 inches wide. Choose one that turns on nylon bearings and has a plastic sleeve, a threaded handle, and short and long extension poles. Roller covers come in lamb's wool, mohair, and synthetic fiber. Synthetic covers work well with most paints, especially latex. Lamb's-wool covers are best for oil-based paints, and mohair produces fine results with high-gloss enamels and clear finishes. Use a short-nap (¼-inch) cover for smooth surfaces, ½-inch nap for textured surfaces, and ¾-inch nap for rough surfaces such as stucco or concrete block.

Specially designed rollers are made for corners and small areas. Save your money: Use a brush for the edging, and standard rollers for the main areas.

Power rollers pump paint to the roller as needed, so you don't have to dip the roller into a tray. These approximately double productivity.

## Sprayers

The best sprayers consist of an air compressor, spray gun with an adjustable nozzle, and large-capacity paint source (3 to 5 gallons). Some painters prefer airless sprayers. Sprayers are extremely fast for woodwork, siding, and walls, and especially labor-saving on intricate gingerbread and moldings. Preparation, including careful masking of areas not to be painted, is crucial. Once this is done, one person can spray a 1,200-square-foot house, inside or outside, in six to eight hours.

Because of the difficulty in cleaning up, spraying oil-based paint is not recommended for nonprofessionals. Latex paint is easier to clean up.

Spraying uses more paint than brushing or rolling, so be sure to have enough to finish the job. If you are painting outdoors, be aware that the spray can drift quite a ways. Latex paint overspray generally does not adhere tightly.

Oil-based paint dries more slowly, so is more likely to stick to whatever it lands on.

You must use protective gear, which includes a respirator, goggles, head covering, gloves, petroleum jelly on any exposed skin, and old clothes.

## Preparation

Proper preparation means creating optimum conditions for the paint to bind firmly to the surface and look cosmetically acceptable. There are some differences in preparation techniques for old and new surfaces.

### Preparing New Interior Surfaces

New wallboard is usually primed, but you can prime it with regular latex. If wallboard walls are to be left smooth, remove any residual sanding dust. This isn't necessary with textured wallboard.

Do all caulking and fill all holes before painting. If staining trim, paint the walls first, then stain the trim before installing it. If painting trim, seal any knots with white shellac or stain-locking primer.

Consider painting new walls before installing electrical fixtures and devices, cabinets, floor coverings, and trim. You will need to take care not to damage the new paint when installing these items, but many professionals find this an effective procedure. Protect electrical devices from paint if you install them before painting. Building inspectors can require you to clean or replace any outlet or switch with paint on it.

## Preparing New Exterior Surfaces

Make sure the surface is dry and that the weather conditions are favorable. Paint on the shady side of the house and follow the manufacturer's recommendations.

The backside of trim can be primed before installation to seal the wood. This is not necessary in many regions, and should be done only to dry wood. Moisture that is trapped in wood will work its way out, destroying most paint films in the process.

With solid-wood siding, countersink nails and putty the holes. Nails in plywood or hardboard siding should be snug but not countersunk.

Redwood or cedar should be painted with a stain-locking primer. This prevents the tannin in the wood from bleeding through and discoloring the paint. Ordinary primers are not effective for this purpose. Some paint suppliers recommend waiting three months to a year before painting redwood siding.

Wood that will be painted or stained usually does not need any other preservative. Exceptions are areas exposed to water, such as the base of porch pillars or posts, steps, railings, and the junctions of walls and decks. Treat the end grain of these pieces by brushing or dipping in wood pre-servative, making sure it is compatible with the paint you are using. Make all cuts before treating the wood. If possible, let the treated wood dry before handling it.

Galvanized metal should be allowed to weather for a year before painting. The next-best method is to treat it with an appropriate galvanized-metal primer. Washing the surface with a mild acid such as vinegar will help. Do not use alkyd paints on galvanized metal; use an acrylic or vinyl acrylic paint instead.

## Preparing Old Interior Surfaces

If the old paint is adhering firmly and is not suffering from alligatoring, checking, cracking, or blistering, the surface is suitable for repainting. Gloss surfaces should be roughened (also called giving tooth to the new paint) with a light sanding or by washing with trisodium phosphate (TSP). Rinse off the residue before you paint. Use TSP or a similar solution for kitchen cabinets or any painted surface that has a grease accumulation. Even years of handprints can leave a residue that will inhibit paint.

Patch any cracks (see page 51 for wallboard or page 59 for plaster). If the surface is too deteriorated, it may be easier to cover it with new wallboard than to repair it.

Remove doors and paint them on sawhorses if possible. Take off hardware, cover plates, and light fixtures. Tape together all screws and small parts to avoid losing them. Light fixtures can sometimes be covered with a plastic garbage bag and left in place.

Seal water stains with white shellac or stain-locking primer. A water stain will bleed through latex paint over and over again unless it is sealed. Eliminate the source of any moisture penetration before painting.

Wash off mildew with a 1:3 solution of laundry bleach and water. Mildew will grow under a new coat of paint and eventually discolor it.

Do not paint over old wallpaper with an oil-based paint. If the paper is smooth and well glued to the wall, a latex primer and paint will probably cover it satisfactorily. Test a section; if the wallpaper blisters or the paint doesn't adhere well, remove the wallpaper (see page 98).

## Preparing Old Exterior Surfaces

Today's paints last from four to seven years, depending on the exposure (sunny exposures fade more quickly), the color (darker colors fade faster), and the surface preparation. Do not paint a house too often; the thick layers of paint will peel away. Most paint wears slowly, through a process called chalking. In many cases removing the chalk by scrubbing will renew a dull painted surface.

A house needs a new coat of paint when the existing paint has almost worn off or if it is peeling, blistering, cracking, or alligatoring. Start by removing as much old paint as possible with a paint scraper, wire brush, or power sander. If you use a scraper, keep it sharp; using a dull scraper is like digging with a brick. Always wear a respirator—old paint often contains lead. Cover the ground with drop cloths to catch the mess,

and dispose of the waste material quickly and properly.

Wash the surfaces with a solution of TSP and water or any strong household cleanser. Concentrate on soffits, porch ceilings, and areas under the eaves. Rinse the surfaces with a hose. A rented power washer can speed the cleaning process. Be careful not to remove paint with the power washer; this will damage the wood.

If the original paint showed signs of peeling, especially on attic or uninsulated walls, eliminate the cause of the problem—moisture that seeps through the wall. Provide vents in the attic or drill the top of each stud bay and install ¾-inch minilouvered vents. Also consider coating the affected walls with primers specified as vapor barriers.

Set protruding nail heads, then fill and sand the holes. Caulk all seams, cracks, and joints. Sand down high spots and lightly sand any shiny spots to give tooth to the new coat of paint.

To prepare masonry, scrub the walls with a wire brush and strong detergent. Masonry walls may have a crystalline powder, a deposit that remains as moisture evaporates from the masonry. To remove this powder, known as efflorescence, scrub masonry with a mixture of 1 part muriatic acid and 3 parts water. Never add water to acid; always pour the acid into water. If the wall is too slick for paint to adhere, scrub again with a stronger acid solution. If the wall is too porous, prime the surface with a block filler.

## Preparing Windows

Scrape away all loose paint with a putty knife or scraper. Remove loose putty around the glass and replace it with new glazing compound. Paint the exposed wood first with linseed oil or primer.

If layers of old paint have sealed the window, cut through the paint with a putty knife or scoring tool so that the window moves freely.

Look for damaged or rotten wood. If the damaged area is extensive, replace the window; if it is small, dig out the decaying wood and patch with epoxy filler, smoothing it while it is still pliable. If the wood is spongy, try a marine-rot epoxy. This material is absorbed by the spongy wood, filling the spaces and killing or immobilizing the fungus that is doing the damage. Patch and sand all holes. Spot-prime patches and bare wood.

## Painting Techniques

Although painting may seem self-explanatory, especially when using brushes and rollers, there are specific techniques that will make the work go faster and produce better results.

### Brushes

Use the largest brush you can comfortably handle and which is appropriate for the area to be painted. Small brushes should be used only for molding. Trim any wild bristles before you start painting.

Dip the brush into the paint no farther than half the

## Roller and Brush Techniques

length of the bristles. Lift the brush straight out of the paint and shake it or tap it against the inside of the can. Do not draw the brush over the rim; this will fill the sealing surface of the can and cause the bristles to clump.

Hold the brush at a 45-degree angle and apply paint in long, light strokes. Do not jab the brush straight in to paint a difficult spot. Work in small sections, about 3 feet square, and slightly overlap previously painted areas. Make sure the entire tip of the brush touches the surface. Always brush into the section most recently painted, which is called the wet edge, to avoid lap marks. To avoid brush marks, work quickly. Thinning the paint a little will also help it to even out.

After laying on the paint with two or three strokes,

spread it evenly. Use vertical strokes on flat walls and ceilings, horizontal on board siding. Work the paint toward uncoated areas. To produce a thin, feathered edge, finish each stroke by lightly lifting the brush from the surface.

Do not leave a brush standing on its bristles. To keep a brush from drying out if you take a break, wrap it in plastic or cover it with the rag you keep handy to wipe up drips. You can also suspend the brush in water (for latex paint) or thinner (for alkyd paint). Drill a hole through the brush and pass a rod through the hole. On hot days don't leave a brush with latex paint in the sun, and plan on washing it out every few hours. Wash a latex brush every four hours any time you use one.

Do not paint directly from a new gallon can. The paint will dry out and need to be

thinned by the time you reach the bottom. Pour some of the paint into a smaller container.

### Rollers

Rinse a new roller cover to remove lint; use water for latex, thinner for alkyd. Shake out the roller, let it dry a bit, then roll it out on a towel or paper. To load the cover with paint, roll it back and forth in a paint tray or on a grid suspended inside a 5-gallon bucket. The nap should be full but not dripping.

Always start with ceilings. First use a brush to paint corners and around trim, fixtures, and other obstacles. Then paint the rest of the ceiling. Use an extension pole on the roller and wear a billed cap or goggles to protect your eyes. When you finish the ceiling, paint the walls from top to bottom.

To apply paint with a roller, spread the first few strokes with a zigzag pattern. To cut down on drips, make the first stroke an upward one. Rolling slowly will cut down on spattering. Increase pressure to spread the load evenly.

Then, without lifting the roller, spread the paint across the zigzag pattern. Use even, parallel strokes; take care not to roll too fast. As the zigzag disappears, begin to feather the paint into adjacent areas, painted or unpainted. Lift the roller at the end of each stroke.

## Sprayers

For large areas use a sprayer that draws paint from a 5-gallon container. Airless sprayers work at very high pressures, and can inject paint under the skin if you accidentally pull the trigger while someone is touching the opening. Such injuries cause almost no pain or loss of blood, but they can result in severe tissue damage and blood poisoning. If you have an accident with a sprayer, seek medical attention at once.

To prevent injuries, make sure the sprayer has a safety lock and guard, as well as a protective shield to keep fingers away from the tip. Never point the gun toward anyone, including yourself. Unplug the sprayer before trying to unclog the tip. Store the sprayer in a locked cabinet when it is not is use.

Cover adjacent areas with drop cloths or masking paper, since nearly all sprayers produce some overspray. Thin and strain the paint. Spray a large piece of cardboard and adjust the spray so that the paint will spread evenly, without spattering. To avoid lap marks, spray in an elliptical pattern that is wide in the center and tapered at the ends. Hold the gun about 12 inches from the surface and move it back and forth horizontally, bending your wrist to keep the direction of the spray perpendicular to the wall. Don't spray one spot too long, or the paint will sag. It is better to spray several thin coats than one thick coat. If the sprayer clogs, unplug the cord immediately. Follow the manufacturer's instructions to release pressure and clean the tip.

## Cleaning Up

Cover paint cans tightly and store them in a cool, dry cabinet away from heat sources and out of reach of children. Label cans well. Do not dump thinners or solvents down the drain or into a sewer. Store them in tightly sealed containers and ask the local waste-management agency for disposal information.

When you finish using a brush, apply as much as possible of the remaining paint in it onto a surface. Pour any

## Painting the Outside of a Window

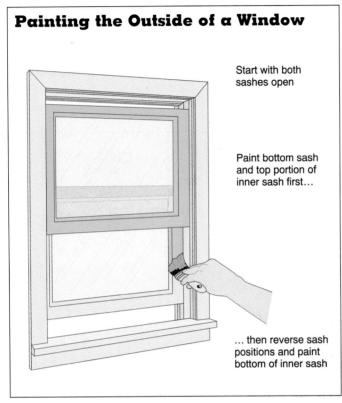

Start with both sashes open

Paint bottom sash and top portion of inner sash first…

… then reverse sash positions and paint bottom of inner sash

## Painting a Door

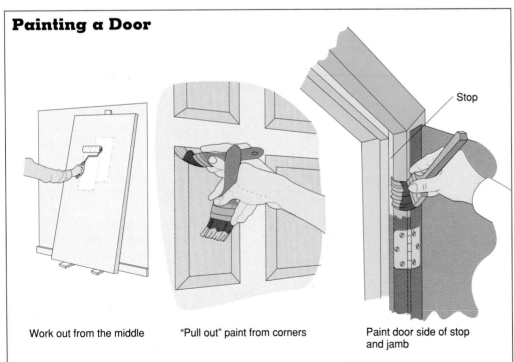

Work out from the middle

"Pull out" paint from corners

Stop

Paint door side of stop and jamb

## Using a Sprayer

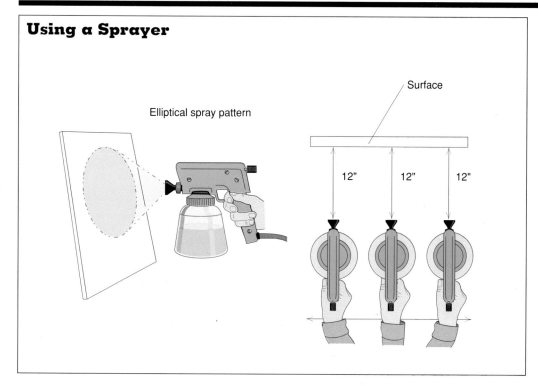

Elliptical spray pattern

Surface

12"  12"  12"

## Cleaning a Brush

CLEANING AGENT

extra paint in the small container back into the paint can.

Latex paint can be cleaned in the sink, using warm water. Dishwashing liquid will speed the process. Wet the brush, then work it under the water until paint stops coming out. Spin the brush with your hands or with a spinner inside a box or bucket.

Cleaning up oil-based paints is a bit more difficult. Do not use the old standby of paint thinner and newspapers. The resulting pile of paint- and thinner-soaked paper is a perfect setting for spontaneous combustion.

To clean up oil-based paint, pour about ¼ inch of thinner into a small clean container. Work the brush in the thinner, bending the bristles sideways but not splaying them out. Pour the thinner into a 5-gallon bucket and shake out the brush inside the bucket.

Spin the brush between your hands inside the bucket (see illustration). Goggles or safety glasses are advisable. Start slowly and spin the brush faster as more thinner comes out. After the thinner stops running off, pour another ¼ inch of thinner into the small container and work the brush some more. Shake and spin the brush inside the bucket as before.

Repeat this procedure four or five times. Little or no paint will be left in the brush. Rinse and wash the brush with warm water (not hot) and soap. Rinse out the soap, then comb the bristles if they are tangled.

Pour the used thinner into a suitable container, label it, and allow it to settle. After a day or two you can use it for the first couple of washes the next time you clean a brush. Eventually, the reused thinner will become sticky; when it does, dispose of it properly.

Once the brush is washed, wipe it with a clean rag and wrap it in paper (not plastic).

If you are using expensive rollers, clean them up right away. Latex paint can be rinsed out of the roller with water. To remove oil-based paint, put some thinner in a paint tray and work the roller back and forth. Rollers can be spun to remove moisture with a tool that works like a child's top.

Wash latex paint from your hands with soap and water. Clean oil-based paint from your hands with vegetable oil; vegetable oil can be removed with soap and water. Don't wash your hands with thinner.

# FLOORS

*Flooring is usually the final finish surface to be completed in a remodeling project or an addition. Floors must endure the most wear and tear of any surface in the house. Almost any conventional flooring material will provide satisfactory results if properly installed and maintained. Just as significant are the floor frame and subfloor.*

## Anatomy of a Wood-Frame Floor

Most floors have a wood-frame construction that spans a crawl space, a basement, or downstairs rooms. The main framing members, which are called joists, are held up by primary structural components such as foundation mudsills, girders, and bearing walls. The size and spacing of the joists depend on the floor load and distance they have to span.

The subfloor is the main platform; it can be made of plywood, dimensional lumber,

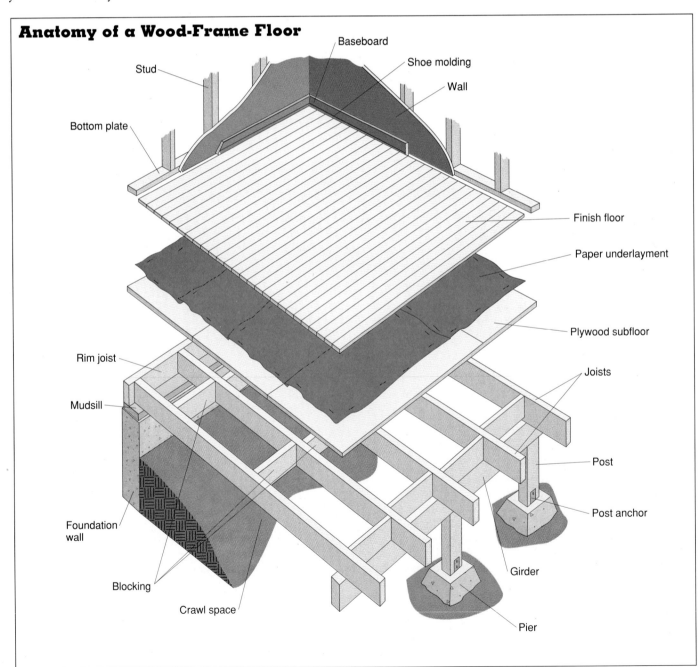

**Anatomy of a Wood-Frame Floor**

Stud
Baseboard
Shoe molding
Wall
Bottom plate
Finish floor
Paper underlayment
Plywood subfloor
Rim joist
Joists
Mudsill
Post
Post anchor
Foundation wall
Girder
Blocking
Pier
Crawl space

## Anatomy of a Concrete-Slab Floor

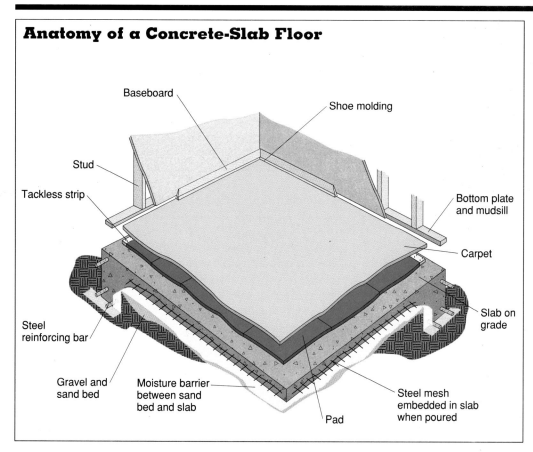

Baseboard

Shoe molding

Stud

Tackless strip

Bottom plate and mudsill

Carpet

Slab on grade

Steel reinforcing bar

Gravel and sand bed

Moisture barrier between sand bed and slab

Steel mesh embedded in slab when poured

Pad

or tongue-and-groove boards. Some subfloors also double as the finish floor, such as ¾-inch tongue-and-groove hardwood or softwood, but most subfloors are covered by finish floor material. A thin underlayment of smooth plywood or particleboard is sometimes installed over the subfloor, depending on whether the finish floor covering requires it.

## Anatomy of a Concrete Slab

Floors of concrete slab are hard and unyielding, but they can be covered with carpet or a wood subfloor. They make an excellent surface for thin or brittle floor coverings, such

as tile and resilient flooring, which are glued directly to the concrete slab. Concrete is not a waterproof material; it can wick moisture up from the ground. To prevent this, a properly constructed slab will have a moisture barrier under it or be adequately sealed before flooring is installed.

## Choosing a Floor Covering

Because the floor is such an integral part of the look of a room, select new floor coverings carefully. Your tastes may change, so the simpler the floor treatment, the more flexibility you will have in the design and use of the room over time. It is much easier

and less expensive to change the color of the walls or to introduce new furnishings than it is to install a new floor.

As a general rule, the best design is a simple one—although simplicity is not always easy to achieve. Most often, floors play a background role, pulling together the other elements of the room. Whether the design is simple or bold, it should complement the rest of the house.

The most common types of floor covering are wood strip, woodblock, resilient tile, resilient sheet, ceramic tile, and carpet. Wood is a traditional favorite that can add

quality, permanence, and livability to any room. The grain gives texture to a floor. Wood-strip floors, especially wide planking, create a strong linear pattern. Wood-block and parquet floors have a dynamic pattern.

## Resilient Tile and Sheet Flooring

This type of covering comes in a wide range of colors and patterns. Resilient flooring is durable, comfortable, and easy to maintain. Sheet materials come in room-sized widths that create broad expanses of color and pattern.

## Masonry Floors

Ceramic tile and other masonry materials, such as brick and stone, create a feeling of permanence and substance. This effect can be either rustic or formal. Grout lines create a strong pattern. Choose a color and width for the grout lines to either accentuate or subdue this pattern.

## Carpet

Wall-to-wall carpet or area rugs offer the advantages of softness, warmth, comfort, and a wide choice of colors and patterns. Carpet is suitable for both open expanses and intimate spaces and can be used in any room. It needs regular maintenance and is not as permanent as other floor materials. However, carpet is the best choice for concealing an imperfect subfloor. It can even be installed over existing carpet.

97

# WALLCOVERINGS

*In addition to the traditional paper, wallcoverings include a number of other materials. Many modern wallcoverings are easy to apply; the most difficult aspect of the job may be choosing an appropriate pattern or material.*

## Types of Wallcovering

The best choice of wallcovering for a novice is pretrimmed, prepasted vinyls. Vinyl is the most durable wallcovering. It is available in strips that can be removed in minutes if you want a change later. The best vinyls are entirely vinyl rather than vinyl-covered paper. Both types tend to stretch when stressed, but will not tear. Because they are not porous, fungus-resistant adhesives should be used to prevent the growth of mildew.

Commonly available wallcoverings are machine-printed in widths ranging from 18 to 27 inches. Most are pretrimmed and many are prepasted. In addition to vinyl, wallcoverings include foil, cloth, and cork veneers. They can be flocked, embossed, or multistrip murals. Consult the dealer about specific installation techniques or adhesives that are required for the covering you choose.

## Estimating Needs

Wallcoverings are priced by the roll (usually 36 square feet) and come in packages of two or three rolls, called bolts. Standard widths range from 18 to 27 inches, with some materials available in widths up to 54 inches. The wider the material, the more difficult it is to work with. If you choose an exceptionally wide, delicate, or expensive material, consider having the job done by professionals.

The easiest way to estimate is to sketch the room, noting all the dimensions and openings, and take the sketch to a dealer. To make your own estimate, assume that a 36-square-foot roll will cover 30 square feet. For European rolls, which are generally 28 square feet, assume coverage of 20 square feet. If you choose a pattern with a large repeat, allow for even less coverage. For each window or door, deduct one third roll from the total needed.

## Preparing Walls

Remove obstructions and repair cracks and holes. Smooth out any roughness or texture; if necessary, remove the existing wallcovering or attach an underlayment. Bare, unpainted walls must be sealed with either oil-based paint or a latex primer-sealer specified for wallcovering preparation. Latex-painted walls should also be primed before wallcovering is applied. Do not use a latex sealer; it may separate from the wallboard and allow the wallcovering to sag.

Existing wallpaper (but not vinyl wallcovering) can be used as a base if it still adheres tightly to the wall. To test, run your fingertips over the wallcovering. If it crackles or moves, the panel is loose and must be removed. Another test is to pick at a seam with a putty knife. If large areas peel off easily, remove all of the old covering. If only small areas peel off, remove them. Fill the exposed areas with wallboard taping compound, then sand them smooth after the compound dries.

## Removing Existing Wallcoverings

It is possible to pull off the surface layer, if not all, of many strippable wallcoverings. To strip the wall, lift up a bottom corner with the scraper, then pull up and away from the wall. Remove all the covering, wash the walls with warm water, and scrape off the remaining glue with a broad knife. Rinse the walls with clear water and allow them to dry thoroughly.

For non-strippable wallcoverings, chemical removers soak covering off the wall by dissolving the underlying paste. Removers may be sold as a ready-mixed solution or you may have to dilute them with water. Follow the manufacturer's instructions about wearing gloves, safety glasses, or other protective clothing. After soaking the wallcovering with remover, use a broad knife to lift the covering away from the wall. Rinse the walls with a TSP solution, and allow to dry before continuing.

If you need to remove several layers of wallcovering, rent a steamer. Lift the covering away as you steam; work on a small section at a time. If the wallcovering is vinyl, score it first to let the steam penetrate to the adhesive, and it will separate from the wall much more easily.

## Tools

Have the following tools available before starting the job.

- Plumb bob or level—a chalk line can be used instead of a plumb bob.
- Ladder or scaffolding—chairs or jury-rigged stools are dangerous.
- Utility knife with extra blades, and shears—professionals may go through hundreds of blades on a large job. They cost much less if you buy them in bulk. Use a quick-change knife; if you must unscrew the knife body to change blades, you probably won't do it often enough. As an alternative, keep a whetstone handy to dress the blade after every few cuts. Use shears for rough cuts.
- Water box—used with tepid water to quickly soak wallcovering, which is then applied directly from the box to the wall.
- Seam roller—this is used to ensure that seams stick well. If you are applying paste, a roller helps spread it toward the edges. Don't press too hard, and don't use a seam roller with flocked wallcovering or grass paper.
- Sponge—for wiping up excess adhesive.

• Soft-bristle smoothing brush—used to flatten the covering to the wall, even out the adhesive, and force out air bubbles. Use a squeegee or vinyl-smoothing blade for heavy paper or vinyl wallcoverings.

The following tools are necessary if the wallcovering is not prepasted.

• Pasting table—the table should be smooth and washable. The surface should be as wide as the wallcovering and at least 6 feet long. Do all the cutting on a smooth piece of wood so that you don't cut the table surface. If you don't have a suitable table, use a piece of plywood covered with plastic or paper (not newspaper). Support it at about waist height.

• Paste brush or roller—use a roller with vinyl paste. Use a paste brush for wheat paste. Ask the wallcovering dealer for recommendations on the weight of the roller nap.

• Clamps—large padded clothespinlike clamps can be used to secure the paper to the table while it is being pasted. These are commonly used by woodworkers and are available from tool-supply outlets.

• Six-inch taping or putty knife—for guiding trimming cuts, and pressing and manipulating pasted wallcovering.

## Planning the Layout

Chances are the ends of the wallcovering will not match when they meet. Try to locate the mismatch over an inconspicuous area.

One of the best places to start the layout is down one side of a door frame. This way the mis-match at the finish will occur above the door.

Another inconspicuous place is where bookcases, fireplaces, or other features that will not be covered jut out into the room. If a bookcase or mantel extends from floor to ceiling, plan to finish on each side of this feature.

## Aligning the Pattern

Lower parts of the wall are often obscured by furniture. The most critical visual elements of the pattern usually appear near the ceiling. If the walls are out of plumb (a common condition in older houses), placing a prominent part of the wallpaper design at the ceiling edge will make the uneven condition more noticeable. That is why professionals usually plan ahead so that a relatively open area (between design elements) is placed at the edge of the ceiling. In any event, avoid trying to make a pattern look straight by lining it up with the ceiling.

## Planning the Layout

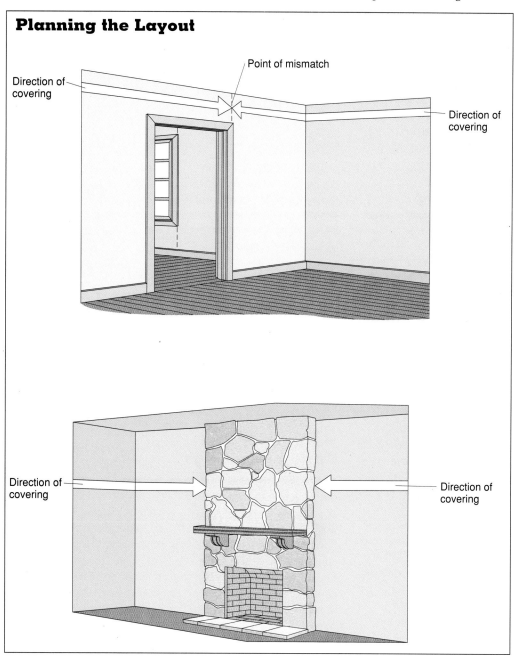

Direction of covering

Point of mismatch

Direction of covering

Direction of covering

Direction of covering

## Laying Out Plumb Lines

Individual strips of wallcovering must be hung perfectly plumb. Even if the pattern is forgiving, crooked seams will look unsightly. Correct alignment is especially necessary for the first strip because this will affect all the subsequent ones. A small skew on the first strip can amount to several inches by the end of the run.

To get the first strip plumb, snap a vertical chalk line or use a straightedge, a level, and a pencil. The chalk line should be about ¼ inch away from the edge of the first strip so that you can use it as a guide when you place the strip.

## Installing Wallcoverings

Assemble all tools and materials. Remove switch plates and cover furniture if necessary. Set up a pasting table if you need one.

### Pasting Wallcoverings

Prepare the paste and let it sit according to the directions on the package. Mix it thoroughly so that there are no lumps. Hand-mixed paste should last all day; premixed paste dries more quickly. While you are waiting for the paste to set up, rough-cut several strips of wallcovering about 4 inches longer than the wall and reroll them with the face out. This will help counteract some of the tendency to curl when you apply paste to the strip.

Place the first piece face-down on the table and apply paste. Clamp the top end of

### Booking a Strip

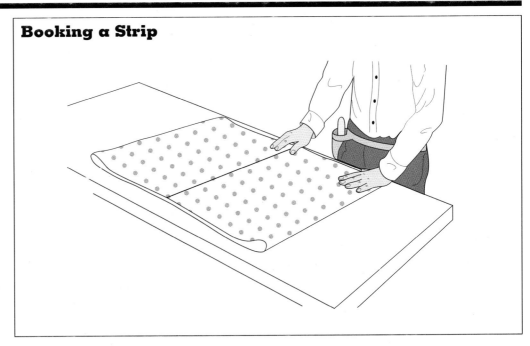

the wallcovering to the table. Apply paste to the top half of the strip, starting in the center and working toward the edges. Wipe up any spilled paste from the table immediately so that it won't accidentally come in contact with the pattern side. When you've finished the top half, unclamp the strip and fold the pasted part back against itself until the end is at the middle of the strip. Clamp the other end of the strip and paste the bottom half.

### Booking and Curing Coverings

When you've finished pasting the strip, unclamp the end and place it at the middle so that it meets, but doesn't overlap, the other end. Align the edges but do not crease the folds. This process, called booking, helps spread paste evenly and reduces evaporation while the wallcovering cures. Curing takes about 10 minutes and allows the strip

to soften and expand. If the wallcovering has a selvage, trim it off while the paper is booked, using a straightedge and a utility knife. Use a fresh blade every time.

### Using a Water Box

Prepasted coverings require moistening, which can be done in a plastic or metal trough. Fill the trough halfway with lukewarm water, then place it on the floor in line with the area to be covered. When you measure out covering from the roll, always add 2 inches excess at both the top and bottom of a strip. Cut a strip and reroll it, from bottom to top. Immerse it, soaking according to the manufacturer's directions, and pull it out from the top.

Some professionals use paste even with prepasted coverings to guarantee long-term adhesion. To do this, mix 2 parts premixed vinyl adhesive with 1 part water.

### Hanging the First Piece

This is easier if you work from a scaffold, but a ladder or non-folding chair will do. To start, carry the booked panel to the wall (the second strip should be curing now). Unfold the top half but leave the bottom folded. A common mistake with some patterns is to hang one piece upside down. Make it a habit to check for this. Marking the top with a small dot will help.

Align the vertical edge of the wallcovering with the plumb line you placed on the wall earlier. Tack the top by pushing it gently against the wall. Slide the paper until it is positioned as precisely as possible. Keep 2 inches excess at the top for the moment, and smooth the center of the upper half, working from the top down, then out to the edges. Smooth out any wrinkles or air bubbles. Use a damp sponge (except on flocked coverings). If you can't remove

100

## Hanging the First Strip

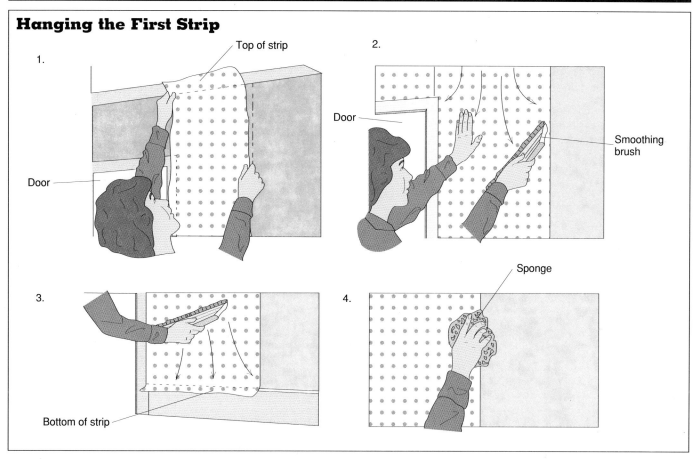

1.
Top of strip
Door

2.
Door
Smoothing brush

3.
Bottom of strip

4.
Sponge

a bubble from vinyl paper, make a pinhole or tiny slit in it, then squeeze out the air. Gently crush any lumps of paste that show through. If the problems can't be corrected, pull the strip from the wall. Usually, it is possible to reapply the strip. If not, clean adhesive from the wall with a damp sponge and proceed with another strip.

When you reach the center of the strip, unfold the bottom and secure it to the wall. Recheck the alignment. When you are satisfied, smooth the remainder of the strip. Go over the strip and clean any stray paste and make a last check for bubbles or wrinkles. Hang the second strip before trimming the first.

## Trimming the Edges

To trim the pieces, use a 6-inch broad knife as a guide and make the cuts with a utility knife. Hold the utility knife in your right hand (unless you are left-handed) and the broad knife in your other hand. Pressing the broad knife flat against the wall and into the corner, pull the utility knife along the edge of the broad knife. Then, without lifting the utility knife from its cut, leapfrog the broad knife to its next position. Continue leapfrogging until you complete the cut. Remember to change blades after every long cut. It's normal to use 30 to 40 blades per room. Changing blades is

much cheaper and less frustrating than tearing wallcovering.

## Making Seams

The butt seam is most common, but it is not suitable in corners or for all-vinyl wallcoverings. There are specific seams for these situations.

### Butting the Panels

Generally, individual panels of wallcovering are joined with butt seams. To make a butt seam, slide the new strip tightly against the previously installed one until the edges form a tight ridge but do not overlap. Be sure the pattern matches, and don't try to stretch the panel.

Flatten the joint with a seam roller. Use a cloth or sponge on

flocked or embossed coverings to prevent crushing the raised pattern. Press the roller lightly to avoid a glossy streak. Remove excess paste and air bubbles with a sponge. Trim the top and bottom edges before or after rolling the seam, using the broad knife and utility knife.

### Making Lap Seams

These overlap the adjacent strip. They are used at corners to deal with out-of-plumb walls. This type of seam creates a slight pattern mismatch, but it was commonly done on older walls and will prevent gaps from appearing later. To do a lap seam, simply lap the first strip over the second.

### Double-Cut Seams for Vinyl Wallcovering

Use this type of seam for vinyl, which won't stick to itself. Overlap the two panels about ½ inch. Then, using a straight-edge and utility knife, cut through both layers. Lift up both edges, remove the waste, then flatten the seam with a roller. Never make a double cut when applying over existing wallcovering—it may cause the old covering to lift.

### Covering an Inside Corner

Because corners are rarely plumb, take extra care when covering around one. In most cases wrapping a full width of wallcovering around a corner is inadvisable; you are likely to end up with wrinkled covering and an edge that is severely out of plumb. The solution to this problem is to cut the first strip about ½ inch after it turns the corner, then continue with another panel. If the piece you trimmed off is more than 6 inches wide, you can continue with it; if not, use a new strip. The key is to plumb the leading edge of the overlapping strip. Treat this piece like the very first one you installed; if necessary, snap a plumb line on the wall. Don't use a butt seam at the corner. It will show a gap eventually. Use a double-cut seam for vinyl wallcovering and a lap seam for all others. Try to keep the overlap less than ½ inch.

---

## Butting Panels Together

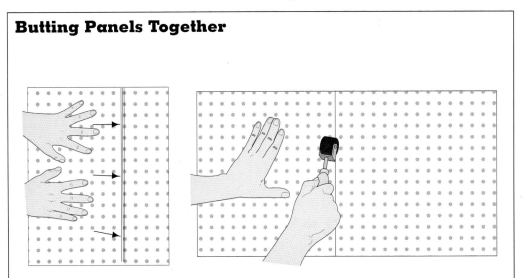

---

## Covering an Inside Corner

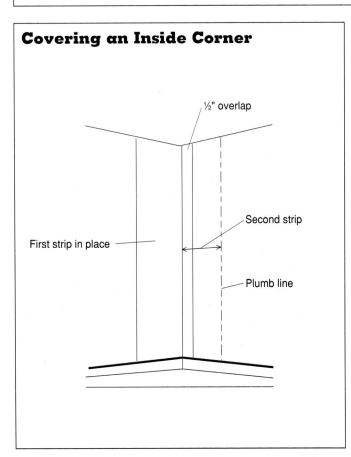

½" overlap
First strip in place
Second strip
Plumb line

## Covering an Outside Corner

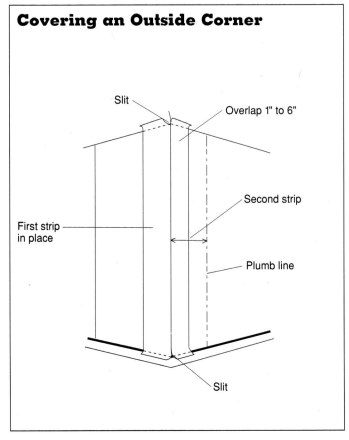

Slit
Overlap 1" to 6"
First strip in place
Second strip
Plumb line
Slit

## Covering an Outside Corner

This is basically the same as for in inside corner, but the covering must be lapped or double-cut at least ½ inch from the corner to prevent fraying and pulling off. If the material is very stiff, carry it 4 to 6 inches around the corner or it may not stick well. Slit the top and bottom of the strip at the corner so you can bend the strip around it. Snap a plumb line on the uncovered wall to guide you as you hang the first strip after the corner.

## Covering Around Beams

Position the wallcovering at the ceiling with the normal 2-inch excess and smooth it against the side of the beam or rafter. Make a slit in the covering, cutting from the lowest edge to the top edge at a slight angle. Smooth the covering into place against the wall, but do not open the strip if it is booked. Slit the covering at the other side of the beam (a mirror image of the previous cut). Smooth the entire panel into place, then trim off the excess around the beam.

## Covering in and Around Arches

Cover the area above and around the arch as you would any wall, allowing the strips to hang into the archway opening. When the full width of the arch has been covered, trim the excess so that it overlaps the edge by 2 inches. Make small triangular snips all around the edge, spacing them more closely where the arch is sharpest. Turn the edge under,

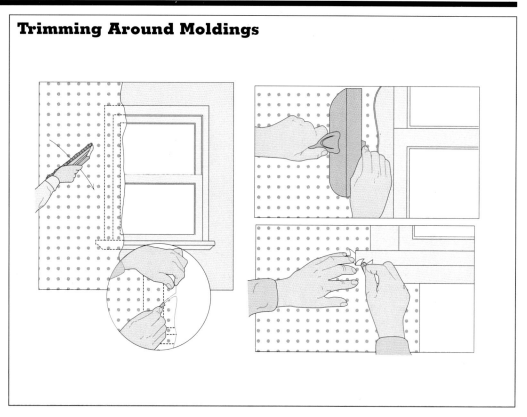

**Trimming Around Moldings**

smoothing the "teeth" firmly against the inside of the arch. Using a new blade, trim them to ½ inch. Cut a strip of wallcovering slightly narrower than the width of the arch (to avoid peeling). Paste it into place, covering all of the teeth.

## Covering Around Switches and Outlets

Be sure the power is off and that all cover plates have been removed. Cover the slots in any receptacles with masking tape to keep out glue. Cover the electrical box and then cut an X across it, stopping about ⅛ inch from the corners. Cut off the flaps, so the hole in the covering is slightly smaller than or the same size as the box.

## Covering Around Fixtures

One method is to remove the fixture and treat the opening like that for an electrical receptacle or switch. Another method is to cut a slit to the fixture location from the end or side of the covering, whichever is closer to the fixture. Cut an X from the point in the covering that corresponds to the center of the fixture, then trim back the covering until it lies flat around the fixture and the slit can be butt-seamed.

## Covering Around Raised Trim

Cutting wallcovering around door, window, or other raised trim is easiest if done after the covering is up. For example, to trim the wallcovering around a window, hang the first strip that overlaps it, and smooth it

loosely onto the wall areas. Cut away all but a few inches of the overlapping wallcovering. Then cut diagonal slits into the corners but don't snip beyond the corner of the window. This cut releases the covering so that it lies flat on the wall.

Press the wallcovering against the window molding with the smoothing brush and then the broad knife. Trim the excess. Cut rounded or irregular parts by hand as you press the covering tightly to the wall with your fingers.

## Covering Around Recessed Windows

The simplest method is to treat the recess like a small room. The strips that cover the recess are folded over onto the main wall. The overlap is covered by the primary wall panels.

103

# FINISH ELECTRICAL AND PLUMBING

*Some of the simplest remodeling jobs—changing light fixtures, plumbing fixtures, and appliances—can bring about major improvements in appearance and convenience with relatively little time and effort.*

## Changing Light Fixtures

This is an excellent remodeling task for homeowners. It requires few tools and can be done bit by bit as time allows. Except for troubleshooting problems, a very basic knowledge of electricity is adequate.

## Precautions

In addition to the normal precautions you should take when working with electrical wiring, there are some safety considerations unique to lighting. Recessed fixtures generate heat that will build up if trapped. Do not cover such fixtures with insulation; allow at least 3 inches of clearance all around. Observe the limit the manufacturer places on the maximum wattage a fixture can accommodate.

Closet lights pose a fire hazard if clothing or other combustible material is too close. Lights should be installed on the ceiling or on the wall above the door. A surface-mounted fixture must have unobstructed clearance to the floor and be at least 18 inches from stored items. A recessed fixture must have a solid lens and at least 6 inches of clearance. A fluorescent fixture must have 6 inches of clearance.

Lights in the bathroom should have moistureproof housings. Switches should not be beside the tub or shower.

The lights in children's bedrooms should be at a safe height, so they won't be broken during normal play. Avoid lamps in the room of an infant or toddler.

Illuminate stairwells and entrances sensibly. Many low lights are better than one light, which may cause shadows.

Observe all code requirements for locating, switching, wiring, and grounding light fixtures. They were written for your protection.

## Track Lighting

These fixtures consist of pieces of track, available in different lengths. The track must be connected to a power source and, to avoid trailing wires, the usual connection is to a ceiling receptacle (you can also get track that plugs into a wall outlet). The individual light units that snap or clip onto the track are purchased separately.

### Installing Track Lighting

Turn off the power and remove the old fixture from the ceiling box. See if the screw holes in the canopy box line up with the corner tabs of the ceiling box. If not, use the adapter ring as an intermediate bracket.

Thread the wires from the canopy box through the square plastic cover plate (and the adapter ring, if needed). Connect the wires by joining black to black, white to white, and ground wire to ground wire. Screw the canopy box into the ceiling box, carefully tucking the wires out of the way. Drill holes for toggle bolts in a section of track, slide the end into the canopy box, and screw the bolts into the ceiling.

Attach the light fixtures to the track and secure them with the locking levers. Turn on the power, switch on the lights, and position them as desired. If necessary, unlock the levers and move the fixtures until they are ideally positioned. Relock the levers.

## Installing a Ceiling Fixture

Make sure the power is off. Attach the mounting strap to the ceiling box in one of two ways, as shown (opposite page). Attach the strap with screws if the fixture weighs less than 30 pounds. Attach the strap with a stud and nut

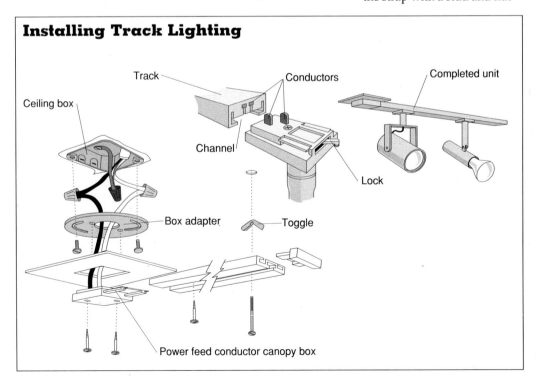

**Installing Track Lighting**

Track · Conductors · Completed unit · Ceiling box · Channel · Lock · Box adapter · Toggle · Power feed conductor canopy box

if the fixture weighs 30 pounds or more. If the box is plastic, the strap must be grounded.

Connect the wires by joining black to black and white to white. (Note that the proper hot wire may actually be red or a white wire made black.) If the fixture is metal, run a short pigtail from the ground screw to the ground wire.

Screw the fixture base to the mounting bracket, carefully tucking the wires out of the way. Screw in the bulb and attach the globe.

## Installing Pendant Fixtures

Pendant or swagged fixtures are mounted in much the same way as ceiling fixtures. Feed the wire through the center of a threaded nipple and connect it. Attach the canopy. If the fixture hangs from a chain, thread the wire through the chain to make it less conspicuous.

## Installing Toilets

Before you install a toilet, the floor and flange should be in good condition. The floor flange should be recessed no more than ¼ inch below the finish floor. The finish floor should extend under the rim of the toilet base. A ½-inch water supply line should be stubbed out of the wall the appropriate distance for the new toilet.

The center of the flange should be the correct distance from the finish wall (double-check the instructions or specification sheet supplied with the toilet). The center of the flange is usually 12 inches from the wall, but on some wall-hung toilets, which have a separate tank mounted on the wall, the distance is 14 inches. A 14-inch rough-in toilet is necessary for this situation to prevent a gap between the tank and the wall.

## Removing the Old Toilet

To remove an old toilet, refer to the illustration below. Guard against back injury; if the toilet is hard to remove, have someone help you lift it. Be sure to block the closet bend (drain) with rags or newspaper to keep sewer gas from escaping into the house.

## Installing a Ceiling Fixture

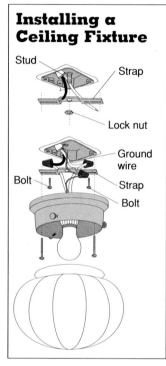

## Installing a Pendant Fixture

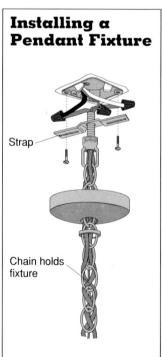

## Removing an Old Toilet

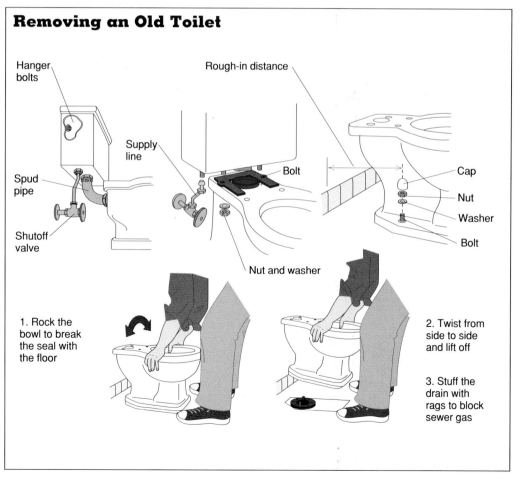

# Setting a Toilet

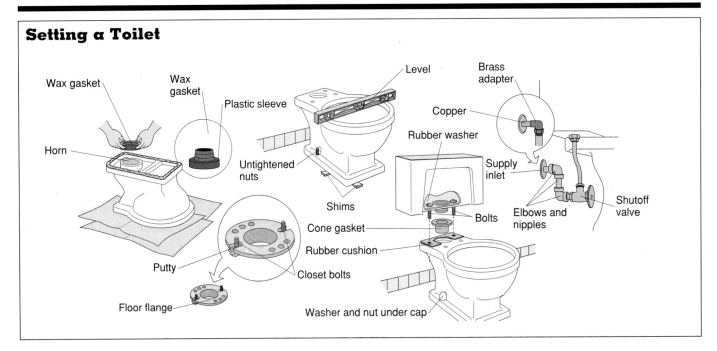

Labels: Wax gasket · Wax gasket · Plastic sleeve · Level · Brass adapter · Copper · Rubber washer · Horn · Untightened nuts · Supply inlet · Shutoff valve · Shims · Bolts · Elbows and nipples · Putty · Cone gasket · Rubber cushion · Closet bolts · Floor flange · Washer and nut under cap

## Setting the Toilet

Take the new toilet out of its box and lay it on a clean tarp or other such surface. Grit will scratch the vitreous china, so take precautions.

Check for packing paper inside the bowl, from below as well as from above.

Place new hold-down bolts into the flange, using plumber's putty to hold them in place if necessary. Spread a thick layer of plumber's putty on the bottom edge of the toilet base.

If the floor flange is flush with or higher than the finish floor, a wax gasket without a plastic sleeve can be used. If the floor flange is recessed below the floor, use a wax ring with a plastic sleeve.

The wax gasket must be soft enough to deform quickly under the weight of the toilet in order to seal properly and to reduce the chance of cracking the porcelain as the hold-down bolts are tightened. Keep the temperature of the ring at 70 degrees for at least 20 minutes before setting the toilet. An old plumber's trick is to place the gasket, wrapped in its paper, inside your shirt. Be careful not to deform the ring if you do this.

The toilet must be placed accurately into the flange. If the toilet is shifted after the wax gasket is compressed, the toilet is likely to leak. Either have an assistant guide you as you position the toilet, or use tape to make alignment marks on the toilet and floor. The flange bolts aren't a precise enough guide.

Pull the rags or newspaper out of the closet bend. As with removing the toilet, be careful not to injure your back. Have someone help you lift the fixture if necessary.

Position the wax gasket on the flange, then position the toilet on the ring. Twist the toilet slightly back and forth to force the gasket down and against the flange. Place a level across the top of the bowl. Check level from side to side and front to rear. Shim the base if necessary to level the toilet, using metal or plastic shims.

When the bowl is level and stable, carefully tighten the hold-down bolts. They should be snug, but it is easy to overtighten them and break the base at the point of attachment. A crack in the china will render the toilet unreturnable to the dealer and unacceptable to the building inspector.

After tightening, check again to make sure the bowl is level.

Install the tank on the bowl (see illustration above). Be sure to install the rubber washers on the anchor bolts before you install them.

Connect the plumbing. If the old water supply line is too high on the wall, install elbows and nipples to bring it down. Install the supply stop (see illustration above) and connect it to the tank with a steel-jacketed flexible line.

## Installing Sinks and Lavatories

Both sinks and lavatories have drains and faucets with hot and cold water. Sinks have larger drain holes with strainers, whereas standard lavatories have pop-up stoppers. Both are supported by counters, legs, pedestals and brackets, or a combination of these.

There are four steps to set and plumb a sink or lavatory: Assemble and install the hardware; set the sink and fasten it securely; make the supply connections; and connect the drain. Kitchen sinks are more complicated than lavatories or laundry basins, but all follow this sequence.

New sinks come with instructions and often with templates for necessary holes and brackets. A novice will take about one to five hours to set and plumb a kitchen sink (add an hour if the sink cutout isn't already done). Bathroom countertops with integral lava-

# Installing a Bathroom Sink

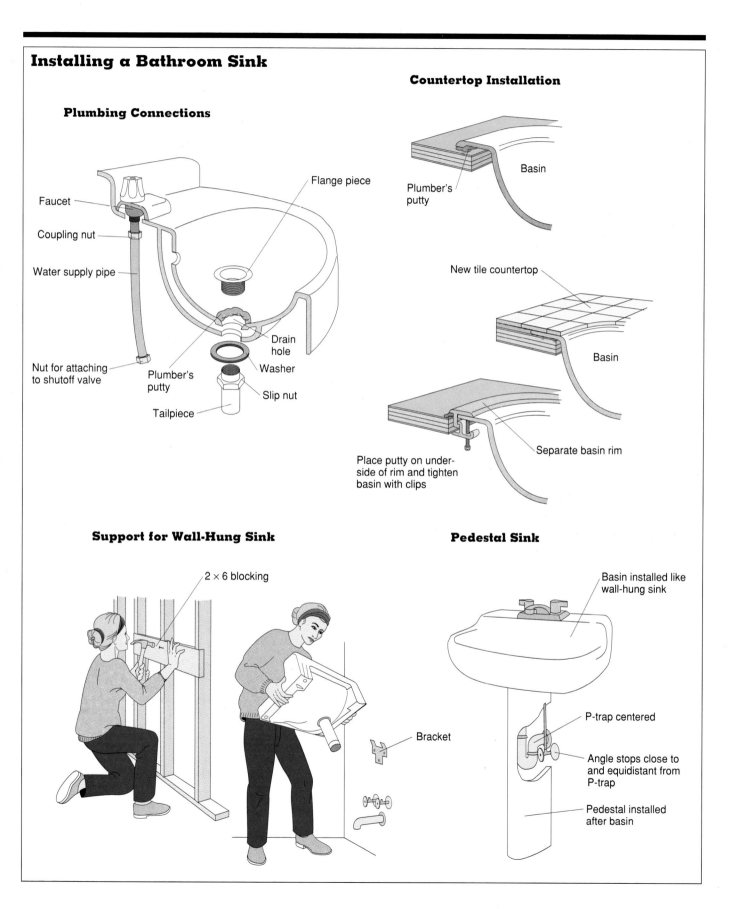

## Plumbing Connections

Faucet

Coupling nut

Water supply pipe

Nut for attaching
to shutoff valve

Plumber's
putty

Tailpiece

Flange piece

Drain
hole

Washer

Slip nut

## Countertop Installation

Basin

Plumber's
putty

New tile countertop

Basin

Separate basin rim

Place putty on under-
side of rim and tighten
basin with clips

## Support for Wall-Hung Sink

2 × 6 blocking

Bracket

## Pedestal Sink

Basin installed like
wall-hung sink

P-trap centered

Angle stops close to
and equidistant from
P-trap

Pedestal installed
after basin

tories take about as long, but are generally heavier.

## Assembling Hardware

Protect the sink from scratches before starting. Almost all modern sinks have a standard 4- or 8-inch space between the faucet holes to accommodate standard assemblies. Most faucets have single handles. Many kitchen faucets have flexible supply lines attached.

Plan which holes in the sink you want to use for various hardware. If there are not enough predrilled holes, an air gap can be installed directly in the counter. New holes can be cut in stainless steel sinks.

Slip sealing gaskets over the supply tubes before inserting them through the holes in the sink. If no gasket is supplied, apply plumber's putty around the base of the faucet and fasten it to the sink by tightening the locknuts on the bottom. Check the alignment before completely tightening the nuts. Put any other items to be attached into the appropriate holes.

Install the strainer and tailpiece. The body of the strainer goes over a gasket or a thick coat of plumber's putty. Press the strainer into place and tighten its retainer or locknut from beneath the sink. If the strainer turns during tightening, insert the handles of a pair of pliers through the strainer to hold it, then insert a screwdriver through the pliers to hold them.

Garbage disposers can be attached at this point, but they make the assembled sink quite heavy. If you prefer, attach the disposer bracket to the strainer now and install the disposer after the sink is in, following instructions supplied by the manufacturer.

If code permits connecting a garbage disposer and a tailpiece on a double sink, you will need to install a directional tee. Code may require a separate drain connection.

If both sink compartments discharge into a continuous waste line, assemble the line as a separate unit. Standard lengths of line can be assembled to fit common sink dimensions. The waste lines should fit into a central tee or an elbow on the side closest to the drain stub. Attach the completed assembly to the sink strainers.

## Setting Wall-Mounted Sinks

This is simply a matter of hanging the sink on its bracket. However, the bracket must be securely attached to blocking framed into the wall. If the existing blocking is not adequate, nail a 1 by 8 board directly across two or more studs so that it will be exactly flush with the surface of the wall after the wallboard is applied. Look at the manufacturer's diagram to see how high from the floor the 1 by 8 board must be to hold the sink at the desired height. The top of a standard sink is 31 inches; it can be installed as high as 35 inches, however.

## Setting Self-Rimming Sinks

To set this type of sink, apply a bead of plumber's putty or caulk all around the rim, then place the sink in position. A cast-iron enameled sink will compress the sealant with its own weight; in some cases no other fastener is needed. If clamps are provided, attach two at each corner and one at the midpoint of front and back. If there are extra clamps, space them around the sink about 8 inches apart.

## Setting Rimmed Sinks

These sinks, also called surface-mounted sinks, have a separate stainless steel rim. Lay a bead of silicone sealant around the cutout opening. Set the sink and rim into the opening while temporarily supporting it. Before tightening the clamps, seal the rim-to-sink joint with a bead of silicone or plumber's putty placed on the sink.

## Setting Recessed Sinks

A recessed sink mounts on a routed ledge and is held in place by tile. Either the bull-nose edging locks the sink in place, or the tile and sink edge are flush.

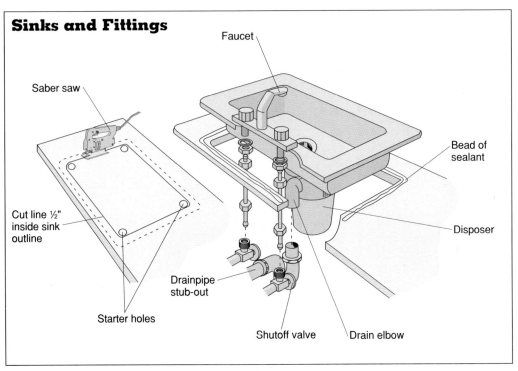

**Sinks and Fittings**

Faucet

Saber saw

Cut line ½" inside sink outline

Starter holes

Drainpipe stub-out

Shutoff valve

Drain elbow

Disposer

Bead of sealant

## Connecting Faucets and Drains

Use a length of supply tubing to connect the faucet to each angle stop. Tighten all the nuts with flat wrenches.

Apply plumber's putty around the drain opening, install the strainer bowl, and tighten the locknut. Hook up the P-trap assembly, connecting it to the drain stub-out and the strainer tailpiece with slip nuts. Tighten the nuts by hand; they will break if over-tightened.

# Installing Appliances

The key to installing appliances in a remodeled house is to make sure they are level. Appliances installed on an uneven floor that are not leveled may vibrate, operate noisily, or wear out prematurely. Cooking on an uneven range or cooktop is dangerous.

## Installing Ranges and Ovens

Gas slide-in ranges have a recess in the back panel. The gas cock must fit into this recess. Connect the range to the gas cock with a length of flexible gas tubing. Plug in the range (if it has a clock or light) and slide it into position.

Electric slide-in ranges are even easier to install. Simply slide the range into place carefully so that you don't damage the floor, then plug it in. A freestanding range comes with a cord to connect it to a dedicated 240-volt circuit.

Built-in ovens require an appropriate cabinet with a

cutout and shelves of the correct size. The specifications supplied with the appliance describe exactly where the gas and electrical outlets should be roughed-in. If the gas or electrical outlet is placed correctly, simply connect the gas or plug in the unit. Some built-in ovens have securing screws or clips.

Cooktops are set in place just like sinks. They use gas or electricity. Most cooktops simply drop into a cutout in the countertop and have a regular base cabinet below. Some cooktops are recessed and sit on a dropped section of the counter, so the cooking surface is flush with the countertop. This requires custom cabinetwork, and tile or other noncombustible material for the countertop and the wall behind the cooktop. Some cooktops include downdraft vents.

## Installing Dishwashers

It is usually best to have the finish floor installed before the dishwasher so that the dishwasher can be removed without tearing up the floor.

A hose with a ⅝-inch inside diameter comes with the dishwasher. It is usually 6 or 7 feet long. If it is not long enough, buy more hose and join it by slipping a short length of copper tubing inside both hose ends. Secure the hoses to the tubing with clamps.

Most codes require that the drain hose have an air gap to prevent overflow from a clogged sink drain from siphoning back into the dishwasher. If code does not require an air gap, you should still loop the drain hose up to

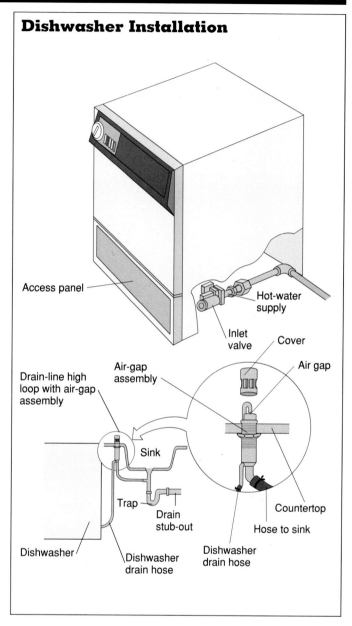

## Dishwasher Installation

Access panel

Hot-water supply

Inlet valve

Cover

Air gap

Air-gap assembly

Drain-line high loop with air-gap assembly

Sink

Trap

Drain stub-out

Countertop

Hose to sink

Dishwasher

Dishwasher drain hose

Dishwasher drain hose

the bottom of the countertop and attach it there with a clamp. Then run the hose into the disposer or sink drain.

The hot-water supply should have a tubing outlet of the size specified by the dishwasher manufacturer. It will be either a flare or a compression fitting. You can also use pipe-joint tape on the threads that will be sealed by the nut, but do not put any around the compression ring or under the

flared tubing. Leave an extra loop of tubing and be careful not to kink it.

Most local codes require that a dishwasher have a dedicated 20-amp circuit, although some may allow you to use the disposer circuit. Dishwashers can be connected to electricity by plugging a cord into an outlet or by connecting a flexible conduit directly to a junction box. Check your local code.

# INDEX

*Page numbers in boldface type indicate principal references; page numbers in italic type indicate references to illustrations.*

## A

Adhesives
  for paneling, *58*, 58–59
  removing, 89, *89*
  for tile, 81, 82–83, 85, 86–87
  for wallboard, 46, *46*
Air-conditioning, ducts for, 36, 37
Air-gap assembly on dishwasher, 109, *109*
Alkyd enamel, 90
Anchor bolts, 19, 23
Appliances
  clearance for, 72, *72*, 73
  installing, 109, *109*
Arches, covering, 103
Asbestos, 16, 17

## B, C

Backsplash
  dimensions of, 72
  installing, 73, 76, 77
  laying tile on, *88*, 89
Balloon framing system, 20
Band joists, 20
Baseboards
  installing, 64, *65*, 66
  removing, 48
  uses for, 60, *61*
Bathroom lavatories, installing, 72, 106, *107*, 108
Bearing walls, 20, 96, *96*
Bids, competitive, 12
Block casings, 63
Blocking
  in floor frame, 20, 23
  in roof frame, 23, *34*
  under wallboard, 56, *56*
Blueboard, 44
Booking, of wallcovering, 100, *100*
Brushes, paint
  cleanup, 94–95, *95*
  techniques with, 93, *93*, 94
  types of, 91
Brushes, paste, 99
Brushes, smoothing, 99, *101*, 103, *103*
Building codes
  on asbestos, 17
  electrical, 40, 104, 109
  on flashing, 48
  on plumbing, 38, 109
  on skylights, 30
  on stucco, 34
  on tile backing, 81
  on wallboard, 45, 46, 49, 52, 56
Building permits, 13
Bullnose beads, 46
Bullnose tiles, 80, *80*, 85
Butt-jointed casings, 62, *63*, 64
Butt joints, 62, 63, 64
Butt seams, 101, *102*, 102, 103
Cabinet installation, *70*, **70–72**
  doors, drawers and shelves, 71, 72

Cabinet installation (*continued*)
  finish panels, 72, *72*
  over island, 71
  measuring and laying out, *69*, 69–70
  preparing for, 68–69
Cabinets, 68–72
  dimensions of, 68
  for ovens and cooktops, 109
  refacing, 68
Carpets, advantages of, 97
Ceiling beams, wallcovering around, 103
Ceiling joists, 22
Ceilings
  attaching wallboard to, 45, 48, 49, *50*
  framing of, 47
  painting, 93
  paneling, 55
  replacing, 6, 7
  trim for, *57*, 67
Chair rails, 60, *61*, 66, *66*
Chalking, paint, 92
Circle, cutting of, *44*, 82
Circuit breakers
  *See also* Ground fault circuit interrupter (GFCI)
  conversion to, 40
Cleanout fittings, 38
Closets, lights in, 104
Concrete
  applying wallboard to, 48
  in foundations, 18, *19*, 23
  paneling walls, *56*
  tiling floors, 81
Concrete block, painting, 90, 91
Contractor. *See* General contractor
Cooktops
  in countertop, 74, 87, *88*, *89*
  installing gas and electric, 109
Coped joints, 62
Corner bead, 46, *46*, 49, 50
Corner clips, 46, 48
Corner moldings, *57*, 58
Corner posts, 20, *21*, 22
Cost estimates, 13
Countertop installation
  cast polymer, 77, *77*
  laminate, 73, *73*–74
  slab, solid-surface, 72, 76, *76*, 77
Countertops, **72–77**
  edging styles, 77, *77*
  measuring for, 72, *72*
  refacing, 68
  tiling of, 81–82, *87*, 87–88, *87–89*
Crawl space, 18, *21*, 41, 96, *96*
Cripple studs, *21*, 22, 26
Cross-bracing, *34*
Cross-connection, defined, 38
Crown molding, 60, *61*, 67, *67*
Curb, for skylight, 30, 31–32

## D, E

Debris box, 16, 17
Demolition, **16–17**
Dishwashers, installing, 109, *109*
Door openings
  checking for plumb, 23
  cutting wallboard for, 50–51

Door openings (*continued*)
  framing, *21*, 22, 26
  wallcovering around, 103
Doors
  *See also* Jambs, door
  installation checklist, 32
  installing casings, 62, 64
  ordering, 26
  painting, 92, *94*
  prehung, installing, 26, **26–27**
  removing frames and, 17
  removing trim and casing, 48
  sliding glass, installing, 27, *27*
Double-cut seams, 102, 103
Downspouts, 24, *33*
Drain holes
  blocking while working, 86, 105
  in sinks, 106, *107*
Drain hose for dishwasher, 109, *109*
Drainpipes, *33*, 38
Drains, sink and dishwasher connections, 109
Drain-waste-vent (DWV) system, 23, 38
Drip cap, *33*
Drywall. *See* Wallboard
Drywall joist. *See* Jacks, wallboard
Dust, protection from, 16, 30–31

Earthquake, impact on foundations, 19
Edging
  for countertops, 77, *77*
  for wallboard, 44, 46, *46*
Efflorescence, 92
Electrical connections
  behind cabinets, 68, 69, 72
  for cooktops and ovens, 109
Electrical receptacles, 23
  cutting wallboard for, 51, *51*
  placement of, 40
  tiling around, 81
  and wallboard taping, 52
  wallcovering around, 103
  when to install, 91
Electrical service heads, 39, *39*
Electrical system, modernizing, 6, 7, 9, 39–40
Electrical work
  rough wiring, **39–40**
  safety concerns, 40, 104
  simple finish, 104–105
Electric radiant heating systems, 36, 37
Enamel, latex and alkyd, 90
End caps, 73–74
End splash, 73, *73*
Excavation for foundation, 18
Expansion bolts, 18, *19*
Exterior, protective overlaps on, *33*

## F

Fascia, *33*, *34*
Fasteners
  for cabinets, 69
  for wallboard, *45*, 45–46, 48, 49
Faucets, connecting, 109
Fire safety
  and paint cleanup, 95

Fire safety (*continued*)
  and skylights, 30
Fire-taping, 52
Fire walls, 45
Flashing
  installing window, 29, *30*, 33, 35
  at roof valleys, 24
  for skylight, 31, 32
Flexible arch bead, *46*
Flooring
  types of, 97
  when to install, 68, 109
Floors, 96–97
  aligning new with old, 20, *21*
  concrete-slab construction, 97, *97*
  hold-downs for, 20, *21*
  levelness of, 23, 26, 56
  tiling, 81, 83, *84*, 85
  wood-frame construction, 20, *20*, 23, 96, 96–97
Foundations, *18*, 23
  joining new to old, 18, *19*
  reinforcing, 19
Framing, **20–23**
  correcting, 47, 47–48
  for skylight, *31*, 31–32
Furnaces, types of, 36–37
Furring
  with paneling, 55, *55*, 56, *56*
  with siding, 35
  in wallboard preparation, 48
Fuses
  types of, 39
  upgrading, 39–40

## G, H

Garbage disposers, assembling, 108, *108*
Gas lines, altering, 38
Gas outlets, for cooktops and ovens, 109
General contractor
  hiring, 12–13
  homeowner as, 12, 16
Girders, in floor frame, 20, *20*, 96, *96*
Glazing for skylights, 30
Greenrock, 44
Ground fault circuit interrupter (GFCI), 40
Grout
  applying, 83, *83*, 88
  elastomeric, 80
  intervals in wall tile, 86
  removing, 89, *89*
Gutters, 24, *33*
Hardware
  attaching surface for, 23
  cabinet, 71
  for kitchen sinks, 108, *108*
  removing, 16, 17, 92
  with windows, 30
HDG nails, 27, 45
HDG screws, 45
Headers, 22, 26, *31*, 32
Heating systems, **36–37**, *36*
Heat pump systems, *36*, 37
Hot mud. *See* Joint compound

Hot-water heating systems, *37*, 37–38
Hybrid heating systems, *36*
Hydronic heating systems, 36–37

# I, J

Inspections
    cracked toilet, 106
    paint on outlets, 91
    schedule of, 13
    wallboard, 45, 52
    wiring, 40
Insulation, 30, 37, **41**
    and cost control, 9
    cutting, 41
    as soundproofing, 48
Insurance
    of contractors, 16
    and remodeling under
        permit, 13
Investment, returns on, 6, 7, 9
Jacks
    padded, 69
    rolling foot, 49, *50*
    wallboard, 45, 49
Jambs, door, *26*
    bow in, 27
    extending, 55
    leveling, 60–61
J-bead, 46, *46*
Joint compound, 52, *53*, 54, 59, 81
Joints
    cold, in joining foundations, 23
    in countertop substrate, 73
    cut in for pipes, 38
    in interior trim, 61–62
    lock-nailed, 64, *64*
    taping and filling, *53*
Joint tape, 52
Joists, floor, 19, 20, *20*, *21*, *96*, *96*

# K, L

King studs, *26*
Kitchen cabinets, installing, **70–72**
Kitchen islands, 71, 87
Knife, broad, 101, *103*
Knife, inside- and outside-
        corner, 54
Knife, utility
    for wallboard, *44*, 50, *51*, 52
    for wallcovering, 98, 101
Knob-and-tube wiring, 39
Knockdown texturing, 54
Laminate
    applying on-site, 74, *75*, 76
    cutting, 73, 74, *75*
Laminating, for tile backing, 81
Lap seams, 101, 102, 103
Latex paint, 90, 91, 95
Lath
    patching, 59
    in stucco, 34
Lath and plaster walls, 22
Layout rod, *85*, 86
L-beads, 46
Light fixtures
    ceiling, 104–105, *105*
    changing, 104–105
    pendant, 105, *105*

Light fixtures (*continued*)
    removing, 92
    track, 104, *104*

# M

Main or service line, in plumbing
        system, 38
Masonry
    floors, 97
    installing exterior, 35
    moisture behind, 55
    painting, 90, 92
Mildew, 92, 98
Mitered casings, 62, *63*, 64
Mitered joints, 62, *63*, 64
    marking and cutting, 62, 64,
        *65*, 66
Moisture
    under painting surface, 92
    tiling walls exposed to, 81
Moisture barriers, *56*, *97*, 97
Molding. *See* Crown molding;
    Trim
Mortar bed, applying tile to,
    81–82, 87, *87*
Mosaic tile
    installing, 83, *86*, 86–87
    types and uses of, 80
MR wallboard, 44, 81
Mudding. *See* Taping and
    texturing
Mudsills, 20, *20*, *21*, 34, *96*, *96*
Muntins, window, *28*, 33

# N

Nail guards, 40, 48, 72
Nailing fins, 27, 29, *29*
Nailing schedule, in wall
    framing, 23
Nails
    filling dimples, *53*, 54
    hot-dipped galvanized (HDG),
        27, 45
    in paneling, 58
    ring-shank, 27, 45
    for wallboard, 45–46, 50
National Electrical Code®
    (NEC), 40

# O, P

Oil-based paint, 90, 91, 95, *95*
Orange peel texturing, 54
Ovens, built-in, 109
Paint
    estimating amounts, 90, 91
    stirring, *91*
    types of, 90
    waste disposal, 94, 95
Painting, **90–95**
    cleanup, 94–95, *95*
    estimating time required, 90
    exterior surfaces, 91–92
    interior surfaces, 91, 92
    interior trim, 61
    techniques for, *93*, **93–95**
    of walls, planning for, 68
Paneling, **54–59**
    advantages and disadvantages
        of, 54–55, *55*

Paneling (*continued*)
    fitting problems, 56, *56*, *57*,
        *58*, *58*
    layout and installation, *57*, *58*,
        58–59
    preparation for, 55–56, 58
    repairing and replacing, 54, 59
Paste, for wallcovering, 100, 101
Pavers, 80, 81
Picture rails, 60, *61*, 66
Pilasters, *20*
Pipe penetrations, insulation
    for, 41
Pipe runs, codes on, 38
Plaster
    covering with wallboard, 48
    painting, 90
    repairing, 59
Plate rails, *66*
Plates, in stud wall, 20, *21*
Platform framing, 20
Plinths of base cabinets, 71
Plumb, checking for
    in cabinet installation, 68
    in door openings, 23
    in hanging wallcovering, 100
    in walls, 23, 85, *85*
Plumbing, **38**
    checking DWV lines, 23
    cross-connections in lines, 9
    insulation of, 18, 41
    reuse of old fixtures, 38
Plumbing connections
    behind cabinets, 68, 69, 72
    tiling around, 81
Plywood
    floor, tiling, 81
    as siding, matching patterns, 35
    as tile countertop backing, 87
Primers, 90, 91, 92
P-trap assembly, *107*, 109

# Q, R

Quarry tile, 80
Rafters
    new connected to old, 24, *25*
    in roof framing, 22, 34
    in skylight framing, 31, *31*, 32
Ranges. *See* Cooktops
Rebars, 18, *19*, *21*
Resale value, 6, 7, 13
Resilient channel, 45, 48
Resistance wiring, 37
Ridge boards, 22, 24, *25*
Rim joists, 20, *20*, *21*, 34
Ring-shank nails, 27, 45
Rollers, paint, 91, *93*, 93–94, 95
Rollers, paste, 99
Rollers, seam, 98, 101
Roofing, 7, **24–25**
    checklists, 23, 24
Roofing material
    removing, 17
    staggering old and new, 25
    types of, 24
Roofs
    cutting skylight opening, 31–32
    framing, 22, 23, 24
    joining new and old, 24, *25*
Rough construction, defined, 15

# S

Safety on job, 9, 16, 23, 104
    and insulation fibers, 41
    paint cleanup, 95
    with paint sprayers, 94
    in removing wallcovering, 98
    in skylight installation, 30–31
    with wallboard panels, 49
Sanders, pole and hand, *44*
Sanding
    and joint compounds, 52
    of plaster repairs, 59
    of wallboard, 54
Scarf joints, 62
Scheduling, 6–8, 13
    of interior trim, 62
    of wallboard taping, 54
Screws, types of, 45, *45*, 52
Septic systems, 38
Set-back limits, 6
Shear walls, defined, 19
Sheathing, 24, *25*, 34
Sheetrock ™. *See* Wallboard
Shutoff valves, 38, *105*, *108*
Siding, *33*
    installing, 5, **34–35**
    materials, 33–35
    painting, 92
    removing, 17, 33, 34
Sinks
    installing, 106, *107*, 108
    installing in countertops, *73*, 74,
        76, 77, 87
    marking bases for pipes, 72
    setting various types of,
        108–109
    tile layout around, 87–88, *88*, *89*
Skip-trowel texturing, 54
Skylights, **30–32**, *31*, *32*
Slate roofs, removing, 17
Sleeping rooms, codes on, 30
Soffits, *33*, 35, 71
Soilstack, 38
Solar heating systems, *36*, 37
Soleplates, 20, *21*, *26*
Soundproofing, 48
Spacers
    in laying out tile, 85, 86
    for tile grout, 82, *82*, 83, *84*
Sprayers, paint, 91, 94, *95*
Stains, 90
Stove duct, measuring, 70
Stove hood, installing, 70
Stovetop. *See* Cooktop
Stucco
    installing, 35
    painting, 90, 91
    removing, 17, 34
Studs
    applying paneling over, 56,
        *56*, *58*
    correcting, 23, 47–48
    cuts in for pipes, 38
    locating, 55–56, 70
    placement of, *21*
    sizes of, 20
Stud walls
    described, 20, *21*
    double, 48
Subfloors, 34, *96*, 96–97

## T

Taping and texturing, wallboard, 52, *53*, 54
T-brace, 49, *50*, 69, *70*
Termites, detecting, 16, 17
Texturing walls, 54, 59
Tile, **80–89**
- backings for countertops, 87
- cutting, 82, *82*
- on floors, 81, 83, *84*, 85, 97
- laying out, 83, *84*, 85, 86, 87–88, *87–89*
- manufacturer's seconds, 80
- preparing surfaces for, 80–82
- removing, 88–89, *89*
- repairing and replacing, 89, *89*
- on roofs, removing, 17
- setting, 82–83, *83*, *84*, 85, 86
- trim, 80, *80*, 85
- types of, 80
- wallboard used with, 44
- on walls, 23, *85*, 85–86

Toe kick, 71, 72, *72*
Toilet
- installing, 105, 106, *106*
- removing, 105, *105*
- tiling floor around, 81

Tools
- for cabinet installation, 69
- for interior trim, 60
- for painting, 91
- for paneling, 56, *56*, 58
- for wallboard, *44*, 45–46, 49, 50, *50*, *53*, 54
- for wallcovering, 98–99

Track lighting, installing, 104, *104*
Trap, in drain system, 38
Trim
- painting, 91, 92
- removing and saving, 16
- tile, 80, *80*, 85
- wallcovering around, 103, *103*

Trim, exterior, **35**
- installation, 35
- removing, 33

Trim, interior, **60–67**
- installation, 60–61, 62
- materials, 60

Trim boards, 34, 35
Trimmer studs, 22, *26*
Trisodium phosphate (TSP), uses for, 92, 98

## U, V

U-beads, 46
Utilities
- notification of changes in, 16
- shutting off, 16

Utility expenses, lowering, 9
Vapor barriers, 41, *41*
Vent pipes and stacks, 38
Vents
- behind cabinets, 69
- on exterior surfaces, 92

Vinyl flooring, applying tile to, 81
Vinyl-surfaced wallboard, 44
Vinyl wallcovering, 101, 102

## W, Z

Wainscoting, paneled, *66*
Wallboard, 44–54
- backing for, 56, *56*
- edging for, 44, 46, *46*
- estimating, 49
- fasteners for, *45*, 45–46, 48, 49, 50
- painting, 90, 91
- repairing, 51–52
- soundproofing with, 48
- tiling over, 81
- types of, 44–45
- use of pieces of, 49, 51, 59

Wallboard installation, **48–51**
- cutting, 50–51, *51*
- gluing, 46, *46*
- hanging, 49–51
- layout, 47, 48–49
- nailing, *45*, 45–46
- preparation, 46–48, *47*
- taping and texturing, 52, *53*, 54

Wallcovering, **98–103**
- on corners, *102*, 102–103
- estimating amount needed, 98
- hanging, 100–101, *101*
- installing, **100–103**
- layout and alignment, *99*, 99–100
- painting over, 92
- preparing walls for, 98
- removing, 98
- seams in, 101–102, *102*, 103
- trimming edges, 101
- types of, 98

Walls
- checking for plumb, 23, 85, *85*
- framing, 20, *21*, 22, *34*
- matching surfaces, 22
- preparing for wallcovering, 98
- tiling, 81, *85*, 85–86
- wallboard installation on, 48–50, *49*
- wallboard taping and texturing, 52, *53*, 54

Warm-air heating systems, 36, *36*, *37*
Water stains, sealing, 92
Water supply lines, 38, 105, *105*, 106, *106*, *107*
Wax gasket, 106, *106*
Wind, reinforcing against, 19
Windows
- casings for, 62, *63*, 64
- cutting wallboard for, 50–51
- installing, **29–30**, *30*, 32, *33*
- leveling jambs, 60–61
- measuring and ordering, 28
- painting, **93**, *94*
- removing, **28–29**, *28*, *29*
- removing trim and casings, 48
- roof and exit, 30
- size and framing of, *21*, 22
- trim for, 35, 62
- wallcovering around, 103, *103*

Wiring. *See* Electrical work
Wood preservative, 92
WR wallboard, 44
Zoning restrictions, 6


## U.S./Metric Measure Conversion Chart

| | Formulas for Exact Measures<br>Symbol | When you know: | Multiply by: | To find: | Rounded Measures for Quick Reference | | |
|---|---|---|---|---|---|---|---|
| **Mass (weight)** | oz | ounces | 28.35 | grams | 1 oz | | = 30 g |
| | lb | pounds | 0.45 | kilograms | 4 oz | | = 115 g |
| | g | grams | 0.035 | ounces | 8 oz | | = 225 g |
| | kg | kilograms | 2.2 | pounds | 16 oz | = 1 lb | = 450 g |
| | | | | | 32 oz | = 2 lb | = 900 g |
| | | | | | 36 oz | = 2¼ lb | = 1000 g (1 kg) |
| **Volume** | pt | pints | 0.47 | liters | 1 c | = 8 oz | = 250 ml |
| | qt | quarts | 0.95 | liters | 2 c (1 pt) | = 16 oz | = 500 ml |
| | gal | gallons | 3.785 | liters | 4 c (1 qt) | = 32 oz | = 1 liter |
| | ml | milliliters | 0.034 | fluid ounces | 4 qt (1 gal) | = 128 oz | = 3¾ liters |
| **Length** | in. | inches | 2.54 | centimeters | ⅜ in. | = 1.0 cm | |
| | ft | feet | 30.48 | centimeters | 1 in. | = 2.5 cm | |
| | yd | yards | 0.9144 | meters | 2 in. | = 5.0 cm | |
| | mi | miles | 1.609 | kilometers | 2½ in. | = 6.5 cm | |
| | km | kilometers | 0.621 | miles | 12 in. (1 ft) | = 30 cm | |
| | m | meters | 1.094 | yards | 1 yd | = 90 cm | |
| | cm | centimeters | 0.39 | inches | 100 ft | = 30 m | |
| | | | | | 1 mi | = 1.6 km | |
| **Temperature** | ° F | Fahrenheit | 5⁄9 (after subtracting 32) | Celsius | 32° F | = 0° C | |
| | | | | | 68° F | = 20° C | |
| | ° C | Celsius | 9⁄5 (then add 32) | Fahrenheit | 212° F | = 100° C | |
| **Area** | $in.^2$ | square inches | 6.452 | square centimeters | 1 $in.^2$ | = 6.5 $cm^2$ | |
| | $ft^2$ | square feet | 929.0 | square centimeters | 1 $ft^2$ | = 930 $cm^2$ | |
| | $yd^2$ | square yards | 8361.0 | square centimeters | 1 $yd^2$ | = 8360 $cm^2$ | |
| | a. | acres | 0.4047 | hectares | 1 a. | = 4050 $m^2$ | |


Proof-of-Purchase
0-89721-269-X